BULGARIA

BULGARIA:

A Travel Guide

Philip Ward

PELICAN PUBLISHING COMPANY
GRETNA 1991

First published in the United Kingdom by The Oleander Press, 1989

Pelican edition, January 1991

Library of Congress Cataloging-in-Publication Data

Ward, Philip.
    Bulgaria, a travel guide / Philip Ward. -- Pelican ed.
       p. cm.
    "First published in the United Kingdom by the Oleander Press,
1989"--T.p. verso.
    Includes index.
    ISBN 0-88289-827-2
    1. Bulgaria--Description and travel--1970- --Guide-books.
I. Title.
DR54.W37 1990
914.9704'24--dc20   90-45357
                                                         CIP

*Cover photos: Thracian Tomb at Kazanluk, Veliko Turnovo,
and Rila Monastery in winter.*

Manufactured in the United States of America

Published by Pelican Publishing Company, Inc.
1101 Monroe Street, Gretna, Louisiana 70053

CONTENTS

ACKNOWLEDGMENTS

To start at the beginning, my wife and daughters provided me, as always, with the time and silence, tea and sympathy, in which to write *Bulgaria* Andrew Poulter generously provided me with the latest archaeological results from Nicopolis ad Istrum.

Among my Bulgarian friends at home and abroad, it may seem churlish to pick out some names and omit others, but I first talked over the book with Lyubomir Hajistoyanov and Angel Angelov, and my longest discussions in Bulgaria were with that boundless source of energy and knowledge, Yordanka Nikolova Kotseva. Grigor Gyurov, like me an enthusiast for all things Finnish, instinctively understood my sympathy too for the Bulgarian land and people. My gratitude to Radoslav Radoulov is boundless. Alexander Levkov helped me to appreciate Sofia, Etura, and Koprivshtitsa. Kostadin Majarov shared with me his knowledge of Hisarya, where he is Curator of the Archaeological Museum. Nikola Gyochev spent valuable hours teaching me Rhodope folklore at Shiroka Luka's Ethnographic Museum. Vesela Stambuliiska showed me virtually every corner, hall and work of art in Sofia's National Palace of Culture. Hristo Yosifov, Secretary of the Bulgarian Football Association, offered companionship and a great deal of information, though we met purely by chance in Veliko Turnovo. Nedyalko Iliev rescued me, stranded in Tryavna's winter snows when my car failed to start, and got me to Kazanluk. Sister Evdokia allowed me to feed her tame deer, Adam, at the Holy Trinity Monastery across the Yantra from Preobrazhenski. Sister Pavlina entertained me in flawless English at the S. Nicholas Monastery in Arbanasi.

And in case the reader thinks I am exaggerating the courtesy and kindliness I met everywhere, ponder this. I arrived one evening just as the last visitor had left Sofia's Zhivkova International Foundation Art Gallery. All the lights were extinguished, the staff had vanished, and the building was being patrolled by a lone security guard. I was leaving the country next morning, and my crowded itinerary had caused me to arrive so late that I should have lost forever the opportunity to see this interesting new gallery. I explained my predicament to the incredulous security guard in a manic half-Bulgarian half-polyglot frenzy which readers of Euripides will recognise from *The Bacchae* and my friends will recognise as typical of me at moments of comic stress.

He thought for a moment, then unlocked the door, put on the lights, and welcomed me in, presenting me – free of charge as the cashier had gone home – with a catalogue and portfolio of posters. To this day I find it hard to believe that a man would risk his job to permit a foreigner and total stranger the run of the gallery he was paid to protect, but such is in fact the immediate reaction of many Bulgarians you are likely to meet. That is one of the many reasons why I suggest you take the trouble to learn a little Bulgarian, and in any case to master the Cyrillic alphabet. Any hours spent in these adventurous ways will greatly enhance your pleasure while travelling throughout Bulgaria, and show respect to hosts who make your sojourn endlessly rewarding.

PHILIP WARD

INTRODUCTION

Fifteen years ago I was browsing in David's Bookshop, near King's College Chapel in Cambridge, when my eye was caught by a large-format, full-colour album called *Bulgarian Monasteries*. A quick glance revealed that Bulgaria possessed seventy-six monasteries at least (all illustrated in Georgi Chavrukov's study) and that because Bulgaria at that time was still virtually unknown in Western Europe, the glories of these monasteries, together with the forests, mountains, hills and valleys in which they are situated, appeared to be unknown. Indeed, travelling in Bulgaria seemed to be the privilege of a tiny few: two thousand in all in 1957, 250 thousand in 1961, two million in 1969. I dismissed the dream of seeing these monasteries, and the rest of the mysterious land known vaguely to the Romans as Thrace and environs, and lazily continued on my lifetime's travels to more familiar destinations: the U.S.S.R., Italy, Japan, Austria, Peru.

In the meantime Bulgaria had modestly and deftly built roads, expanded airports, created a tourist infrastructure of hotels, restaurants, information bureaux and ancillary services, and risen in the tourist industry to a position where 7½ million foreign visitors had been welcomed in 1987, and Balkan Bulgarian Airlines had affiliated, in 1988, to IATA. I feared, exploring from one end of the country to another, that I should find Costa del Sol crowds paying Monte Carlo prices, and hosts by now disaffected by hordes of strangers. Nothing could have been further from the truth.

Whereas certain other Eastern bloc countries fester in sullen resentment against their Soviet neighbour, Bulgaria welcomes Soviet visitors as liberators (twice over) of their small and vulnerable nation, its socialist allies as friends, and visitors from Western countries or Japan as guests. This openhanded trust is shown by unaffected hospitality, a willingness to chat (providing you have a common language), and the easy wave of the hand a foreigner sees when he drives anywhere he likes, and photographs whatever he sees. The scenery is completely unspoiled, except for the industrial areas of a few cities such as Pernik, which you are unlikely to see, and the pollution of a few rivers, which are unlikely to inconvenience you.

The water is drinkable everywhere, violent crime is almost unknown, petty crime quite rare, and as if this were not inducement enough, the cost of living for a foreigner from Western Europe seems extraordinarily low, except for a handful of great hotels, the scheduled air fare from Frankfurt or London, and car-hire. You can get round the first expense by preferring private accommodation booked through Balkantourist; you can circumvent the second by selecting one of the many package tours available; and the third can be overcome by using public transport or bringing your own car.

My book is based on the reader's access to a car, whether self-driven or chauffeur-driven, because so many of the delights of this greatly under-rated tourist destination are to be found well away from big cities (I think of Rozhen Monastery or the late Roman tomb at Silistra), or in unexpected locations, such as the Neolithic tomb beautifully preserved in the hospital grounds in Stara Zagora or the new Museum of Icons above Tryavna.

A huge proportion of Bulgaria's summer visitors never see more than their Black Sea resort, which strikes me as even less sensible than a tree, rooted in the midst of woodland, complaining of being unable to see the beauties a few miles off. Eighty thousand Britons (a number larger than any other nationality) enjoyed the skiing in Bulgarian winter resorts in winter 1987-8. But the best times to explore the Danube from Vidin to Silistra, or the historic heartland near Veliko Turnovo, or the dozens of fascinating monasteries, scattered about the map of Bulgaria like leaves on a rectangle of Roman mosaic at Sandanski, will be spring and autumn, when the press for accommodation relaxes. For one thing, spring blossoms and the roses in the Rose Valley turn the whole country into a festival of colour and light. For another, autumn tints offer especial appeal in a country seventy per cent mountainous, with a dense tree cover reminiscent of mediaeval England.

Bulgaria: a Travel Guide starts with the historic fulcrum of the Bulgar nation as it finds its roots, self-confidence, and destiny: at Pliska, Preslav, Madara, and Veliko Turnovo, with the Preobrazhenski and Sveta Troitsa monasteries and the museum-town of Arbanasi. Then to Tryavna, the undiscovered Balkan art centre,

Bozhentsi, Sokolski Monastery, Gabrovo, Etura Open-Air Museum, the Rose Valley and Hisarya.

Sofia, the capital city, possesses the most important museum in the country and the most active cultural life: galleries, theatres, opera and operetta, ballet and cinema. After visiting Vitosha we travel north to Vratsa, Milhailovgrad, Belogradchik, the Magura Cave and Vidin, before beginning the eastern drive through Pleven and Lovech to Ruse and Tolbuhin.

The Black Sea Coast is a paradise for sunworshippers and hedonists, but it possesses too a rock-cut monastery at Alaja, and the surprise of Nesebur's mediaeval peninsula, with the fine cities of Varna and Burgas, and the attractive little port of Sozopol.

Crossing the country westward brings you to mountain towns and villages such as Kotel, Zheravna, Medven and Katunishte, as well as cities like Sliven, Stara Zagora, Haskovo and the impressive Plovdiv, once Philippopolis. Ascending the Rhodope mountains you pass the fort and rock church above Asenovgrad, Bachkovo Monastery, the agglomeration of Smolyan, Pamporovo's health and ski resort, and the unspoilt enclave of Shiroka Luka.

From the tragic town of Batak and Velingrad you emerge into Pirin and the undiscovered art town of Bansko, the health resort Sandanski, the museum-town Melnik and its isolated Rozhenski Monastery before exploring Blagoevgrad and the greatest wonder in all Bulgaria: the fantastic monastic stronghold of Rila. The route through fertile Kyustendil, exquisite Zemen, historic Samokov and snow-capped Borovets leads back to Sofia.

Such an itinerary might take upwards of three weeks if done all at once, with three nights in Sofia and at least two each in Veliko Turnovo and Plovdiv, and would allow, such is my almost reluctant suggestion, no more than an hour or so for lying on a beach or wandering in a forest. You can save a great deal of time by using internal flights, which are extraordinarily cheap, and convenient because airports are near town-centres (except for Veliko Turnovo), but they do lack that all-important ingredient in the appreciation of beautiful Bulgaria: the landscape.

It may seem odd that the book steers clear of the political minefields inherent in meetings between people from different socio-economic and polical milieux. But the function of this book is not to exacerbate such differences, neither is it to pretend that Bulgaria and its system is either 'right' or 'wrong', if any such facile categorisation could be made, which is self-evidently absurd in its stark simplicity. It is to enable the reader, by exploring Bulgaria from end to end, to see so much of the country and its people that he or she will be in a much better position to come to a series of partly subjective, partly objective opinions based on personal observation, with a background of historical data drawn from texts acquired in Bulgaria, such as *Bulgaria's Past* (Sofia, 1969) by Moutafchieva and Todorov, and abroad, including R.F. Hoddinott's *Bulgaria in Antiquity* (London, 1972), *Thrace and the Thracians* (London, 1977) by Fol and Marazov, and R.J. Crampton's *A Short History of Modern Bulgaria* (Cambridge, 1987). Many Westerners may be prejudiced against Bulgaria because of having read one-sided propaganda: I suggest that such prejudice be set aside before the journey, in the interest of fair play.

PHILIP WARD

LIST OF ILLUSTRATIONS

Acknowledgements

Thanks are due to Balkantourist Tourist Publicity Centre for permission to reproduce maps, and for their courtesy in allowing the use of some photographs for which they hold copyright.

1: THE HISTORIC HEARTLAND

Pliska — Preslav — Shumen — Veliko Turnovo — Arbanasi —
Nicopolis — Dryanovo Monastery — Bozhentsi — Gabrovo — Etura —
Sokolski Monastery — Tryavna — Shipka — Kazanluk — Kalofer —
Karlovo — Hisarya — Sopot — Troyan Monastery — Koprivshtitsa —
Etropole

The warlike, nomadic people from the East known as Bulgars settled in the country now named after them in 681 A.D., inaugurat-
ing the First Bulgarian State under Khan Asparuh, having defeated
the Byzantine Emperor Constantine IV Pogonatus (668-685) and
overrun Scythia Minor, that is Dobruja, and reaching the Balkan
Range (the Roman Haemus) without encountering any resistance.

Pliska
Pliska, an earlier Slav settlement, became the first capital of the
proto-Bulgarians from 681 to 893, when that status was conferred
on Preslav until the fall of the First Bulgarian State in 972. Then
followed a period of Byzantine rule, when the Bulgarians kept their
hopes alive in the far west at Ohrid (in present-day Yugoslavia), and
it was not until 1185 that Veliko Turnovo (Great Turnovo, as
opposed to Little Turnovo near the modern border with Turkey)
could be recognised as the seat of a Second Bulgarian State, which
lasted there until the Ottoman yoke descended on the Balkans, at
Turnovo in 1393 and at the last redoubt, Vidin, in 1396.

So the three capitals of Pliska, Preslav, and Veliko Turnovo
constitute the real heartland of historic Bulgaria, and any traveller
will want to discover them in that sequence. Not that Pliska ruled
an area like modern Bulgaria: it extended only between the Stara
Planina and the Danube, stretching northeast along the Black Sea
coast far into present-day Romania but touching neither Sofia to
westward nor Nesebur to eastward. Pliska was the capital of
Asparuh, third son of the mighty Khan Kubrat who had adopted
Christianity during his childhood in Byzantium. Khan Asparuh

was succeeded by Tervel (701-718), with whose help Justinian regained his throne. Byzantium sharpened internecine strife between the heirs of Khan Tervel, taking advantage by a 'divide and rule' policy of dissension to raid through the Balkan range, and it was not until 777 that Khan Kardam could by firm rule guarantee a generation of peace and strength. Kardam was succeeded by Khan Krum, who extended his imperial sway to Avar and other Slav possessions beyond the Danube, including his own Bessarabian homeland, and then resumed hostilities against Byzantine possessions such as Serdica (now Sofia), which he demolished. Emperor Nicephoros I retaliated by despatching an army across the Haemus Range in 811, sacking Pliska and refortifying Serdica, before retreating in the conviction that it had won a lasting victory. Meanwhile, Krum's armies had assembled and, barely six days after their defeat at Pliska, surrounded the Byzantine forces in a precipitous, narrow pass with wooden palisades to cut off escape in such a way that Nicephoros is reported to have cried: 'Even birds could not escape from such a ravine'. The might of the Byzantine army, its generals and its very Emperor perished on that day, and Krum exhibited the head of his rival on a wooden stake for several days before having a goblet carved from it, lined with silver to toast his guests at newly reconstructed Pliska. He relied on Slav boyars both in his own court and beyond to keep control of the increasing lands, with huge numbers of peasants, swollen by immigrants, prisoners-of-war, and landless peasants. Khan Krum (803-14) was succeeded by his son Omurtag (816-831), who replaced the original tribal structure based on clans by a regional administrative system, with governors of provinces responsible only to the Khan. It is the ruins of Omurtag's Pliska we see today; his marble palaces modelled on those of Byzantium, his temples, and his stone walls, defending a triple fortification system. The first defence was an earthwork and ditch; the outer defensive stone walls protected the peasants, barracks and stables; the inner brick walls provided further security for the wealthy and powerful boyars, with the Palace of the Khans, and its pagan temple probably dedicated to the Sun and Moon, honoured by animal sacrifices.

The first line of defence was a moated earthwork. Between the earthwork and a circuit of stone walls lived the Khan's army and its horses, its artisans and peasants. Beyond this, as if to dissociate himself from his pagan predecessors, Tsar Boris erected his first

Cathedral in 865, a basilica with its column bases still in position. I pondered the life of Boris in his new monastery and cathedral church, following voluntary abdication in 893. The adoption of Christianity changed much. For one thing, Boris had suffered weakening military defeats and urged a peace treaty on the menacing Byzantine Emperor Michael III (842-67), which the Christian made dependent on the pagan's renunciation of his tribal faith. Boris forced his loyal boyars to adopt the new religion, though his subjects proved less pliable, mistrusting the addition of the clergy as a new stratum of potential oppressors. Furthermore, Boris found it easier to treat with other European sovereigns within a common Christian framework. His position was enhanced by the doctrine of the divine origin of kingship and a new code of secular laws to complement new spiritual doctrines. The Thessaloniki-born brothers Constantine (later called Cyril, when he took monastic vows) and Methodius, of Slav origin, created a new Glagolitic alphabet, based on Greek italic writing with new letters for non-Greek sounds occurring in Old Bulgarian. Patriarch Photius intended to send these brothers throughout Slavonic lands as missionaries to Christianise the pagan Slavs, and approved their use of a new alphabet in evangelisation. Cyril died while in Rome in 869, and Methodius in 885, but their disciples were welcomed by Boris, who objected to the pro-Byzantine clergy officiating in Greek. Their disciple Kliment (after whom Sofia University has been named) modified Glagolitic into the Cyrillic alphabet, and in 893 became bishop of Ohrid. Their disciple Naum remained to preach and teach in Pliska until Kliment's elevation, when he too moved to Ohrid.

So I moved into the sanctum sanctorum of Pliska with the resonance of Christian and pagan histories burning like the midday sun on the back of my neck. Within the brick wall stands the ghost of the Lesser Palace of two storeys, the lower floor with four large rooms and a number of anterooms or servants' quarters, obviously a good deal earlier than the Greater Palace of Omurtag's reign which stands outside the brick-walled enclosure. The site museum presents a picture of daily life, rather than imperial splendour, with tools and weapons, and baked-clay jars for storing flour, water and wine.

I drove quickly off towards Madara, where the rock-carved 'Madarski Konnik' attracts the same kind of public in Bulgaria that

Map of Bulgaria

Käläraš

Konstanca

Oltenica

N

Srebārna

Silistra

Dunav

Tutrakan

Gjurgevo

Ruse

Kubrat

Tervel

General-Toševo

Isperih

Razgrad

Tolbuhin

Šabla

Kavarna

Rusalka

Bjala

Pliska

Novi Pazar

Balčik

Aladja
manastir

Albena

Popovo

Kaspičan

Pobiti
kamāni

Zlatni pjasāci

n. Kaliakra

Târgovište

Šumen

Madara

Družba

Ljaskovec

V. Tārnovo

Omurtag

Preslav

Provadija

Devnja

Varna

Kamčija

vo
na

Elena

Prchod na
Republicata

Kotel

Žeravna

Bjala

Obzor

n. Emine

rohod

Karnobat

Slančev brjag

Ravda

Nesebār

Sliven

Pomorie

Nova Zagora

Jambol

Burgas

Sozopol

Stara Zagora

Radnevo

Grudovo

Ropotamo

Primorsko

Kiten

Elhovo

Mičurin

Marica

Topolovgrad

Ahtopol

Malko Tārnovo

Veleka

Harmanli

T Ü R K İ Y E

Svilengrad

umovgrad

Edirne

Arda

S

ivajlovgrad

Isolated rock and earth pillar Rocher et dolmens Einzelner Fels und Erdpyramiden mit Deckstein Rocce e rocce fungoidi Peñas y peñones	**Cave** Grotte Höhle Grotta Cueva	**Picturesque settlement** Site pittoresque Malerische Ortschaft Centro pittoresco Lugar pintoresco
Canyon Gorges Bergschlucht Gola Desfiladero	**Mineral source** Source minérale Mineralquelle Sorgente minerale Fuente mineral	**Museum** Musée Museum Museo Museo
Natural stone bridge Pont rocheux Natürliche Steinbrücke Ponte di roccia Puente de roca	**Mountain resort** Station de montagne Gebirgskurort Stazione montana Centro montañeros	**Historical and cultural monuments** Monuments historiques et culturels Historisches und Kulturdenkmal Monumenti storici e culturali Monumentos históricos y culturales
Rocks Formations rocheuses Felsenkomplex Gruppi rocciosi Formaciones rocosas	**Corst source** Source karstique Karstquelle Sorgente carsica Fuente cársica	**Sea resort** Station balnéaire Seebad Stazione balneare Centro de veraneo marítimo	**Tomb** Sépulture antique Grabmal Tombe Sepulcro histórico

itude mark
te d'altitude
ofel - Kote
na e quota
na con cota

in France brings out the visitors to Carnac; in England to the White Horse of Uffington, one of sixteen such. But Madara, on the other side of the main road to Shumen, is a warren of monastic cells, tombs, kitchens, churches. The picture in the centre of the rocky frame is a worn bas-relief of a rider and horse facing right, with a faithful dog following behind, lean and hungry as Cassius' hound, and a spear transfixing a beaten lion. The rider lifts in his other hand a goblet likely to indicate a toast to his victory. This is one of fifty rock carvings ordered by Khan Omurtag: a badly-eroded Greek inscription names himself, with his predecessors Tervel (701-18) and Kormisoch (721-38). The immense monastery possessed at least a hundred fifty cells, and pre-Christian evidences are everywhere, with votive tablets to the Thracian horseman, that god-king-hero with which each succeeding ruler was all too eager to be identified. Circling eagles scrutinised the grass for an elusive hare. Lizards scattered like leaves in a gale as I climbed up 671 steps to the cliff top, for an eagle's view. Binoculars showed me tractors working in sunny fields, ruins, canals, simple modern

Madara. The Horseman

homes and ancient villas and temples. I ran my fingers over the yellowy-brown sandstone as over ancient parchment; indeed, if you thought of Madara's rocks as more permanent than that it is sobering to see new fissures run like shivers through the body of (Khan Tervel's?) horse. Archaeologists have recently suggested that the Madara Horseman represents the God of Heaven venerated by the proto-Bulgars, a view not excluded by the vaguer concept, all too convenient among autocrats, that gods and heroes and kings and valiant horsemen all partake of the same superhuman status, to be venerated without question by their servants, the common people.

Preslav

Madara Museum exhibits finds from the cells and especially from the Great Cave, such as Getic votive plaques, Roman finds, proto-Bulgarian pottery, and mediaeval objects left by monks and visitors to the hermitage in the rocks.

With my reservation already secure at Shumen's Hotel Madara, I drove in the warmth of an early afternoon to Preslav, a town of ten thousand inhabitants famed for its delicious grapes, then continued southward to the ruins, parking by the site museum where I studied the plans and model of the Royal Palace to get my bearings before walking out. Preslav, a town founded from Pliska by Khan Omurtag in 821, became capital of the First Bulgarian State in 893 under Tsar Simeon. Like Pliska, its plan was concentric, defending an inner palace and churches described by the Exarch Yoan as decorated 'with stone and wood, and in many colours; within, they are adorned with marble, copper, silver and gold. Visitors can find nothing in the rest of the country to compare with these wonders, for elsewhere houses are roofed only with thatch'. John saw Simeon wearing 'a garment studded with pearls, with a chain of medals round his neck and bracelets on his wrists, a purple girdle round his waist and a golden sword by his side'. On his head was a gold crown encrusted with precious stones and pearls, and he held a sceptre in his hand.

The outer town, also defended by stout walls, had a 'Golden' Church of 907, with twelve marble columns, and polychrome ceramic tiles. Yosif, the Archbishop of Bulgaria, resided at Preslav, which became known as Veliki (Great) because of its prestige and size, with a peasant settlement of thatched huts extending in all directions. Simeon may have insisted on splendour at court, but he invited to Preslav many scholars including his schoolmate Ioan, the monk Hrabr, Bishop Constantine and the Presbyter Grigorii, together leading the Preslav school of Bulgarian literature which concentrated on Christian teachings, secular subjects such as geography and natural history, and specialised in translation, mainly from the Greek. They enriched the vocabulary of Old Bulgarian, paving the way for the spread of Slavonic among the literate classes and the future evolution of Bulgarian, Russian, Macedonian, Serbo-Croat, Ukrainian, Byelorussian, Slovenian, Czech, Slovak, Polish and Lusatian (or Wendish). Some of these languages kept a version of Cyrillic and others adapted the Latin alphabet to conform roughly to their own phonetic values but, as a family, the six chief characteristics of the Slavonic tongues are their variable word order; a high degree of inflection (like Latin, but unlike English); verbal aspects corresponding to the completed or habitual nature of the action; few diphthongs; agglomerations of consonants; and varying degrees of palatalization. Learning Old Slavonic is as practical and useful for picking up the modern Slavonic languages as learning Latin is for the easy learning of modern Romance languages, and Preslav – for all its present ruins – can be viewed as Tsar Simeon's intellectual centre, taking over from Pliska and Ohrid from the tenth century to the twelfth. The Asen dynasty occupied the palace at Veliki Preslav too, in the 13th century, but its power and excitement had evaporated by that time, and when the Turks demolished Preslav they reused some of the building materials in the limekilns on the site of the capital's former glories and the Tombul Mosque at Shumen stands proudly in stone retrieved from Preslav.

A few km outside Veliki Preslav, on a wooded slope high above the river Kamchiya, is the ruined Patleina Monastery, concealing the name of S. Panteleimon. Founded by Knyaz Boris I at the end of the ninth century, it too saw the flowering of scholarship, under Kliment and Naum. Boris, weighed down with responsibilities of office and the horrors of war, spent his last years here, and died here. In the 11th century the monastery was robbed, looted and destroyed by wandering tribes such as the Cumans and the Pechenegs, but its traces were discovered during excavations in 1909-14 and we now know that its interior was frescoed and an icon of coloured glazed ceramic tiles, depicting S. Theodore Stratilates, has been rescued, partially restored, and displayed in Sofia – a rare work of the 10th century. Preslav and its surroundings were so wealthy and populous with churches, chapels and secular buildings, that even up to the 19th century, as Turkish caravans were continuing to transport its stone to build their new city of Shumen, Veliki Preslav's shadow of its ancient majesty was still known to the Turks as 'Eski Stambul': 'Old Capital'.

Preslav architects must have been men of wide culture, judging by the 'Golden' Church with its gilded dome and gilded mosaics found below the supporting walls; so must the sculptors of excavated sheep and lions; and the artists used dominant ochre, greens, olive reds, violets and light-browns on tiles with a cream background. We can trace artistic development to the early 11th-century frescoes of the Church of S. Sophia in Ohrid, and then to Bachkovo, with a sudden rapid efflorescence at Boyana, near Sofia.

Shumen

Shumen (known as Kolarovgrad briefly from 1950 after the revolutionary figure, Vasil Kolarov) has a truly magnificent mosque: the Tombul (1745), a creation of Sharif Pasha. The ablutions fountain with its courtyard could be anywhere from Meknes to Hama, and though few worshippers were using the mosque for customary prayers during my visit, I reckoned them fivefold at least for Friday worship, and so upwards of a hundred likely to face Makkah al-Mukarrimah. Heavy chandeliers glowed Rembrandt-gold, and the blue and gold ceiling reached up to an impressive dome. A Turkish religious school or *madrasah* in the mosque precinct now sports an Ethnographic Museum. The Regional History Museum can be seen at 10 Ul. D. Blagoev. You can get to the Art Gallery westward along Ul. G. Dimitrov, giving you some feeling for spacious new Shumen. The old town is, as in Plovdiv, much more interesting, with vestiges of its quaint Turkish past, huddling beside the river Poroina below an 18th-century clock tower destined to fall foul of the developers. Taking advantage of chances to look inside blank walls instead of simply walking alongside them, I entered the former home of Lajos Kossuth, the great Hungarian revolutionary who lived in Shumen for three months in 1849 before being interned in Turkey. No. 35 Ul. Tsar Osvoboditel, lovingly restored, displays furniture of the period in panelled rooms, silent with dust, clammy with history, echoing with dying footfalls. At No. 87, further along the same street, I enjoyed the books and

Shumen. Ploshtad 9 Septemvri

portraits, the pictures and furniture, of the dramatist Dobri Voinikov (1838-78). Having spent formative years at the French school
in Bebek, outside Istanbul, he could be forgiven for writing com-
edies in the style of Molière, but then this son of Shumen startled
everyone by writing plays such as *Civilisation Misunderstood* (1866)
and *Princess Raina* (1866). Still considered by some to be the father
of Bulgarian drama, Voinikov is dismissed as 'without artistic
merit' by Mercia Macdermott who accords the 'father' epithet to
Vasil Drumev (1841-1901), also of Shumen, author of the historical
play *Ivanko, Assassin of Asen I* (1872) and a realistic story of some
interest: 'An Unhappy Family' (1860). Drumev assumed the name
of Kliment as Metropolitan of Turnovo and took an active rôle
politically as a pro-Soviet.

If you are beginning to feel at home in 19th-century Shumen,
another step in the city's intellectual history can be followed
through the rooms of Vasil Kolarov's House. Kolarov was actually
a transnational figure, deriving from the middle class, possessing a
university education (in Geneva), and taking Soviet citizenship

after the abortive rising of 1923, returning home after the Soviet liberation of Bulgaria to watch over the ideological purity of the Communist Party and its virtual monopoly of post-war power (the Agrarian Party having minimal impact). Kolarov's home and his rise to power as deputy party leader can be examined at No. 11 Ul. Ikonomov.

Shumen's Drama Theatre (1956) celebrated the inauguration of Bulgarian drama with the 1856 production of a play by Sava Dobroplodni, yet another Shumen native.

At dinner in the Hotel Madara, I made friends with a group of Bulgarians on holiday from Sofia. Over sarmi (vineleaves stuffed with minced veal and pork, seasoned with paprika, mint and parsley), I explained the differences between a writer's life in England and abroad, as far as my experiences allowed.

In the fug of cigarette-smoke, growing so dense that I wondered about calling for a fire-extinguisher, I quizzed Stefan and Dimitur about themselves. If there is such a thing as 'national character', what are Bulgarians like? 'Steadfast, loyal, honest', replied Dimitur. 'Calm, thrifty, patient, quiet', countered Stefan. From the next table a stocky figure in a black leather jacket added, 'good drivers: I just came back from Italy (I'm a truck-driver) and couldn't stand the klaxon and the dangerous overtaking'. 'We believe in the unity of the nation first, after so many foreign invasions,' interposed Stefan. 'We work hard, sometimes two jobs to make extra. We don't like it when so many rich foreigners in big cars flash around lots of Deutschmarks.' After a lull, Dimitur ventured as if hesitant. 'The foreign women come here not dressed in a modest way, want a good time, then some of our boys are told to get lost. They are what: flirtish?' Yes, I thought, British girls used to Corfu and the Costa Brava may well be inclined to the flirtish. Whenever I found a common language in which everyone could express themselves fluently, the Bulgarians made straightforward points. Leather Jacket considered Romanians dishonest, and Stefan viewed Russians as drunkards: 'We Bulgarians take food with our aperitifs; we never get drunk. The Russians just swish cognac and vodka down their throats: they want to get drunk very quick'. Dimitur angrily sent back his meat balls to the kitchen, disgusted that some bread had been included in their composition, and was given a fresh portion. The smoke thickened, as if in the heart of a gipsy encampment. I could imagine the gipsies retiring to the wings after *Il Trovatore*'s Anvil Chorus and settling down to a quick game of cards before their next entrance.

Veliko Turnovo

My pulse quickened next morning as I headed west to Great Turnovo, capital of the Second Bulgarian State from 1185 when Petur and Asen rebelled against the Byzantines to 1393, when the Ottomans captured the citadel and set fire to the city which had become celebrated as 'second after Constantinople'.

However, like Amalfi or Ronda, Veliko Turnovo exceeds its reputation in beauty, grandeur, strangeness. Ivan Vazov memorably described its houses, huddling on the hillside over the raging Yantra, as like a 'flock óf frightened sheep', and no matter where you stand near the riverbends, fresh images strike you at every level. You might be living within a kaleidoscope of colours, tones, ridges and precipices. Of course such a picturesque site was inhabited by early man, as attested by palaeolithic finds from the Bacho Kiro Cave near Dryanovo and a multitude of neolithic sites witness Copper and Bronze Age settlements. A Roman fortress of around the fourth century has been excavated on the hill known after it as Momina Krepost, and Tsarevets Hill became a stronghold of the Byzantines in the 5th-6th centuries under Justinian, but it was seized by the Slavs in the 7th century, after which little is known until the declaration of the Second Bulgarian State by the new Tsar Petur in 1185.

Taking advantage of the fact that the Seljuk Turks had robbed the Byzantine Comnenus dynasty of much of its territory in Asia Minor, the Serbs and Magyars had cast off their allegiance in 1183 and two years afterwards the Normans had captured Thessaloniki, the Asenids – as the new Bulgarian dynasty became known – declared their own sovereignty. The boyar brothers Petur and Asen found no shortage of allies rallying to their succour when the Byzantine Emperor Isaac Angel II mounted a first, second and eventually even a third attack. His troops won a number of battles, forcing Petur and Asen to flee beyond the Danube, and the town of Lovech to withstand a three-month siege in 1187. But finally the Byzantine forces retired, leaving the boyars with the lands between the Danube and Stara Planina. Petur abdicated in favour of his brother in 1187, retiring to Preslav, from where he ruled Dobruja. Asen planned to claim Macedonia and Thrace and succeeded in capturing Sofia and parts of Macedonia, but rival boyars disputed Asen's authority and a boyar named Ivanko slew Asen in 1196. A few months later, Petur fell to the feuding aristocrats too, and his young brother Kaloyan ascended the throne with Cuman mercenaries helping to recapture virtually all the lands previously annexed by Byzantium. In 1205 he took Thrace, then immediately marched west to take the whole of Macedonia, falling victim to a Cuman assassin one night in 1207. The boyar conspirators chose the Asenid nephew Boril to succeed him, but Asen I's heirs (then minors) eventually returned to Bulgarian soil with Russian and Cuman mercenaries and young Asen became Tsar Ivan Asen II (1218-41), bestowing on his great new kingdom more than two decades of relative peace, during which Bogomil heretics were left largely alone to practise their faith.

We do not know when the Bogomil world view took root in Bulgaria, but S. Kozma had written *Against the Heretics* in Slavonic in the tenth century, and certain aspects of their teachings seem to have come from the East, because the word 'bogomil' derives from the translated name of the Syrian sect of Massaliani, in Greek Euchites. The sect is known also as Paulicians, in Bulgarian Pavlikeni, and enjoyed toleration under the Ottoman yoke, agreeing to join the Roman Catholic Church in 1650 at least in the persons of Plovdiv sectarians, and those living near Nicopolis. Vigorously disseminating their views throughout Europe, their affiliates arose in different regions and at different times. In northern Europe the Waldenses and Anabaptists spread a Bogomil message, in Russian the Dukhobors and Strigolniks identified with them, and the Cathars or Albigensians of France have been minutely studied in Emmanuel Le Roy Ladurie's evocative *Montaillou* (1975; English translation 1978). In 1223 the French Catholic hierarchy declared the local Albigensians 'Bulgars' or 'Bougres', a term of abuse later also to enter English.

We cannot understand the hidden spiritual life of Bulgaria, running as a parallel strand with feudalism and the Orthodox Church, without appreciating such Bogomil tenets as denial of the divine birth of Christ, of sacraments and ceremonies, of the personal coexistence of the Son with the Father and the Holy Ghost. Strigolnik, preaching in the 14th century, repudiated churches (prayer should be in private homes), priests (believers should instruct each other), and infant baptism (the rite should not be literally by water, but spiritually by self-abasement and the singing of prayers and hymns). Each member of the congregation could become perfect, like Christ. Bogomils rejected the monastic life, crucifixes, icons, and the worship of saints or relics. Taking as their texts apocryphal Biblical tales, doctored where needful to substantiate their body of belief, the Bogomils taught that God had two sons, the elder being Satan'il and the younger Miha'il ('il' being the 'el' of Semitic religions). Satan'il rebelled against God and was deprived of his divine title, creating the lower heavens and earth, where he tried but failed to create man. Miha'il (our Michael) was identified with Jesus in the form of a man and was 'elected' by God after baptism in the Jordan. He then vanquished Satan, who according to the Bogomils then invented the whole Orthodox community with its panoply of vestments, ceremonies and priesthood. Each Bogomil community elected its own twelve 'apostles', and allowed women to join the 'elect'. Their vigorous, fanatical teachings led to equally vigorous persecution; it is said that the Empress Theodora had more than a hundred thousand of them murdered. The doctrines offered comfort to the poor and landless, threatening the status quo everywhere from Serbia, whence they were expelled at the end of the 12th century; to Bosnia, where they were called 'Patareni' but subsequently embraced Islam; and throughout Western Europe, especially in German and France. The Quaker movement in England resembles the Molokani in Russia, themselves like the Dukhobors who emigrated to Canada when persecuted in Orthodox Russia.

So we must see Veliko Turnovo during the Second Bulgarian State as a place of toleration towards the Bogomils; a time when Ivan Asen II extended his borders and sphere of influence by dynastic marriages to scions of Epirus, Serbia and the engagement of his youngest daughter Elena (then eleven) to Baudouin II, Emperor of the so-called Latin Empire, which incorporated more or less the same territories as the old Byzantine Empire. Ivan Asen himself married the daughter of the King of the Magyars, and minted his own coins, the first Bulgarian king to do so, stimulated by trade with Venice through the Republic of Dubrovnik. Pope Gregory IX, worried about the growing influence of Bulgaria in the Balkans, broke off Elena's engagement and appointment as regent of the Latin Empire in place of Elena's father the then King of Jerusalem, one Jean de Brienne. Elena was married to the son of a new ally, the Nicaean Emperor, who recognised the Bulgarian

Church as independent from the Church of Rome.

After Ivan Asen II's death in 1241, his heirs struggled for the throne, and the bloody succession reminds one of the sanguinary battles of Scottish chiefs dramatised by Shakespeare in *Macbeth*. But then, much the same occurred throughout the rest of feudal Europe. Internal boyar struggles were exacerbated by invasions, such as that of the Tatar Khan Nogai (1271), or by peasant rebellions like that of the swineherd Ivailo (1277), who became Tsar in 1278 and married the widowed Tsaritsa. Ivailo, deposed by the Byzantine puppet Ivan Asen III, sought refuge with Nogai, who promptly beheaded Ivailo and sent his head to Byzantium. The Cuman boyar Georgi Terter reigned as Tsar between 1280 and 1290, a puppet of the Tatar Khan banished by the Khan in favour of the boyar Smilets (1290-98). Georgi Terter's son Svetoslav seized the throne (1300-22), repudiated Tatar suzerainty, reduced boyar power, and made peace with both Serbs and Byzantines. New turbulence broke out and Tsar Mihail Shishman (1323-30) had to fight a series of wars to regain lands lost to the Byzantines after Svetoslav's death. Shishman was killed fighting against invading Serbs at the Battle of Velbuzhd (today called Kyustendil) west of Sofia. Shishman's nephew Ivan Alexander (1331-71) was placed on the throne by the boyars and soon won back Thracian districts snatched by the Byzantines after Velbuzhd, signing peace treaties with Serbs and Byzantines alike.

Ivan Alexander's reign is notable for dazzling architectural achievements: S. John at Ohrid, and several churches at Nesebur, characterised by alternate courses in brick and stone, polychrome glazed ceramics and vaulted niches. Painting reaches new heights at Ivanovo and Zemen, and crafts emerge that will remain forever identified with the Bulgarian spirit: woodcarving, gold and silversmithing for church vessels and icon-covers; miniature painting shown at Rila Monastery Museum, and the Four Gospels of Ivan Alexander in the British Museum, where the book is known as the Curzon Bible. Patriarch Euthymius (1374-93) founded his own school at the Holy Trinity Monastery near Turnovo.

The Second Bulgarian State fell during the reign of Ivan Shishman (1371-93), who knew nothing but strife from the siege of Adrianople (Edirne) in 1371 by Sultan Murad I (1362-89), to Murad's capture of Macedonia (completed in 1375), of Yambol, Sozopol, Ihtiman, Samokov and Sofia. Isaiah, a monk on Mount

Athos, could write of Macedonia in those days as a land 'deserted, deprived of all that was good, people perished, cattle and fruit-trees disappeared, and the living envied those already dead'. The end was signalled when allied Serbian and Bosnian armies defeated the Turks at Plochnik in 1387 with the assistance of Ivan Shishman, for the Ottoman Empire sent an army 30,000 strong to punish the rebellious Ivan Shishman, who was compelled to surrender. Sultan Murad died, like Lazar of Serbia, at the Battle of Kosovo (1389) but Sultan Bayazid I (1389-1402) determined to end the resistance of his neighbour to the north, and took Veliko Turnovo in 1393, after a three-month siege. The brave besieged were enslaved or massacred: which was worse? The end of the Second Bulgarian State had arrived after more than two centuries of wavering fortunes, and with it the long night of the Ottoman yoke.

So when we explore Turnovo, it is as though we turn back the pages of history more than six hundred years. We scent desperation in the air, as harvests burn, women are raped and children sent into Anatolian bondage. Looting, murder, and sacrilege were of daily occurrence, for the invaders respected neither the Christian religion of their new subjects, nor their Bulgarian language. Civic leaders had to choose between the chains of slavery or the curved dagger (*yataghan*) for rejecting Islam.

But the glory of the city is its Bulgarian remains, lovingly restored where possible, and still being excavated. You cross over to the hill of Tsarevets by a narrow stone bridge replacing the original drawbridge. The ramparts rise in a near isosceles triangle, with the Frankish Gate and Baudouin's Tower at the south-east corner in the short side. The summit (above romantic mist, like Heidelberg above the Neckar) is crowned with a new church which has been painted with a 'Pantheon of Bulgarian Spiritual Culture' by Teofan Sokiarov, which I admit I found profoundly depressing in its crudeness, representational without genius, expressionistic without taste. A tape-recording of the Ioan Kukuzel Male-Voice Choir, poignant in its sombre golden glow, floats above and through the hasty paintings from the acceptance of Christianity (865) in the narthex to the northern wall's sketches of Asen and Petur rebelling; the victory of Tsar Kaloyan in 1205; and the Monk Simeon giving his *Chronicle* to Ivan Alexander. On the apse wall Ivan Asen II extends the domain of Bulgaria. The southern wall depicts Theodosius of Turnovo, Cyril and Methodius, and their pupils Kliment, Naum and Sava.

An old woman from Varna, heaving herself up hundreds of stone steps, called out to her friend on the coach-trip: 'My daughter-in-law would be astonished to see me climbing up these steps so quickly!' Orange marks on the walls indicate the level of the original masonry. Below the church extends the palace, at least in plan, exposed by archaeologists, with the open-air opera stage close by. Exploring the palace and the 15th-century mosque to the north of it, made with stone from the earlier buildings, has been made all the more pleasurable because the local council have laid out the area as a public park, conscious that civic pride will ensure that none of the archaeological treasures will fall victim to vandalism or destruction. The main part of the Great Palace was the audience hall, where the enthroned Tsar would receive deputations. About thirty-five metres by sixteen, it was divided into three aisles by carved columns, with a tiled floor and frescoed or mosaic walls portraying royal figures or historical scenes.

Tsarevets is almost completely enclosed by a loop in the river Yantra: across to the south spreads the second largest university in Bulgaria: the Cyril and Methodius, to the east Momina Krepost, to the north Arbanasi, and to the west Trapezitsa, stronghold of the feudal aristocracy of the Second Bulgarian State, led by the boyars and the higher clergy, who enjoyed access to Tsarevets by a road running past the Church of the Forty Martyrs. Nowadays, you can reach Trapezitsa from the Hotel Yantra's steps and cross the railway line by footpath. Many churches were identified in excavations, all with a single apse and aisle. Regrettably Trapezitsa bore the heaviest brunt of Ottoman depredation and of the seventeen private chapels in this district we have only pitiful architectonic fragments, and buried jewels, pottery, coins and crucifixes.

The Asenovo district, by contrast, offers a different impression of the Second Bulgarian State, its life and churches, spreading at the riverside below the rocky outcrops of Trapezitsa and Tsarevets. This is where the merchants and craftsmen plied their business, the last mediaeval buildings wrecked by earthquake in 1913. I gained only limited access to the vast Church of the Forty Martyrs (ask for Sveti Chetirideset Muchenitsi), because it was undergoing restoration at the time, but you may be luckier. Constructed in 1230 by Ivan Asen II, partly from classical column-capitals and -bases brought from Nicopolis, the church has wall paintings contempor-

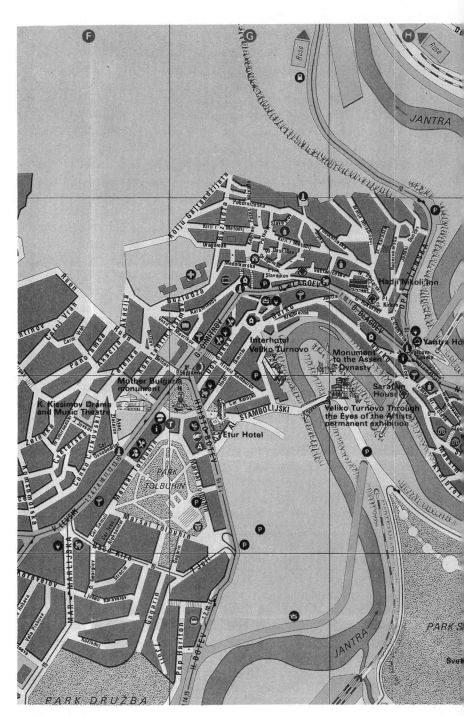

Map of Veliko Turnovo

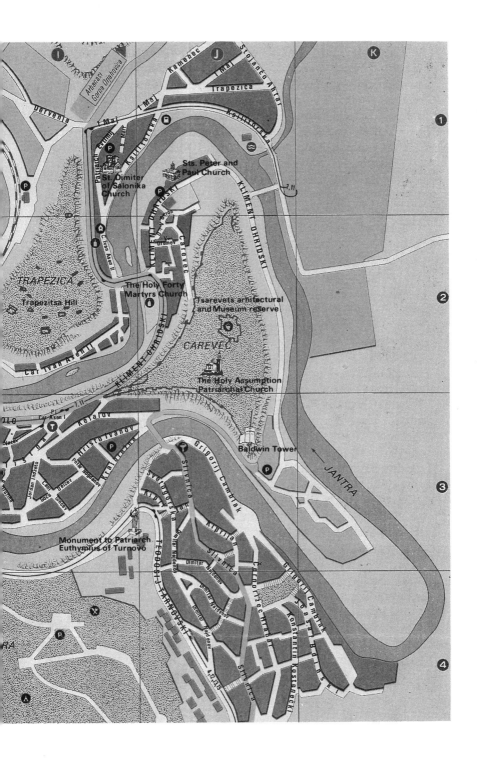

ary with the church, and hence of enormous historical value. Three columns bear mediaeval inscriptions: one is from Pliska, in Greek; another is Omurtag's Column from Preslav, also in Greek; the third is Ivan Asen II's column of victories including Klokotnitsa (1230), in Old Bulgarian. Forty Martyrs became a mosque, with a minaret that fell down more than once, an act attributed by Christians in Turnovo to a vengeful God retaliating for the erection of a mosque on the bones of S. Sava and members of the royal family.

On the other bank of the Yantra I found Sv. Dimitur, built in 1185, to accept the icon of S. Dimitrios of Thessaloniki as protector of the city, but badly damaged by the 1913 earthquake. Archaeologists have uncovered a Thracian sanctuary on this site, and the church was reconstructed in 1985 to the Nesebur pattern. It is in this church that Petur and Asen declared independence and here that Tsars were crowned. Two strata of paintings are found in the apse: the original frescoes from the first Turnovo period, and a 16th-century sequence with Greek inscriptions. Sv. Georgi, on the same bank of the Yantra, has early 17th-century frescoes of the Creation and the Last Judgement, among others.

The Church of SS. Peter and Paul (closed on Mondays like other museums in this museum-city) was the church of the Greek bishops of Turnovo, many times reconstructed and badly damaged by the 1913 earthquake. In the 17th century, when the open gallery was added, the outer wall was demolished revealing the secret private library of Patriarch Euthymius, hidden from the Muslim Turks and burnt by the Greek Orthodox bishops. A squirrel in the church garden bounded ahead of me, as if to show me the way, then darted round the narthex and out of sight. Columns brought from Nicopolis divide the church into three naves. A Tree of Jesse is painted on the first arch, and above it a Dormition of the Virgin, a masterpiece of Bulgarian art. The first square column, facing the single apse, has the original portrait of S. John of Rila copied at Rila. The southern wall has a fine Deiesis, in which the Virgin and John the Baptist beg Jesus to succour mankind. A young Bulgarian girl, about 22, with flowing black hair and eyes like burning coals, transfixed the Deiesis with her gaze as if the two colluded spiritually, not seeking but finding. An older man behind her, shuffling his feet, hands in the pocket of his dark brown leather jacket, sniffed the air as if mistrustful: a juror in the case against Jesus inclined to the prosecution. I turned round, surprised by the

Veliko Turnovo. Tsarevets, seen from Hotel Yantra

whiteness of the pure mountain air, and made out Sv. Dimitur: two beacons against a sudden invasion of heretics. I remembered seeing an x-ray of a Lucas Cranach painting in Leningrad's Hermitage: he had overpainted a view of Turnovo, a town he had seen in 1493. I passed, two hundred metres distant, the Church of the Dormition of the Virgin, rebuilt after the 1913 earthquake on the site of an earlier monastery renowned as that Monastery of the Virgin of the Prisoners where Tsar Ivan Alexander forced the empress Theodora to enter holy orders so that he could take as his second wife the Jewess Sarah.

I felt exhausted by the historical palimpsest of Turnovo, but found no restaurant at hand, so walked the length of Ulitsa Kliment Ohridski and Nikola Pikolo up to the heights of the Yantra Hotel in the old town, taking an early dinner before the last showing at the Poltava Cinema. The Poltava off 9 Septemvri Square has a large, modern auditorium entered below Lenin's dictum that cinema is the most important of the arts, by which he meant that propaganda for his doctrines must take precedence over that horrific concept, 'art for art's sake'. Luckily, independent film-makers like Alexei German and Elem Klimov have challenged censorship imposed by the Soviet state and 'glasnost' has at last permitted some of the best of recent Soviet films a general release, at home and abroad. In Bulgaria, similar views begin to prevail, and I was encouraged by Rangel Vulchanov's spirited *A Sega Na Kude?* ('Where do we go from here?'), in which auditions are held for 26 young men and women on a stage, and we see these aspiring artists behind the scenes, too, and also on the roof! A nude scene (apparently not the first in Bulgarian cinema, like the Indian industry plagued by limitations on physical contact) caused the audience to catch its breath, but there were no love scenes apart from one chaste kiss, making a director's job even more difficult if he tries to portray life and literature (no D.H. Lawrence, no Nabokov, no Tennessee Williams). At the end of the film, the panel of judges says 'we'll let you all know' and the actors feel discouraged. The eight o'clock audience, with many soldiers and young couples, filed out silently from the side of the cinema; I trudged down Ulitsa Tsar Kaloyan to my comfortable corner room in Hotel Veliko Turnovo.

Next morning my view from Room 361 encompassed the Yantra's dark waters far below, magnificent trees shading the flowing river from the sun, and the pink, brown and white houses clustered at so many levels that I saw them poised in descent like the mysterious pack of falling cards concluding *Alice in Wonderland* which proved after all to be 'dead leaves that had fluttered down from the trees upon her face'. Nobody sees what Veliko Turnovo is like, nobody can see it all at once, because of the Yantra's sly swirlings around the limestone rocks.

The Archaeological Museum (Ul. Ivanka Boteva) reveals that Samovodene district was inhabited from the early Neolithic (7th millennium B.C.) but we cannot find remains in the city centre earlier than Copper Age objects of the 5th millennium B.C., contemporary with the gold trove of Hotnitsa, copies of which are shown here. Homer (*Iliad* X) describes a Thracian chieftain of the Iron Age period, fighting on the side of Troy; such a warrior might have come from the village on the hill later known as Tsarevets. The long march of history traverses the Hellenistic period (4th-1st centuries B.C.) with its Greek trade goods, inscriptions and capitals from Nicopolis, a magnificent bronze head of a man from the Roman town of Novae (now Svishtov) on the Danube, ceramics from Pavlikeni (the Bogomil town near Gabrovo) and a fine cameo of Athena, thoughtfully provided with a magnifying glass. On the upper floor, where again all captions are only in Bulgarian, a gold medallion of Khan Omurtag's time exemplifies the powerful migrations of Bulgarian power to Niš in Yugoslavia. Here are the single-headed eagle of Ivan Asen and the double-headed eagle of Ivan Alexander. Nobody disturbed my enjoyment of this indispensable museum, not even a caretaker to protect the mediaeval jewellery, arms and armour, the coins of Mihail Shishman, Ivan Asen II and Todor Svetoslav, and copies of contemporary frescoes from Turnovo and Boyana.

The adjacent old Turkish Konak was demolished in 1872, and the majestic building we see today is a faithful restoration of Kolyo Ficheto's old town hall of the 1870s, which achieved national fame in 1879 as the seat of the Constituent Assembly that produced the Constitution. The assembly elected Prince Alexander Battenberg, and six years later Petko Karavelov and Stefan Stambolov recognised the union of the Principality with Eastern Rumelia. The Museum of National Revival opened in 1985, celebrating the first constitution of 1879 presided over by the Russian Count Dondukov-Korsakov. A second constitution was approved in 1944 and a third in 1971.

Another Ficheto masterpiece is the mansion of Haji Nikoli Minchev: a Haji in Christian Bulgaria was a man who had returned from pilgrimage to the Holy Sepulchre in Jerusalem. Nikoli's shops on the ground floor have been transformed into craft shops for a potter, a weaver, a goldsmith, but the rest of the rooms form an Ethnographic Museum where women knit and chat, sew and chat, welcoming the odd visitor with kindly curiosity. On the stairs I passed Haji Nikoli's great safe, and found elegant bead purses, stamps for ritual bread, regional costumes, Vratsa silk, woven belts, scarves and aprons under the dignity of glass yet similar to those you see in use today. In a museum-city like Turnovo, much of the atmosphere is to be sensed indoors, where wealthy bourgeois would have sought refuge from baking sun and inquisitive neighbours.

A samovar awaits family guests who would sit not on chairs but on long wooden benches around the walls. Architectural photographs allow you to glimpse the wealth of Turnovo in a single survey. On the upper floor festivals are illustrated: Spring 'martenitsa', S. Trifon's Day, for vine-growers, on 14 February, when the oldest man present tugs a twig from last year's vine and pours wine on to the wound, to heal it. S. Lazarus' Day, two weeks before Easter, is celebrated by girls; and S. Basil's Day, on 1 January, by boys. One week before Easter is Flower Day, the name-day of Bulgarians named not after saints but after flowers of the field. The *horos*, or round dance, on S. George's Day, 6 May, is about the last of the festivals before the summer work in the fields. A rhyme runs: 'Red, red Easter, and green, green S. George's means you'll be healthy for a year', which explains why Bulgarian Easter eggs are painted red.

I explored the craft shops along Ulitsa Blagoev, talking with the cooper Tsanko Borisov Petrov, and the turner Kiril Tomanov. Glazed ceramic bowls cost between 3 and 8 leva. Kiril told me how to find the House with the Little Monkey-Man at 14 Ulitsa Vustanicheska, Kolyo Ficheto's inspiration of 1849. Yet another merchant's home and store combined, this building has a façade limited to seven metres and a depth of only seventeen metres, but an effortless appearance of size and grandeur is achieved by corbelling, balconies, with a cheeky carving of a grimacing man providing a gargoyle effect familiar to us from northern cathedrals. Gurko Street is packed with architectural incident, a jack-in-the-box of sudden encounters, foam-white depths of the Yantra, cars racing on one track, trains on another, the Art Gallery like a neo-Renaissance Cathedral, scaffolding at your elbow zooming up, rickety as Jack's beanstalk and as close to the sky.

Kolyo Ficheto's creativity looms wherever you turn your head: Sv. Atanas at 31 Ulitsa Kiril i Metodii, and in particular Sv. Konstantin i Elena at 11 Ulitsa Donchev, near the Church of the Blessed Saviour (Sv. Spas), Fichev's last church at Turnovo, finished in 1872. This manual of good design for sensitive lovers of the past (National Revival was always looking over its shoulders) corresponds to the Arts and Crafts Movement in England – Fichev's church is perhaps spiritually kin to Lord Grimthorpe's new west façade of St Alban's Cathedral (1879). Whether you concentrate on the ingenious lighting, the free-spinning columns at the church entrance to minimise subsidence, or the clean harmony of in-built columns and blind niches, everything demonstrates masterful simplicity.

A Museum of 19th-Century Life has been set up in the Sarafki House at 88 Ulitsa Gurko, a winding street facing the Art Gallery in Asen Park and the 1985 Monument to the Asen Dynasty. Dimo

Saraf (the name *sarraf* means 'moneylender' in Arabic and cognate languages) built this extraordinary house in 1861 on five floors to profit from the steep slope – and to suffer from landslides. Three lower floors, facing the Yantra, were used as store-rooms, and the two higher floors facing the street now called Blagoev were used as living quarters. A typical National Revival wooden ceiling in carved squares and angled panels surrounding a central leafy boss displayed bourgeois opulence while it was still respectable. Splendid wrought-iron grilles and lattices decorate staircases, vestibule, doors and windows.

Konstantin Paustovsky, that greatest of all Russian autobiographers after Gorky, spent three days in Veliko Turnovo, yet years later he looked back on his experiences with some degree of amazement. 'It is as if ancient plays were staged here a long time ago,' he mused, 'after which the actors and spectators died, leaving behind only the setting of this fairy-tale city, overhanging the precipitous, meandering ravine of the Yantra. Turnovo is a city of houses rising above one another amid chasms, of bridges and tunnels unexpectedly spanning the river, a magnificent museum with ancient inscribed columns, monasteries with rich murals, astonishing chimney-stacks, wooden balconies, its nights filled by the unceasing, even flow of the river on which lights are reflected.'

Ulitsa Gurko palpitates with historical resonance, with Baba Mota's House at no. 35 and Ana Harieva's at no. 55. Baba Mota gave refuge to Vasil Levski, Bacho Kiro, and colleagues in the anti-Ottoman resistance movement, and quite a few other houses in this delightful narrow street date back to Ottoman times, though subsidence has required many a new strut, joist and balcony in place of the old.

From the Hotel Veliko Turnovo I crossed the bridge from Ulitsa Stamboliiski on to the island-peninsula of Asen Park, jutting into the Yantra below Sveta Gora, pronounced 'Hollywood' by a Bulgarian friend, though the name means 'Holy Wood'. I dislike the Art Gallery as a building, for it floats out of scale like a scenic effect in Lilliput. The closer I approached the more it seemed to be made of cork. Closed on Mondays, the Gallery presents a permanent exhibition of Bulgarian townscapes, predominantly scenes of Turnovo itself, for example by Todor Hajinikolov (1981), an artist born in 1920. Women attendants drooping at the end of a long day presided over my search for floppy overshoes, then followed me around at a discreet four paces like interpreters behind a foreign head of state suspected of sabotage. I forgave Alexander Terziev's histrionic, arid 'Asen and Petur' (1981) for his portrait 'Baba Elizaveta' (1981) and undated 'Portrait of Boris Bogdanov'. His stolid, unimaginative 'Followers of Ivailo' (1969) represents life-size, long-nosed, grim-faced peasants with swords, poles and axes, and I sighed with disappointment, yearning for a half-solemn, half-humorous treatment of the subject in the Flemish mode, as Pieter Breughel might have done it, bristling with telling detail, but nothing here dilutes the stern nationalistic message. Vasil Stoilov (b. 1904) shows 'Patriarch Euthymius' (1964) proudly unflinching before sneering Turks in a manner faintly reminiscent of Bosch's 'Christ Crowned with Thorns' in the Escorial; his 'Bogomil Propoved' (1969) refers to a religious leader of the heretical group already discussed. Georgi Maslev's 'Tsar Simeon entering Preslav' looks alarmingly like the lean and hungry Don Quixote of Doré's engravings. An effective Portrait of 'Panayot M. Velchev' (1855-1910) was painted by Arno Novak (1874-1914) in 1905-8. Boris Denev (1883-1969) is represented by drawings of soldiers embroiled in World War I.

A prominent notice in the three-star Hotel Veliko Turnovo announced, 'Dear Guests, For your safe stay at the hotel, the guidance asks you do not carry in the hotel and use your own electrical appliances. Smoke only at the appointed. Do not cause lifts! Do not use panic! Please, report any unusual or suspicious situation to the front.' More fretting about sabotage? Bulgarian television was showing Pleneno Yako ('Captured Flock'), a propaganda film made about 1960 and set towards the end of World War II, concerning a group of Communist revolutionaries sacrificing all for their beliefs. In sharp contrast, the Kino Poltava showed Emir Kosturnica's pungently ironic Bashta v Komandirovka ('Dad's Away on Business', that is, in jail) a Yugoslav movie which managed to treat politics as a three-dimensional problem, affecting real human beings in living situations.

Seven km outside Turnovo on the road to Ruse, that follows the bends of the Yantra like a horseman being pursued by a snake, in a high grove of lime trees rises the Monastery of the Transfiguration of Our Lord (in Bulgarian Preobrazhenski), a 14th-century foundation of Tsar Ivan Alexander which suffered terribly at the hands of Muslim invaders. The buildings we see now, a little to the north, date from 1825, when the monk Zotik obtained permission to start a new church and the services of master-builder Dimitur Sofiyaliyata, master-builder Kolya Ficheto, master-artist Zahari Zograf (1849-51) and others, who saw a potent symbol in this monastery, in its sublime situation glowing red-tiled below the Belyakovski Cliffs overhanging the Yantra, the railway line, and the sliver of road. You need to know that the revolutionary hero-martyr Vasil Levski hid here and in the caves nearby, and that the monastery sheltered and nursed Russian troops in the War of Liberation. The overwhelming impression is of mediaeval art and architecture, but in fact Preobrazhenski dates from the time of the Colt revolver and Darwin's discoveries on Galapagos. Zahari's 'Wheel of Life' adopts the age-old imagery of teaching the illiterate, admonishing them to use time wisely, for it is soon gone. Zahari's 'Last Judgement' could be studied for its iconography alone: we see here the people of Turnovo in 19th-century dress, Patriarch Euthymius of Turnovo, Sv. Ivan Rilski and Russian saints such as Boris and Gleb. His typically unequivocal morality appears in his depiction of sinners in Hell: not only thieves, traitors, adulterers, smugglers and witches, but also millers (then notorious for giving short measure in flour), and innkeepers, disreputably inclined to fleece customers, water wine or overcharge. The esonarthex has a portrait of Zahari Zograf, and another of Levski. Roses bloomed in the monastery garden, their tender fragrance suddenly suppressing pervasive *Lindenduft*. On these slopes, even more abruptly than at Turnovo itself, subsidence nags the spirit, and empties the maintaining purse. Scaffolding braced the Transfiguration against fresh shocks, and will always be required: crutches for the aged ailing. The underground chapel of S. Andrew (1834) recently vanished in a tremor. Only five monks remain in these shattered premises, shored up for the time being. The women's section of the church is decorated with paintings of female martyrs such as Catherine and Barbara, as well as Cyril and Methodius, those presiding geniuses of Bulgarian religious faith. For the monks, pilgrims had left presents (shirts, napkins) hanging near the candelabra, sputtering candles needed at noon to dissipate ancient darkness. The presents for the monks are not always needed, and those surplus to requirements are auctioned off to the faithful on feast-days, the monks using such proceeds for their keep.

Across the Dervent Gorge you can just make out the red tiles of the Patriarchal Monastery, equally isolated in appearance, but actually just as easy of road access, on the other side of the Yantra, 5 km off the road from Turnovo to Arbanasi. During the reconstruction of the 17th-century church, an inscription was found dating the original monastery to 1073, during the Byzantine period, when the hesychast Theodosius of Turnovo settled here. It earned the honorific 'patriarchal' when Euthymius (whom the Bulgarians call Eftimi) established himself in this secluded corner below limestone crags about 1370. If you have some time to spare you can explore cells and grottoes in the rock face carved by hermits choosing the path of solitude. The Ottomans ransacked the monastery and massacred its monks, but one elusive, persistent monk after another maintained the tenuous identity of this shrine until its best restoration, under Master Fichev (affectionately known as 'Ficheto'), in 1847, a church with two domes and paintings by Zahari Zograf. This masterwork crashed into the valley and river after the 1913 earthquake, but workmen are now slowly and patiently restoring it to its pre-Fichev plans, with three domes. When I met the only nun (the former monastery had long since become a convent), she pointed over the radiant, sunwashed chasm, and explained that here anyone could live and die in perfect peace. She herself came from a Romanian convent in 1945, spending the next three years at Sv. Nikola in Arbanasi before arriving at the Convent of the Holy Trinity ('Sveta Troitsa') more than forty years before. Her round black bonnet held her hair in place while gardening; a metal buckle on a wide belt held her lightweight black cassock firm. Sister Evdokia introduced me to her black and white cat and tame deer, called Adam (the first male allowed into the convent in many years, apart from workmen restoring the church). Adam's mother had been killed on the main road in the valley, and the orphan had been rescued and brought for tending to Evdokia. There is no other nun to keep her company, among her oranges, quinces, olives, and lemon trees, but she keeps fish in a tank, enough running water and well-water, and kind women come from Turnovo once in a while with gifts of food, or soap and suchlike. A male watchman ensures her security, and she sent her greetings with me to Sister Pavlina at Arbanasi.

Arbanasi
Where to find Sister Pavlina? I drove into Arbanasi and was told of

two convents: Sveti Nikola (where Evdokia had once resided) and the Assumption of the Virgin, both once inside the town boundaries but now isolated, with the shrinking of the population as they migrate from the museum atmosphere and into the city of Turnovo 4 km away. The Assumption's church is a renewal of 1680, with two narthexes and a large chapel dedicated to the Holy Trinity. The frescoes date from 1762, when the church and chapel were restored. A few icons are attributed to artists of the Tryavna school: Tsanyu Stefanov (1816-1888) and his son Tsanyu. I found Pavlina at Sveti Nikola, and marvelled at her perfect English. In the world Pavlina Dimitrova, she originated from a village near Tolbuhin, and she took early retirement. Just four years ago she had been making reservations for British tourists at Golden Sands, but now her only guiding duties were as the welcoming nun at Sv. Nikola. Her convent, once a monastery, existed as early as the Asenid dynasty of the Second Bulgarian State, but suffered badly in 1393, being rebuilt only in 1680, and after many vicissitudes abandoned in 1798, then rescued by Zotik of the Transfiguration Monastery. The present neo-classical iconostasis is arranged in the Russian Orthodox manner, with S. John the Baptist and S. Nicholas on the same level as Christ. The Bulgarian style is to place an icon of the church's patron saint in the third place on the left next to the Virgin. Russian icons are almost entirely covered with silver or gold, leaving only the painted faces and hands visible. Bulgarian icons occasionally have silver or gold covering haloes or hands, but the rest of the image remains visible.

Arbanasi is much more than its monasteries however; according to one theory it was originally settled by Hellenised Albanians fleeing after the failure of the Kastriotis rebellion of 1466. At all events, Arbanasi reached its apogee of a thousand houses in the 17th-18th centuries, the main activity being trade in livestock, supplying soap manufacturers, butchers and provisioners, tanners, tailors and furriers. Caravans of forty to fifty horses each wended along trade routes to Romania, Hungary and Italy, to Poland and Russia, and of course to Istanbul, Baghdad and Persia. The decline caused by pillaging, plague, and finally the Crimean War (1853-6) ended Arbanasi's prosperity, and incidentally diminished Turnovo's too, for that was the market-place where Arbanasi traders sold silks and spices brought back from the Orient. On Fridays a lively market brought craftsmen and farmers from miles around.

On Sundays the notables of the village (*chorbajis*) and their richly-attired wives (*kokonas*) would make their stately way to any one of five churches and two monasteries, accompanied by servants. Neighbours would take coffee in their homes or promenade near the two majestic fountains: the Bazaar Fountain (17th century) inscribed in Osmanli Turkish, and Kokoni Fountain (1786) erected by Mehmet Said Agha. Two hundred metres beyond Kokoni Fountain stands the oldest and most extraordinary church of Arbanasi: the Nativity of Christ, sonorous with liturgical chant from a hidden tape-recorder. Dimitrov and Draganova's book on the village dates the church buildings and frescoes to the first half of the 17th cen-

Arbanasi. Turkish Fountain

tury, but scientists have recently uncovered even earlier frescoes, of the 1590s, below the major sequence with over a thousand figures, of the period around 1638. A side gallery with stone benches once used to feed pilgrims has a men's section and women's section and gives on to a Chapel of S. John the Baptist with 17th-century murals of the saint's life damaged by the earthquake of December 1986, epicentred at Strazhitsa. The tomb of the donor *chorbaji* Georgi is accompanied by his portrait and those of other donors: Kiratsa, Stoina, Stoiko, Stamo and Niku. A Last Supper painted above the altar belongs to that rare genre with Jesus present in each of two halves. Just inside the door of the men's section I found a moving version of the decapitation of S. John the Baptist. The women's section is fascinating for its gallery of ancient philosophers wearing haloes: Galen, Aristotle, Plato, Plutarch, Solon, Archimedes, even Homer and Jesus in bizarre juxtaposition. The church is now a secular museum, without religious services, so it is permitted to pass beyond the iconostasis, with a Virgin as usual in the apse and a Christ Pantocrator above your head. The Burial of Christ is signed by the artist Ivan Popovich of Elena and dated 1821. Icons on the iconostasis, all inscribed in Greek, deal with the Creation of Man, the snake tempting Adam having a human head.

At the southern limit of the village is the second church in Arbanasi, dedicated to the Archangels Michael and Gabriel, and built in about 1600. It is the largest in the village, with an imposing narthex and a dome concealed by the roof. The paintings date from 1761. Sv. Dimitur, in the centre of Arbanasi, was the parish church after Liberation, but the 1913 earthquake caused fatal damage to the frescoes of 1612 and 1794. Sv. Georgi (1661) offers greater rewards, covering earlier paintings with murals of 1710 executed by Hristo and Stoyo. The icon of S. George is by the Tryavna artist Dimitur Kanchev (1839). Sv. Atanas (1637) at the northern end of Arbanasi was a church frequented by the poor, and is thus smaller and less richly decorated, though some of the frescoes of 1728 by Tsoyo and Nedyo are distinguished in their provincial way, epitomising for instance in the Last Judgement the antique vision of a world still divided quite simply into good and evil. Monastic cells are found in the courtyards of Arbanasi's walled churchyards, so that a monk might seek even greater loneliness from the world and its wickedness. A magpie rose like a soft Concorde from the corner of Sveti Atanas's compound. Beyond the wall sheepbells tinkled comfortably. A Balkantourist Mercedes drew up as I arrived at the largest mansion in Arbanasi to survive intact: the Konstantsalieva House, which belonged to the wife of Dimitraki Bey called Kokona Sultana and built like a fortress for her early in the 18th century following the great fire of 1798. Her husband was a dealer in sheep and cattle, and their marvellous home has been preserved as an Ethnographic Museum. A sentry would have sat before the main door, itself protected within a walled compound. You then climb stairs from the ground floor built of massive stone blocks to withstand tremors, and enter the wooden upper floor, with carved ceilings and low benches round the walls. The summer guest room allows highland breezes to waft through, while the winter bedroom has heavy sliding shutters on the windows, and a great swivel wooden bed above the tiled floor. The sitting-room's fireplace wall abuts on the bedroom to diffuse heat economically. A concealed doorway provides a means of rapid escape in the case of sudden raids in time of upheaval: a feature of all *chorbaji* homes. The merchant's office, spacious and comfortable, is laid out for coffee over negotiations. A kitchen (*hachevo*) and servant's passage is situated close to the toilet (a triangular hole in the floor) and bathroom. Doorways are decorated in plaster. Off the reception room I found a forty-day isolation room for the mother and her new-born child. The summer bedroom faces east (for coolness and brightness) and has a charmingly ornate plaster frieze and ceiling. Another secret door let the family run for refuge down a wooden staircase, across the lawn and through a door into the neighbouring property. But none of these precautions prevailed against such emergencies as bandit raids, general warfare such as the terrible War of Liberation (1877-8), and the awesome quake of 1913.

Two other houses are opened for visitors: the Hajiliev (near Market Fountain), with its magnificent wooden doors; and the Kandilarov, sunning itself below a peerless blue sky, with carved wooden ceilings both simple and exquisite. If you find Tryavna the most unobtrusively lovely of Bulgarian towns, cosily domestic in contrast to Nesebur's majesty thrust like a loaded spring into the Black Sea, then you will be enchanted by Arbanasi, an example to all concerned with conservation of how best to realise a past dream in present materials.

Nicopolis

Nicopolis ad Istrum seems to have been established by Trajan in 106, after his conquest of the Dacians, in a most unpromising situation exposed on all sides. But if you recall that the Romans held Momina Krepost and all other significant Veliko Turnovo hill fortresses, this is a reasonably logical site for a garrison of occupation on the crossroads from the Danube to Constantinople, and from the Black Sea to the west. Bulgarian archaeologists working here have uncovered season by season not only a covered theatre and a reservoir fed by an aqueduct more than 20 km long, but a great forum with many temples and a street system of blocks familiar to all those who have enjoyed Timgad and Leptis, Ostia and Pompei. Devastated in about 251, the revived city was ravaged again by the Slavs and Avars in the early seventh century, so in effect we have two cities: Early and Late Roman. The second century enjoyed a durable peace in Thrace, where many fine public buildings witnessed Roman glory and confidence. Its wealth can be judged from a letter of 198 from Emperor Septimius Severus thank-

Nicopolis ad Istrum. Ruined bull frieze beside cardo maximus

ing the citizens for a munificent gift. In its grid of paved cardo-decumanus and lesser straight streets intersecting the colony, the city was endowed with a magistrates' council-chamber, basilica, market-place, theatre, baths.

Visigoths occupied the lands around Nicopolis in 347-8; it became a bishopric in the 5th and 6th centuries; and was abandoned only after the invasions of the next century.

The early Roman city was abandoned in the 3rd century, and another fortification constructed to the south, thus allowing two adjacent excavation programmes to be conducted simultaneously by a Bulgarian team in the early city and by a British team in the later, beginning in 1985. The British expedition found the defensive enclosure of nearly six hectares had been protected by twenty towers projecting fifteen metres from the curtain walls, as large as any in the Roman Empire, and matching those at Kula (Castra Martis), 32 km west of Vidin, close to the present Yugoslav border. At Kula, a tower stands 16 metres high even today. In this period, walls consisted of roughly-hewn limestone blocks, bonded with soil and with a mud-brick superstructure, whereas the Early Roman city's materials were preeminently tile, stone and mortar. The Late Roman style may seem primitive, but Andrew Poulter has found similar techniques today in the nearby village of Nikyup, and they are provenly effective for keeping warm in winter and keeping cool in summer. Amongst impressive stone and tile buildings, a Christian basilica excavated in 1986 has been dated to the 5th or 6th centuries, and a second was found in 1988. The Late Roman city clearly reused some building elements from its predecessor (columns and architraves for example), much as the later city was robbed by successive waves of occupants. Later Roman Nicopolis seems to have had no paved streets and no civic buildings for drama or gladiatorial games: it seems instead to have concentrated on faith in the Christian church and its almost impregnable defensive walls and towers. We have therefore moved, in this distant imperial outpost, from supreme confidence in the might of Rome to an early mediaeval trust in castle and Christ.

Every road out of Turnovo leads to beauty and adventure, whether you take the southeastern way to Elena, with its beautiful house of 1710 once inhabited by Ilarion Makariopolski (1812-75) and now a Museum of National Revival, via the Plakovski Monastery of the Prophet Elijah; or the southeastern way over the Republican Pass via the Monastery of the Virgin's Nativity at Kilifarevo, with Master Ficheto's Church of Sv. Dimitur (1840).

Dryanovo

I headed southwestward to Gabrovo, making detours to Dryanovo Monastery and the museum-village of Bozhentsi, a favourite haunt of artists and honeymoon couples. Dryanovo (the place of dogwood, as Turnovo is the place of thorns, and Gabrovo the place of hornbeams) enjoys fame as the birthplace of Kolyo Ficheto, photos of whose work we have already seen in Turnovo's Ethnographic Museum. The Fichev Museum (closed on Mondays) can be seen morning and afternoon near the bus-stop for Turnovo or Gabrovo, though if you want only the monastery you should stay on the southbound bus. Dryanovo Monastery was established in 1190, during the Second Bulgarian State, but was repeatedly destroyed in reprisal for dissent by monks who allied themselves with rebels against Muslim rule. After the April Rising of 1876 which failed so disastrously, rebels led by the monk Hariton, Bacho Kiro and Petur Parmakov pitted their few hundreds against thousands of Turkish soldiers dispatched from Shumen, and held out for nine days, but the monastery was gutted by fire and what you see now is a sympathetic reconstruction, built in a curve of the Dryanovski river that flows far below immense limestone crags, the whole area green with dogwood. Dryanovo has always been famed for its silk industry and vine-yards; the latter are being reintroduced after a terrible plague of phylloxera. The monastery museum celebrates the martyrdom of Dryanovo's rebels, and you can ask to see icons such as a splendid gold-haloed Christ of 1816 by Simeon Tsonyuv from Gabrovo. Half a km away is a palaeolithic cave, named for the poet-teacher Bacho Kiro hanged for rebellion. A two-star Balkantourist hotel near the monastery provides ideal relaxation off the beaten track.

Bozhentsi

If you find the heights of Rozhen, at the end of any motorable road, as infinitely enchanting as I did, then you will find the wooded slopes of Bozhentsi equally ravishing, yet only eighteen km from the busy, noisy industrial town of Gabrovo. Bozhentsi seems to doze in a permanent siesta, a compound of tangible flowers and misty legends, one of which tells of its origin. After the fall of

Veliko Turnovo to the Turks, Christian Bulgarians found themselves overtaxed and deprived of many civil liberties, so they would eventually drag themselves away from persecution and hope for a better life elsewhere. One boyar's widow from Turnovo uprooted herself with her nine sons and their flocks of sheep to seek refuge in the mountains. Each morning the flocks would wander off, returning each evening well fed. Curious about their source of satisfaction, Widow Bozhena decided to follow them and found them grazing by springs of fresh water in fertile pastures. She built a house there for herself and for each of her sons, and the great family prospered. Small and isolated as it was, Bozhentsi grew in affluence throughout the 18th century on its wool, sheepskin, honey and beeswax, trading with Romania and Hungary, Italy and Austria. Artisans prospered in metal, embroidery, weaving and dyeing and their houses grew in size and opulence. A hundred lovely homes have been restored, among them those of Doncho Popa and Kalcho Drenkov, opened as museums of crafts and architecture. I found candles being made in the ancient manner, and was invited to visit the school. The whole vision is surrounded by dense woods, with the belfry of the Church of the Prophet Elijah soaring above tiled roofs like a lighthouse over a port.

Gabrovo

Now it is time for Gabrovo, and its House of Humour and Satire. Gabrovians are to the rest of Bulgaria what Kerrymen are to the rest of Ireland; foolishness personified, and Aberdonians to the rest of Scotland: meanness taken to delirious lengths. A Gabrovian asked his wife about the temperature in the room. 'Fifteen degrees', she replied. 'And outside?' 'Twenty degrees'. 'Then open the window and let in the other five'.

Two Gabrovians were congratulating each other on the state lottery results. One said, 'I save fifty stotinki from every draw by not buying a ticket'. His companion said, 'That's marvellous, so you can stand me a drink'. A Gabrovian urchin enquired of a bread-ring vendor, 'How much does the hole in the bread ring cost, uncle?'. 'Nothing, sonny', was the answer. 'Then I'll have the one with the biggest hole'. A new road was built to shorten the distance to Sevlievo by eight km. A notice was put up on the new road out of Gabrovo: 'This is the short cut to Sevlievo. If you can't read, take the old road'. One day a Gabrovian lad missed school, and next day his teacher asked the reason. 'Mother washed my trousers, so I couldn't come', replied the boy. A few days later he was again absent. His teacher now called his bluff, because no Gabrovian mother would wash clothes that frequently. 'I was about to come, sir, but as I passed your house, I saw your trousers on the clothes-line'.

I lunched at the traditional 19th-century inn called Strano Priemnitsa ('Strangers' Reception') at 17 Ul. Opalchenska, and stayed at the three-star Hotel Balkan at 14 Ul. E. Manolov. At the inn two strangers, true to form, joined me at my table, and – helpless with laughter – one of them explained how he had fooled the railway company. He wanted to take the train to Turnovo and back the day before without paying, so he phoned up his friend in Turnovo and asked him to go to the station and buy two platform tickets. The Gabrovian then bought one platform ticket to get on to the station at Gabrovo, joined his friend at the agreed time on Turnovo platform, they both left the station after handing in their tickets, and did the same thing in reverse in the evening.

The short fat stranger gobbled his laughter at the ingenuity like a turkey not yet advised of his destination that Christmas. The thin, swarthy storyteller, observing the success of his tale, expanded his chest and puffed out his cheeks like the West Wind in a fairy-tale, then continued masticating his *bombar*, that home-made sausage peculiar to Gabrovo. 'Now you', beamed short-and-fat, in my direction. I had just finished my shish kebab and white bread sprinkled with herbs, so I pushed my empty skewers to the side of the table and began. 'I once lived in a country of the Middle East where alcohol was prohibited, but diplomatic bags are immune from inspection and discreet packing-cases sent through customs addressed to diplomats are passed without remark. Unfortunately, one such heavy case marked 'Furniture: Fragile' was dropped by a crane and smashed on the airport tarmac. A diplomat for whom the consignment was intended received a phone call from the Head of Customs at the Airport asking him to come and collect the goods fairly quickly. 'I'm afraid to say, sir,' confessed the official, 'that your furniture is leaking'.

Gabrovo's House of Humour and Satire was founded in 1972 as the Louvre of laughter, the Prado of pratfalls. A satirical theatre opened in 1984, and a biennial festival celebrates cartoons, comedy films, TV funnies and humorous books, with a four-yearly national festival every May culminating in a carnival. You can take tea in a 'half-bar' near the theatre. Captions are in Bulgarian and English, ruefully acknowledged as the capital language of fun, though at the bookstall Soviet tourists were ransacking the shelves for the ever-popular Russian edition of *Gabrovo Anecdotes* selected by Stefan Furtunov and Petur Prodanov (Sofia, 1985). Ten galleries are devoted to permanent and changing exhibitions from Bulgaria and abroad, including humour and satire in painting, cartoons, graphics, witty photographs, 'The Roots of Gabrovian Humour', masks, and murals. The Czech artist František Dostal has drawn a bridegroom with a bride on one arm and his double bass on the other. The New Zealander Bob Darroch shows a palaeolithic mother in a cave rubbing out the animals which her weeping son has just painted on the walls. Laihia, the Finnish equivalent of Gabrovo, was honoured during my visit by a special display. The people of Laihia have invented a ladle with a hole in it for dieters and a mousetrap both new and economical, without cheese. The mouse shakes its head in disgust and cuts its throat on a saw.

Yet Gabrovo is not only about fun and games: it is also an industrial town, the Manchester of Bulgaria, and has a National Museum of Education in the Aprilov Secondary School built by Kolyo Ficheto (1835), emulating the Richelieu Lycée in Odessa. As well as a planetarium, Gabrovo has the interesting Church of the Holy Virgin (1865) and a District Art Gallery (10 Ulitsa Kiril i Metodi) with splendid icons by masters of the Tryavna school, works by the Gabrovian Hristo Tsokev (1847-83), and other paintings by Jan Mrkvička, Jaroslav Vesin, and Zlatyu Boyajiev. Dechko's House, a girls' school from 1869, is nowadays the local History Museum.

Etura
Eight km south of Gabrovo off the road to Shipka Pass you can visit one of the most fascinating and picturesque of open-air ethnographic museums anywhere in the world: Etura, beyond which is the Sokolski Monastery.

Situated on the banks of the Sivek brook, it consists of a number of typical houses brought here or reconstructed to give a view of a National Revival village of about 1860, with present-day craftsmen. I bought a sheep's bell (now used by my wife to summon me downstairs to meals) from Ivan for 3 leva 40 stotinki; a candlestick from the village shop cost 1.50 leva, and other visitors in the shop found a copper dish for 28 leva, a woollen jacket for 76 leva and a fur hat for 28 leva. A fountain was built in 1843, the fulling-mill dates from the 1850s, and the water-wheel from 1874. A quality of seriousness, of duty, hung in the air. We enjoyed ourselves in a decorous, permitted fashion. Nobody stomped a foot in a quick flamenco flounce, or ran with heart-bursting exuberance, pointlessly and with shining eyes. Never mind: we shall live fully again in the *Odyssey*, or *The Brothers Karamazov*, one of these days. Marya Miteva sold me two of her tasty simiti, glazed buns of chick-pea flour sold piping hot, and I bought halva before taking hot chocolate in Motko's verandahed coffee-house. Make sure you visit Sako's House (1850), and the contemporary dyeing workshop. You can stay at the Etura Inn, opened in 1981.

Sokolski Monastery
The road to the Gabrovski-Sokolski Monastery, as it is named over the door, winds lonely and wooded, secluded like the Secret Garden at Hampton Court. Now a convent with six nuns, it was founded in 1833 by Archimandrite Yosif (in the world Sokolski), a monk from Troyanski, like his companion Agapi. A tiny wooden church below the main church is situated next to a barred graveyard with the grave of the Nun Makrina (1921-1986). Niches in the rock may have been hacked out by early hermits. The main church (1834) was frescoed in 1862 by a priest called Pavel and his son Nikola from Shipka; the icons are attributed to Zahari Zograf and the Tryavna School. In 1836 Yosif established a school for children of the surrounding villages. The eight-spouted fountain is by Kolyo Ficheto. A pine-tree in the courtyard, planted by Yosif, still wafts its scent over the roses and lawns. A nun emerged with a saucer of milk and food for a clamour of cats, their tails raised to match their urgent yowling. I gave a lift to two decrepit old women in black whom I mistook at first for nuns but found to be domestic helps from the nunnery. One I dropped off very soon; the other regaled me all the way back to Etura with her life story and doings. It takes her an hour to walk to the nunnery, and lifts are rare. She is 73, one of six girls and five boys: now only she and one brother survive. She married in the village next to the nunnery, where a new building has recently been made for a museum celebrating Vasil Levski and a certain Voivod Tsanki Dyustabanov who led the Gabrovo rebel detachment in the weeks following the April Rising of 1876. Kip-

Sokolski Monastery (now a convent) in winter

riana is the name of the abbess at Sokolski, and she knows the name of Mihaila... I did not press her for the other names, because it is usual to exaggerate the numbers of monks and nuns for some unknown reason, and if there were only two nuns at Sokolski Convent, I did not want to press my passenger for four imaginary names. The cabbage harvest was *in* at Etura, piled high on trucks. It was 5 November, and snow began to fall, appallingly early by Bulgarian reckoning, then faster, firmly, densely, evanishing on the grass and tarmac, then in the second act slowly settling, as if making up its mind about an early winter. I shivered as my bent passenger wished me long life: 'another hundred years!' and slammed the door shut again, waving as I sped off towards Tryavna, snow faltering in the fading afternoon light, then gathering strength in the third act with nightfall, streaming into my headlamps, cheerily, ebulliently suicidal.

Tryavna

Dark swept up like a swift witch on a broomstick, and I slowed the car on the narrow roads for safety, as snow blanketed my visibility to a few yards, so that it took forty minutes to cover the twenty km from Gabrovo to Tryavna. Once there, I left my car in Ulitsa Georgi Dimitrov and walked up the snowy slope to the two-star Hotel Ralitsa, which looked deserted, but was in fact fully booked, awaiting groups delayed like me by unexpectedly heavy snowstorms. I had reserved a room on the top floor, to enjoy spectacular views of the Balkan Range, glittering angelic white on that most magical of evenings. I had looked forward to this day since I had studied, with increasing astonishment at my ignorance, Atanas Bozhkov's *Tryavna Art School* (Sofia, 1983), bought at a second-hand bookshop. Why had I never come across, in histories of art, and architecture, this revelation of a village inhabited by hundreds of painters, sculptors, woodcarvers, master-builders? It takes Bozhkov 237 pages to describe and illustrate the most outstanding works of art, windows, balconies, and tiled roofs of the National Revival period in Tryavna and owing to Tryavna masters in nearby Elena, Zheravna, Bozhentsi. There is nowhere like Tryavna anywhere in the world, and I longed to see the subject of Atanas Bozhkov's illustrated album. The foyer of Hotel Ralitsa displays photographs of houses and museums open to the public. The most important, for a visitor out of tune with Tryavna who restricts time there to a minimum, are the Slaveikov and Daskalov Houses in the centre and the Icon Museum above the village, open from about 8 to noon and 2 to 5.30. These same hours apply to the Slaveikov School (now an art gallery), the Ivan Popdimitrov House and the Kalinchev House. On Mondays and Tuesdays the Angel Kunchev and Raikov Houses are closed. The Angelov and Pop Yovcho Houses are opened only on request (tel. 2115, 2426). The churches of the Archangel Michael and S. George must certainly be seen for their icons and wood-carving.

What is the Bulgarian National Revival that reaches its artistic apogee with the hundreds of artists connected with Tryavna? From 1700 to 1760s churches are built and self-confidence grows in craftsmen deriving from guilds and a mastery of professional handbooks. The second stage consolidates existing schools and forms new schools from the 1770s to about 1800, with the growth of individuality and new groupings. From the end of the 1790s to the 1850s the religious icon-painters achieve their apogee and begin to decline as motifs are endlessly repeated without fresh ideas. From the 1850s to the Liberation in the 1870s, secular genres such as contemporary portraits and landscapes compete for supremacy with religious art.

The artists of Tryavna are identified with the National Revival from the earliest times; the hundreds of masters and guild-members worked locally and as far afield as Mount Athos, Vidin, Sliven and Smolyan. One hundred and forty buildings in Tryavna are listed as of architectural merit, and one family (the Vitanovs) produced about fifty artists and craftsmen distinguished, according to the silk merchant Haji Hristo Daskalov, 'by their exceptional talent: the men dressed in expensive apparel and carried jewelled weapons; the women's finery was even more gorgeous than that of the wealthy merchants' wives and they never engaged in agricultural work'. Daskalov advised, 'Give your daughter to the Vitanovs, but don't take one from them'. Some twenty members of the Zahariev became icon-painters, and sixteen Venkovs. Icon-painters would work in harmony with wood-carvers and master-builders, for a commission to create a church would often be seen as a single unified collaboration, and some painters also carved wood, as did some masons. When we see Papa Vitan's iconostasis for the Church of the Archangels in Arbanasi, we recognise the master's integration of his own icons (and those of other artists) with the superb panels, pilasters, lunettes and whorls, the whole concept unified with carved flowers he had noted in the fields of the Balkan Mountains.

It may have been Tsar Kaloyan who commissioned Tryavna's Church of the Archangel Michael, and the churches of the Prisovski and Dryanovo monasteries, but in any case we know that descendants of Turnovians fled the Asenid capital to refuges in the Balkans, where throughout the Ottoman period Tryavna remained a 'defiant zone', rejecting Islam and refusing to allow Ottoman families to live in the town. By a firman of the Sultan, Tryavna was exempt from paying taxes, as a result of its nomination as a settlement of soldiers and sentries safeguarding the road between Rose Valley and the Danube at Ruse. One consequence was that other nationalistic Bulgarians left their suffering districts to create a nucleus of patriotism and Bulgarian consciousness that would lead to rebellion against the Turkish yoke. Vasil Levski visited Tryavna eight times, protected by the master-builder Penyu Oshanetsa. The intellectual Petko Slaveikov and his son the poet Pencho promoted national awareness through literary freedom. Angel Kunchev (1850-72) became a revolutionary inspired by Levski and shot himself rather than betray his secrets, dying with the words 'Long live Bulgaria!'

Old Tryavna is a narrow settlement on both sides of the Trevnenska river, more of a stream perhaps, giving a pleasantly rural appearance to streets close-set with courtyard-style walled houses, two storeys high, with heavy stone tiles to bear the weight of winter snows. Generous eaves, graceful wooden balconies and oriel windows shelter passers-by from summer heat and winter rains. The unity of old Tryavna, sensitively retained by local civic authorities, proves that a sense of aesthetic beauty ran perennially through each

Tryavna. The Trevnenka River frozen over

family like the stream through the town-centre. All is fitting, simple, solid, enduring. Whitewash renewed annually gives a sense of hygienic sobriety. The high church tower (1814) relates harmoniously to that bridge (1845), that old schoolhouse (1837), and the Church of the Archangel Michael (1819). The eighteen-room schoolhouse called after Slaveikov was devoted, during my visit, to a disappointing exhibition by the brothers Kazakov: the painter Dimitur (b. 1933), who fails to evoke originality in 'Diana' and such easy symbols as a threefold fish/horse/bird, cut apple, and sun; and the sculptor Nikola, who belongs to the 'hew-it-out-of-a-tree-trunk' fraternity, and spends much of his time on naive low-reliefs of limited decorative value. Much more interesting is the Slaveikov House-Museum, honouring Petko Slaveikov, who translated the Bible into Bulgarian and thus played much the same rôle in the creation of literary Bulgarian as Luther in modern High German or the translators of the Authorized Version in modern literary English. His museum at 50 Ulitsa Dimitrov is in a house constructed in traditional style in 1830. On the verandah or *chardak* you can see the loom used by Irina Slaveikova, when she wanted to weave *en plein air*. The living-room has an open hearth, with low round table and simple half-moon stools, with characteristic bench-seating. The 'Irinkina-Window' is so-called because that is where his melancholy wife would sit to await Petko's return from Tsarigrad, as the Bulgarians called Istanbul. The adjacent bedroom contains the original table at which the young poet Pencho, born in this home in 1866, first learned to read and write. Petko had arrived in Tryavna in 1849 as a young teacher, and the town's quiet, cultured atmosphere (like Tübingen, Salamanca or Poitiers) encouraged his poetic muse, publishing in 1852, before his marriage to Irina, daughter of Ivancho Raikov, a wealthy merchant who gave the young couple this home as a wedding-gift. It was to remain their home until 1876. His son Pencho started collecting folksongs from his mother, his friends, relatives, and people he met in wanderings through the mountain countryside. He lived here until his tenth year, when he moved to Stara Zagora. Pencho, founder of the National Theatre and National Library, fell into the Maritsa river when it was frozen, and suffered partial paralysis as a result until his death in 1912. His significance in Bulgarian literature is that, like his friend Kracholov, writing under the pen-name of Peyo Yavorov, he repudiated Vazov's nationalistic bias, and sought to 'extricate the human from the Bulgarian', like his hero Nietzsche elevating human personality to the superhuman, and stressing the myth of Prometheus: man challenging the divine. Pencho travelled widely, unlike most Bulgarian writers, and came to sympathise with literary strands from German idealism, Russian scepticism, and English romanticism. His 'Song of Blood' on the April Rising is still quoted today as an exceptional contribution to Bulgarian patriotic literature. I made a note to see his house-museum in Sofia, next to that of Yavorov.

The silk-merchant Haji Hristo Daskalov commissioned a house from the master-builder Dimitur Oshanetsa and took possession in 1808. It has two storeys and two symmetrical wings connected by a spacious verandah with staggering views of the mountains, and its opulence, combined with a central position in old Tryavna, made it an obvious choice for the Woodcarving Museum, to celebrate the art of the panelled ceiling, picture-frame, shepherd's crook, walking stick and such craft masterpieces as the free-standing soldiers in the Gencho Marangosov Collection. Every door and cupboard is carved, and like most of the Tryavna houses, one or more ceilings have a flaming sun carved in wood set in the centre. The merchant Nikola Raikov was the original owner of the Raikov House, started in 1846 by master Dimitur Sergyuv. On the ground floor stands the first iron bed to arrive in Tryavna: it came from Vienna, and one can almost hear the grumbles of disapproval from wood-sculptors. 'How can we earn a living if people are starting to buy these ugly iron beds?' Elsewhere, one need not worry: this classical late-Revival home creaks satisfyingly, and wood is carved and crafted in most rooms, from cupboards to a charming cradle. A wooden bed opens to reveal a drawer for the sleepers' boots. Fireplaces warm two rooms at once, for instance kitchen and bedroom.

In Pop Yovcho's house, once the property of a local historian, I found a permanent exhibition devoted to the painter Ivan Hristov, with landscapes of Balchik, Plovdiv, Lovech and Tryavna; and to the young sculptor Borislav Rusinov.

The Church of the Archangel Michael (1819) exemplifies the Tryavna School's best traits. Twenty cm of snow had covered the town overnight, and everywhere in the churchyard I trod on virgin snow, crackling soft and stable underfoot. Inside the church that Sunday morning, Church Slavonic was being chanted in a near monotone. The service had started in the dark, and would continue for a long while yet, as day knocked on the windows until someone noticed and glanced out. The service receded inexpressibly inward, however. Five celebrants allowed the priest to carry the liturgy onward, candles flickering and spluttering on a round candelabrum. One of the men stood near the throne and assisted with the service. An old woman, four feet ten inches tall and clasped in black like a vertical corpse, half-whispered, half-intoned a message for the other side. A man turned round to look at me, his dark moustache twitching nervously, then reverted to face the iconostasis, where icons of Virgin and Child and Archangel Michael gazed at me impassively with the rigidity of fate. What on earth or in heaven are you doing here, they asked? You, who believe in no gods, nor in angels, nor in saints, nor in the efficacy of prayer? What was it Barth said? 'There is no way from us to God – not even a *via negativa* – not even a *via dialectica* nor *paradoxa*. The god who stood at the end of some human way would *not be God*.' I surveyed the five stone columns on both sides, with wooden beams between them. My eyes grew accustomed to the dim light of the three-naved, barrel-vaulted church that had seen so many thousands of hours of worship, while Bulgaria endured in a Muslim empire, a Christian kingdom, and a socialist state. The chanting in Old Bulgarian drugged my mind into a half-state of receptivity; a simple melody threaded on a line that occasionally snagged, in a style that may be connected with the old Greek musical modes. An old couple came in, placed candles in the brass candelabrum, and spoke to each other, as though no words of ordinary language could possibly interrupt the liturgical flow that would expand, extend, run its appointed course, and allow us the grace to live until we came again. I felt insulted that they should natter and gossip while the service continued, but that of course was my secular preoccupation, seeing the process as a concert where the audience should remain dutifully silent. I was wrong again.

My Renault's diesel fuel had frozen, and after several frustrating attempts to start the car, generously aided by neighbours leaving their warm homes on a bitterly-cold Sunday morning to bring me out kettles of boiling water to thaw the fuel tank, I was offered a lift in a Skoda to the Icon Museum. The catalogue of the Gabrovo exhibition called *The Tryavna School of Painting* (Sofia, 1980) explains some of the innovations of Tryavna artists to mediaeval painting's rigid simplicity. As early as the end of the 18th century, aesthetic qualities of embellishment are added; gold backgrounds are replaced by natural greens and blues, and old hieratic lines soften to human curves, gentle eyes and rosy complexions, reducing the severity of the icon and increasing its tenderness. We have lost the vast majority of Bulgarian icons through fire, Islamic iconoclasm, and the so-called banditry period (1780-1810) when *kurjalis* (plains-robbers) and *daalis* (mountain-robbers) disbanded from the Turkish army roamed the countryside, looting, pillaging, and causing whole villages to empty. Yet a census reveals that 648 icons still exist in the environs of Tryavna. The gallery's central hall shows icons of the Vitanov family across two centuries. Papa Vitan the Elder, also a woodcarver, is known by only one surviving work: his 'Christ' of 1798 which manages to harmonise the ecclesiastical requirement of 'abstract universality' while suggesting an individuality embracing both the serene and the agitated. The original is found with his brother Simeon Tsonyuv's 'S. Nicholas' of 1798 in the annex to the National Art Gallery in Sofia, both obviously intended for the same iconostasis and both characterised by the same small shadowed eyes, with the same blue background lightening towards the lower edge. Simeon daringly scatters stylized flowers over the saint's red robe, but the face, with symmetrically furrowed brow, and symmetrical hair, moustache and beard looks back to ascetic forebears.

In 1821-2 Papa Vitan Koyuv worked on the iconostasis of the Church of the Archangel Michael in Tryavna, and painted several of its main icons, such as the magnificent 'Virgin Hodigitria' which seems to have been based on the face of a contemporary Bulgarian woman, elevating motherly joy to all-consuming compassion, mystical as well as human. The colour tones take on flesh tints. One small room is devoted to original artists' materials, the preparation of wood, and sketches. The last room deals with the late 19th century, when the tradition fades and dies. The 'S. John the Baptist' at the Church of S. Michael, for example, has a merely folkloric value, and 'Christ as a Shepherd' lies outside the church's canon and outside the bounds of artistic development: senility as reversion to childhood. I asked the lady in charge the original purpose of the gallery. It was considered a healthy spot, so the queen of King Boris had a sanatorium built for children, and the museum opened in 1984 in the premises of the sanatorium chapel.

Stranded like a whale on a snowy beach, my Renault refused to budge, so I gratefully accepted a lift with Nedyalko Iliev from Gabrovo, who offered to take me to Kazanluk, where I could pick up another car from Balkantourist. He told me about the Uzana Hunting Lodge near Gabrovo, where each year three or four hunting parties usually from Austria or West Germany hunt wild boar, deer and bear, and fish in the local dam. Game hunting has increased in Bulgaria with the increase in game itself: roe deer are currently estimated at over 106,000, and red deer numbers have increased in the last decade from 4,000 to more than 8,000. The road above ran grey-black like a gutter below a snowladen roof. Children scooted down gentle slopes on sledges, while their fathers looked on. How good to see these warmly-clad infants shouting with delight, growing up slowly like a brook instead of a waterfall.

Shipka

Nedyalko stopped at the Shipka Freedom Monument, to spend a few quiet minutes at the pass where 6,000 Bulgarians and Russians resisted a mighty Ottoman battering by 27,000 soldiers to crush the Siege of Pleven in 1877. After five thousand Turks and allies had fallen, Russian reinforcements came to aid Bulgarian volunteers and the rest of the Ottomans were finally defeated outside Kazanluk.

Far below the village of Shipka glittered in golden sunlight on snow, and gold too shimmered the little domes on the Memorial Church (1885-1902), paying tribute to the fallen of 1877-8. The Russian architect was A.I. Tomishkov, to a design by Pomerantsev, who was responsible also for the Russian Church and the Alexander Nevski Memorial Church in Sofia. Restored in 1957-9, the church rejoices in the heroism that each succeeding generation fosters ferociously: 'never forgive, never forget'. I found the atmosphere stifling, the vacant air in the silent church gripping me by the throat. Seventeen bells for the church had been cast from bullets found on Shipka Pass, the biggest bell weighing nearly twelve tons. How can the two thousand inhabitants of Shipka village breathe under the weight of such bullets? The very pine-trees whistle for revenge. Thirty-four marble slabs are engraved with the names of soldiers who died: thirty Russian and four Bulgarian; in the crypt another seventeen sarcophagi gaped up at me in mute, rigid blankness. What is to be done? The caretaker shuffled past me, with a slight nod of recognition, or of calm welcome.

Kazanluk

Nedyalko explained my predicament to the receptionist expecting me at the three-star Hotel Kazanluk, and she smiled. 'We already have your replacement car, because the Hotel Ralitsa called Balkantourist here'. Nedyalko stayed to have lunch. News came through of Esperantists from the Warsaw Pact countries visiting Black Sea ports; temperatures of -2°at noon and a snowfall in Sofia of 30 cm overnight; Mrs Thatcher has just left Poland after her official visit; CFKA Sredets of Sofia beat Panathinaikos of Athens in the European Cup-Winners' Cup.

Old Kazanluk revolves around the rail station, but very little is left, and the modern town is largely industrial, textiles, machinery and timber being the major activities in addition to the seasonal rose harvest in late May and early June. Rose-pickers must be ready before dawn to avoid losing the unique fragrance, and two thousand rose petals are required for just one gramme of attar of roses. The rose industry began to export in 1860. Weight for weight, attar of roses costs as much as gold and Bulgaria earns valuable hard currency by exporting 70% of the rose oil used by the cosmetics industry. The Rosarium and Museum are open every day from 8 to 5 between May and October, but I found the research institute gardens anonymous with snow: I might have been in a turnip-field.

In addition to the rose industry, with more than two hundred varieties, Kazanluk has a factory called Bulgarian Rose which produces liqueurs, rose-water, fine jams, and Turkish Delight of subtle fragrance which (I shamefully confess) I bought in considerable bulk from a shop in the town. The annual Rose Festival (usually in the first week of June) is an international event, with folksong, dancing, traditional costume, lunch in marquees and souvenirs shown by craftsmen. The whole Valley of the Roses teems with glorious pinks and reds, an aroma like nectar and ambrosia.

West of Kazanluk spreads the Georgi Dimitrov Dam (1947-55) irrigating over a hundred thousand acres of land between Rose Valley and Stara Zagora. Its waters have drowned the city of Seuthopolis, founded in the 4th century B.C. by a Thracian monarch, Seuth III, who imported olive oil and wine from Thasos. The Thracian city, with walls two metres thick, fell victim to fire late in the 3rd century B.C. The time of Seuthopolis is the period of the celebrated Thracian tomb, in the Türbeh (Turkish Mausoleum) Park northeast of the town. 'Celebrated', because of the three hundred and thirty or so tumuli in Bulgaria, no fewer than thirty-seven are concentrated in the zone between Shipka, Alexandrovo and Vetren, in the middle of which lies Kazanluk. Most of the Bulgarian tumuli are Thracian, though some appear to be Celtic. The Kazanluk tomb, one of the very few with paintings (Muglish is another), was discovered by chance in 1944, and has become a Unesco monument. What is shown now, in order to preserve the original, is a faithful replica of the beehive tomb consisting of a wide rectangular antechamber, a narrow sharp-vaulted passage or *dromos*, and a beehive-domed circular burial chamber adorned with magnificent frescoes of the 4th-century B.C. Could the artist possibly have been a pupil of a great master? We know no surviving work by Apelles, but we do know that he painted Philip and Alexander of Macedon, and this painter must surely have been itinerant since there could hardly have been enough work in the Seuthopolis region for a permanent artist.

The paintings in the *dromos* depict the military exploits of the deceased man, who must have been either a monarch or one of the very highest military rank in the 4th or possibly the second quarter

Kazanluk. Thracian Tomb (4th century B.C.)

of the 3rd century B.C. Quick, vivid brushstrokes delineate horses in combat, and infantry with shields and daggers. The burial chamber itself glows with the red we know from Pompei, as well as ochres, yellows, purples and greens. The subject is the funeral feast of the man and his pensive wife, with a procession of maids and menservants. Husband and wife clasp each other by the wrist: the man's red, the woman's flesh-pink, her white and red robes draped elegantly, parts in shadow. Particularly extraordinary is the quadriga, each horse modelled differently and conveying its own character by a tilt of the head or position of its leg. A stable-boy with hair flowing in the wind attempts to bring them under control. Above the major frieze, three *bigae* race eternally round the inner frieze of the dome. Maidservants offer jewels, a tray and a veil. Menservants present a cup and blow horns in a ritual manner suggesting to me that the artist probably enjoyed initiation into Thracian cult practices; the brilliant marriage of architecture with frieze may even suggest that he had more than a little control over the building he frescoed. Dafina Vasileva has stated that 'conservators have not carried out any restoration work,' so that we can see the frescoes (at least in this faithful replica) in the state left by their creator. The original enjoys a constant microclimate.

The Historical Museum in the centre of Kazanluk, a town of 62,000, is situated beneath the Art Gallery on the corner of Ulitsa Iskra. It shows finds from Seuthopolis amid their context. Greek inscriptions are found near huge wine jars of the type we shall find in the courtyard of Hisarya Museum; Thracian weapons and pottery were traded for Greek vases. Coins and small pieces of gold show the prosperity of Seuthopolis, transient though it was. Captions in the Thracian tomb were in Bulgarian, Russian, French and English, but in the Art Gallery we revert to Bulgarian-only captions, despite the fact that the icon collection struck me as precious, if poorly documented. A charming 'Annunciation', restored like all the rest, remains undated, but at least 'The Ascension of Christ' is attributed – to Krustyu Zahariev. Modern paintings worth study include Netko Klisurov's self-portrait (with neatly-curled moustache and trimmed beard) and, as you might expect here, 'Roses'. Stefan Ivanov's tender 'Esen' portrays a woman in mourning black, and I admired Patriki Sandev's 'Still Life' and tiny 'Portrait of an Old Woman'. Ivan Hristov's 'Turnovo' is an image that eluded Veliko Turnovo's own gallery. Vasil Stoilov's 'Shop' depicts one of the hard-headed, quick-witted 'village' types living in and around Sofia, comparable to Cockneys in terms of London. 'After Work' is a Svetlin Rusev painting far superior to anything he showed in Sofia at his 1988 exhibition. Hristo Forev's 'Portrait of Tanya' is a study in grey, black and red, but again I wondered when, if ever, Whistler's atmospheric colourism would arrive to enrich the Bulgarian palette. Nikola Alexiev's 'Morning' possesses an aura of magical enchantment that deserves wider recognition.

Kalofer
I drove steadily westward to join the river Tunja at Kalofer, birthplace of Hristo Botev (1848-76), killed while leading two hundred rebels after seizing the steamer *Radetzky*. The Utopian poet and revolutionary wrote to his wife Veneta while still on board, 'Forgive my not revealing my destination. It was my love for you that made me do it, for I knew that you would cry and I cannot stand seeing you in tears. You are my wife and you must listen and trust me in everything. I have asked my friends to stay with you and take care of you. God will protect me and, if I survive, we shall be the happiest people in the world; if I do not, you should know that I loved you best, after my fatherland.' Botev's birthplace has been rebuilt as a museum.

Karlovo
Karlovo was temporarily renamed Levskigrad, after its leading citizen, Vasil Levski (1837-73), the 'apostle of liberty' who has been compared to Che Guevara as a passionate rebel putting theories into guerrilla practice. Levski's birthplace, now a spotless museum in which whispering schoolchildren tiptoe from room to room in ecclesiastical fervour, describes the ideology of the revolutionary movement, beginning with Rakovski and Karavelov, and lists all the many pseudonyms Levski adopted (most of them Ottoman, such as Asan Agha and Aslan Dervishoghlu) in his travels to and from Romania, the plains of Thrace, and the Balkan mountains. Unlike Rakovski, he taught that the revolution would break out within the country, and toured much of the country to organise subversive committees first from 11 December 1868 to 16 February 1869, then from May 1869 to 1870, when he formed the Central Revolutionary Committee in Lovech. The house itself was poor, for his father died when Levski was young, and his mother had to

support a large family as a dyer.

The History Museum of Karlovo, a town of 26,000 people, has been laid out in a secondary school opposite Sv. Nikola. The best-known local wine is Karlovski Misket, and as well as the local rose industry, activities include carpet-making, tanning, dyeing, leather work and woodcarving. The local hotel is the two-star Rozova Dolina (Rose Valley), but despite its attractive rose-gardens, cypresses and fig-trees, Karlovo is not a town demanding a long stay and I sped southward to the promise of Hisarya, a town deriving its name from the Turkish word for a fortress.

Hisarya

The three-star Hotel Augusta in Hisarya, open throughout the year, offers a balneo-sanatorium with curative massage, herbal treatment, and a range of other facilities, including dietetic meals as well as national and Continental cuisine. Treatment at Hisarya is especially recommended for conditions of the liver and bile ducts, the kidney, pancreas and stomach. We are in Augusta, settled by the Romans for its therapeutic qualities, though the site had been occupied since the fourth millennium B.C. The waters of Augusta are alkaline, slightly mineralised hyperthermal, hydrocarbonate of sodium and fluoric, with a temperature ranging from 37°C to 51°C.

Situated only forty km from Philippopolis (now Plovdiv), the town on the southern slopes of Sredna Gora at an altitude of 360 metres became a countryside resort, with a small theatre, and fourth-century fortress walls bisected by the modern Ulitsa Lenin, erected after attacks by the Goths. Augusta seems to have become even more populous in the 5th and 6th centuries, and traces of 43 towers on the city walls must have impressed Slav invaders seeing the city for the first time, with ten Early Christian basilicas. The Slavs ruled by the Byzantines called the town Toplitsa but it was known to the Byzantines as Diocletianopolis. The Turks seized Toplitsa in 1364, and Anatolian Turks settled here in the sixteenth century, rebuilding the damaged baths in the 17th and creating new baths. Much archaeological work remains to be done in this evocative, charmingly-situated town, with its summer theatre, 'Camel Gate' flanked by watch-towers, late 4th-century basilica (a hundred metres west of Camel Gate), and 6th-century Church of Sv. Stefan, a hundred and twenty metres south of Camel Gate in the modern Turkish cemetery. You might like to find the 4th-century frescoed

Hisarya. 'Kamilite'

Roman family tomb, with a mosaic floor, or the Havuz mineral baths, opposite the Archaeological Museum, but it is the museum which will give you the clearest insight into ancient Hisar, to give the town its Turkish name. Neolithic idols set the stage for the longer perspective, as does a prehistoric settlement shown on the plan just inside the eastern wall. Seven of the ten basilicas were situated outside the fortress wall, showing the remarkable development of population and piety during the Byzantine period. Other finds in Room I include an iron spit for a fireplace, the inscription 'Theodoros' in Greek and Roman oil-lamps. A newly-discovered small bronze of Dionysus was shown me by the curator, Kostadin Majarov. Ceramics have been found to prove continuous settlement throughout the Middle Ages until the fourteenth century, then rifles and pistols exemplify, rather drily, the culture of the fifteenth to eighteenth centuries, when the Sredna Gora was haunted by the irregular soldiers of the Sultan called 'bashi-bazuks'.

They caused trouble everywhere, not only in Bulgaria, as the French traveller Charles Didier records in his *Sojourn with the*

Grand Sharif of Makkah (1854; translated 1985). 'These Reiters of the East, known as bashi-bazuks (which in Turkish means 'broken heads'), are the scourge of the countries to which the Porte sends them as garrisons; in the bazaars they take everything without paying for it, and maltreat any merchants who complain. A man's life is of no higher value in their eyes than a dog's, and of much less than a horse's. One of these brigands meets an unveiled woman. He draws out his pistol, takes aim with it, and blows out her brains in front of everybody, after which he calmly puts his weapon back into his belt and goes on his way twirling his moustache, without anybody standing in his way or looking askance at him. Just imagine the fate of populations that war places at the mercy of soldiery so brutal and lawless!'

Sopot

I returned north through Banya, regaining the Sofia road at Karlovo, and heading for Sopot, once known as Vazovgrad after the national poet, and author of the classic novel *Pod Igoto* translated by Marguerite Alexieva and Theodora Atanasova as *Under the Yoke* (Sofia, 1982). Ivan Vazov (1850-1921) spent his formative years under Ottoman domination, restlessly travelling and writing in Plovdiv, Romania, and back in Sopot as a revolutionary in 1870. The atmosphere of Sopot (the 'Byala Cherkva' of his major novel) is evoked in his pages, as is the April Rising of 1876, following which he fled to Rumania for two years, returning only to find his father murdered in another outrage. His is the voice of nascent Bulgarian belles-lettres, finding a literary power that will stand comparison with his beloved Russian and French models. His birthplace is reconstructed as a museum, with items associated with the period of the National Revival. I did not stay at Sopot's two-star Stara Planina Hotel, but lunched there off shopska salad, vegetable soup, and a 'Srednogorie Hotch-Potch' in which I detected veal, okra, onions, mushrooms, tomatoes, red peppers, potato, parsley and a smattering of rice.

Troyan Monastery

Troyan Monastery, with Rila and Bachkovo, must be one of the most utterly beautiful of all Bulgaria's many superb monasteries. Isolated – the nearest town is not Troyan at all, but Oreshak – the monastery has '200 beds for guests' according to Mihailov and

Smolenov's *Bulgaria: a Guide*, though the chances are you will be told that all cells are full and you will have to return to the two-star Hotel Troyan in Troyan town 10 km away if you find yourself benighted hereabouts.

On the western side of a forested gorge, the monastery rises like a delightful barracks below banks of green. When I was there, white sheets hung out to air on lines across three galleries like banners of truce against the modern world. 'Yes,' they announced, 'to pay our way in the modern world we have to accommodate visitors from Bulgaria and other Eastern countries, but at least we can manage to pay our way.' Water-supply is assured by the Black Osum river; the air is pure and pine-scented; after nightfall the silence reverberates like bellows, if one accepts the wind in the pines as a sound consecrated to the greater glory of silence. The story of Troyan Monastery is very much the story of Bulgaria since 1600, when the first monks sought solitude in these forests, far from Lovech, Plovdiv, Sofia, or Turnovo. The monks built a church to the Virgin, and cultivated lands for their livelihood, subject always to Ottoman permission. Meanwhile, marauders despoiled the unprotected monks of their chattels, murdering any who resisted. Pilgrims and local worthies helped the monks to repair their fortunes, despite attempts at control by Greek metropolitan bishops of the Lovech and Turnovo districts. A delegation from Troyan went to Constantinople to request from the Patriarch exemption from local bishops' jurisdiction and in its place direct rule from Constantinople. This status, known in the church as 'stauropegial', was granted in 1830 probably in some part to recognise the distinguished administration of Abbot Parteni (1817-40), who had achieved religious, literary and social renown as a place of worship, research, scholarship and education. The oldest monastic building still standing is the Chapel of Sv. Nikola the Miracle-Worker, that semi-legendary saint we half-recognise as S. Nicholas of Myra, or 'Santa Claus', but his chapel lies half-an-hour's hike to the south, and the church at the centre of Troyanski Manastir is the 1835 National Revival work of Konstantin, a master-builder from Peshtera (Kyustendil).

The main part of the church is square, dark, with a column and capital at each corner, supporting arches and a dome. The apse is semi-circular, and the nave and two aisles open out into a cruciform shape. An open gallery surrounds the northwestern side of the entrance. 'Qui m'y a mis?' I pondered with Pascal in increasing

Troyan Monastery. Church, from the gallery

anguish. 'Who has here me set down?' Why here? Why now? 'Je m'effraie et m'étonne de me voir ici plutôt que là.' Alternating strata of limestone and baked bricks give an appearance of long weathering, and from within the mediaevalising effect is increased by the traditional frescoes painted by Zahari Zograf, of the Samokov school, commissioned by Parteni's successor, Abbot Philotei, himself an artist. Portraits of the Abbot and Zahari can be seen on the wall of the western window at the northern side, and near the altar stand surveyed all twenty-seven monks then at Troyan. Nowadays the monks in numbers perilously near extinction derive some of their income from pilgrims' offerings, and a steady living from a co-operative farm on monastic land operated by the Government which also purchases the produce.

I confess to a delight in the naive, even childlike exuberance of the frescoes (look at the endearing eight-pointed star above the tiny swaddled Christ in the 'Nativity' of 1847-9), and particularly enjoyed the lozenge-shaped 'Resurrection', with astonished soldiers emerging from the edges as suddenly as a towering Christ issues from the Bulgarian-inscribed tomb. Zahari's identification of the Bulgarian church with the Bulgarian people suggested motifs for the rest of the church: Slav saints such as Cyril and Methodius; warrior saints; martyrs; and Bulgarian patriarchs. The walnut iconostasis immediately conjures up memories of Tryavna, whose carvers produced here yet another masterpiece of their craft, a sinuous vine issuing from the heart of Adam.

The museum has an icon of 'Jerusalem' brought by Abbot Philotei, and a green cloth with the slogan *Svoboda ili Smurt* ('Freedom or Death') from the time of Levski, who often visited Troyan, and hid from pursuers in a secret room reached by the top of a wardrobe. The icons of Sv. Georgi by Koyu Vitanov and 'The Virgin and Child' (1828) by Koyu Tsonyuv look forlorn out of their religious context, like straying sheep, and I returned to the monastery church to see icons, mostly by Dimitur Zograf, Zahari's brother, hence Samokovian. Tryavnian icons from the earlier church depict the Virgin Hodigitria (1818), Sv. Dimitur, and S. John of Rila, which I think sounds much better as Sveti Ivan Rilski. The earlier icon, of 'The Miraculous Three-Handed Virgin', is said to have come from Mount Athos during the 17th century, having been donated by a Romanian monk on his way back from the peninsula who wished to show his hosts at Troyan gratitude for their hospitality. Another story tells how the monk's horse would not stir from Troyan until the icon had been taken from the wanderer's luggage and left at Troyan, which does not show the Romanian monk in such a charitable light. Many Troyan monks went to study Greek and to read in the libraries on Mount Athos. In the revolutionary struggle Troyan played a key part, for its monks Maxim, Kiril and Parteni joined a committee with seventy other men, led by Archimandrite Makari. No wonder that the Austrian traveller Felix Kanitz mused on the purpose of so many weapons and ammunition there...

I pondered the chequered story of the Bulgarian Church, disestablished in 1944, Patriarch Stefan dismissed in 1948, reestablishment in 1951 and the appointment of Kiril as Patriarch in 1953, the death of Kiril in 1973 and the appointment of Patriarch Maxim, who enjoys an extremely close relationship with the state. Maxim had been a novice and monk at Troyan. Troyan had three monks, as far as I could ascertain in 1988, and two priests, the difference between them being that monks must remain celibate and priests are permitted to marry.

I bought grapes from private-enterprise stalls outside the monastery and strolled back towards my car, watching an old man in a brown jacket and baggy blue trousers nodding contentedly with himself, uttering from time to time a few words inclining to doubt or wonderment. I wore jeans to fit in with the predominantly rural dress of the people in the Sredna Gora, as I wore a suit in Sofia or Plovdiv, and felt inconspicuous among Bulgarians who dressed plainly, in dark clothes that might be considered 'drab' on the streets of Paris or New York but clearly correspond to a racial feeling here for the simple, undemonstrative, and unostentatious. Like meals in Bulgaria, like the prose or the domestic buildings, clothes show a steady, functional grasp of everyday life which seems easily offended by frills and fripperies. How relaxing not to suffer from creeps hanging around for tips, for bakshish! Communism, whether in Albania or Bulgaria, has no time for scroungers, loungers and spivs, but treats equality as a totem and work as an unquestioned principle of the virtuous life. I heard no reference to the 'proletariat' of Lenin's time, or the 'peasant' of Stalin's epoch; 'muzhik' appears in the Bulgarian dictionary, but only to refer you to the Russian term for 'peasant': the accepted term now is *selyanin*, roughly translatable as 'villager'.

Oreshak has plenty of such 'villagers' but many earn a good living as craftsmen, mainly in plentiful local wood, and display their handiwork at the national fair. Troyan too has a permanent Museum of Art and Craft, with pottery, wood, copper, textiles. A town of 24,000 people, it straggles around the White Osum river, protecting the road pass which was first made secure by the Emperor Trajan after whom both town and monastery were named. The two-star Hotel Troyan offers accommodation in this bracing mountain resort, where the only building to survive the devastation by fire caused by the Ottomans in 1877, a police station, has been transformed into an interesting District History Museum.

Koprivshtitsa

I headed back south down from Troyan to the valley between Stara Planina and Sredna Gora, making towards Sofia, and after passing through the rose-village of Rozino turned off to Klisura. Here, in April 1876, the feared bashi-bazuks had burned down the little town and murdered about two hundred people, though its sunny tiled roofs and brilliant flowers seem to have forgotten about the massacre. We are approaching Koprivshtitsa, a village of terrible historic resonance, where the first shot was fired on 20 April 1876 to mark the April Rising against the Turks; symbolically, it would be the first village liberated by the partisans, on 24 March 1944. Listen to the words of Lyuben Karavelov, President of the Bulgarian Revolutionary Central Commitee, who made the name of his village famous in urgent, physically expressive prose long before the Rising:

'In Koprivshtitsa you find stones, instead of fertile earth, but for that very reason it is all the more active and vital a place in which to live. To till the unfruitful land you must expend energy, until the sweat pours from your body, but such activity strengthens the body and inspires the mind and will to ever higher aspirations.'

Bulgarians teem in Koprivshtitsa like salmon in a stream, for every house has a story to tell, and National Revival architecture to admire. Every five years (1991, 1996, 2001), a national festival is held nearby at Voivodenets: the 1986 festival attracted twelve thousand performers and three thousand onlookers, to enjoy national costume, instruments, singing and dancing. Like Elena, the village was established by boyars after the fall of Turnovo in the 14th century and became a base for shepherds and sheepdealers. Nowadays it supports a population of around three to four thousand. The first village appeared in stages, up to 1793 when it was pillaged by the *kurjalis*; the second building phase occurred from 1810 to the mid-19th century; and the last important period was from 1856, the date of the Oslekov House, now the noble Ethnographic Museum where every visit should begin. The first type of house, represented by that of Pavlikenski, is made entirely of wood, of one storey, and still primitive. The second type, including the houses of Hajistoyanov, Benkovski and Duchkov, have an open verandah and solid doors against brigands, usually stone walls

Koprivshtitsa. Oslekov House, now the Ethnographical Museum

and a second storey. The third type, which is considered the Koprivshtitsa house *par excellence*, includes the Desyov, Garkov, Markov, Mlachkov, and Topalov mansions, each with many windows, glassed-in frescoed kiosks, discreetly opulent woodcarvings, and those ornamental niches called *alafrangas*. A general ticket covering six house-museums can be bought in the general store or Kupchinitsa, closed on Mondays and Tuesdays in the winter. A typical home of the wealthy *chorbaji* class, in this case a tailor and seller of serge clothes, the Oslekov House is the work of Samokov builders under Master Mincho and has been restored since 1956 as a museum of life before the Liberation of Bulgaria in 1878. Nencho Nikolov Oslekov travelled on business throughout the Middle East: his family photograph in the entrance-hall shows the kind of entrepreneur and paterfamilias we recognise in Victorian poses throughout European and North American industrial cities and towns: the backbone of international capitalism that preceded Lenin's collectivism. Oslekov's charming mansion comprises a cellar, a ground floor, and an upper floor. The ground floor is reached by a wooden staircase protected by a three-arched portico, above which extends a bay window overhung by eaves and a sharply-sloping tiled roof. Snow was falling gently, as in Tchaikovsky's first symphony, *Winter Daydreams*. Everything breathes an atmosphere of wealth, ease, comfort, style. Why, thought Oslekov, should we not enjoy at home in the Sredna Gora the amenities enjoyed by my business associates in Constantinople or my friends in Plovdiv? Murals depict towns and harbours visited by Oslekov; woodcarvings on ceilings and cupboards display technical bravura and realism allied to naive fantasy entirely endearing. Left at the top of the stairs is the women's guest-room, next to a weaving-room and the men's guest room, contents imaginatively recreating the ambience of the epoch, as if the family had just stepped out for a moment.

Next door is the Majarov House, somewhat earlier in date, with typical carved doors and cupboards, splendid bay windows opening to east and west, and floor plan almost identical on each storey.

The Church of the Resurrection (1817) stands on the site of a church razed by the *kurjalis* in 1804. Immediately recognisable by its bright blue, as if to draw attention to itself, the church had no dome, in those days of persecution, and the bell-tower was added much later. Icons are attributed to Yoan Samokovli and the ubiquitous Zahari Zograf, but the church was closed and its windows broken. In the churchyard, the stone figure by Ivan Lazarov refers to the melancholy mother of Dimcho Debelyanov (killed in Greece in 1916), and in general to those Bulgarians – and there have been many – who died for their ideals. If you leave the churchyard by the west gate you come to the house-museum of Todor Kableshkov (1845), with two halls, ten rooms, and a fine kiosk. Ears of corn carved in the ceiling and the sun's rays symbolise fertility. Kableshkov was another of the revolutionaries of Koprivshtitsa and his activities are explained on the second floor, with one of the twenty fatal 'cherry-tree' cannons that blew up in the faces of cannoneers when the linings made from melted-down copper kettles wore away. Here are weapons of the period, a green banner bearing the slogan 'Death or Liberty', and uniforms which they insisted on wearing, despite being much more easily identified and pursued when wearing them. The Bozov House (1859) has two floors on sustaining stone foundations and faces the 'Bridge of the First Shot' over the river Byala, where the first Turkish soldier fell in the Rising of 1876. Nearby is the Kesyakov House (1838), with a beautiful façade on the south side and an iconostasis with wooden sculptures on the north wall.

The Topalov House (also called Lyutov), completed and painted in 1854, is distinguished by its yoked corniche (a reference to the Turkish occupation) and admirably symmetry, lacking in the Oslekov House because the neighbours refused to sell the necessary land for an extension there. Wooden ceilings have exceptional fine carvings, and the frescoes look nearly as fresh as the day that artists painted these baskets of flowers and far harbours. Look for the stout wooden door of the Desyov House (also called Stariradev), which still shows the axe-holes made by attacking bashi-bazuks. The mansion is dedicated to the Bulgarian Academy of Sciences as a quiet place for study and research, but you might be allowed to visit the 'green' and 'yellow' rooms with their charming murals.

You will need more than one day to enjoy the intimate corners of Koprivshtitsa, so my recommendation is to ask Balkantourist for a private room in one of the historic mansions; otherwise the option is Hotel Koprivshtitsa on Ulitsa Benkovski. Next morning I started out from the old pharmacy on the main square (now occupied by the Museum Service), which may be open upstairs, where Kableshkov presided over sessions of the revolutionary council. I took Ulitsa Doganska (which leads to a fir-wood), its thick wooden gates and high stone walls so typical of a village where extended families kept themselves to themselves, and secured their property jealously against the all-too-likely threats of raids, rape, and murder. The birthplace of the revolutionary Naiden Gerov faces the Pranchov House (1820) with a shop on the ground floor and beds for forty tourists on the upper floors. Hajivalkov's house (1832) was expanded later with another wing, and an enlarged balcony. Even earlier is the Duchkov House (1809), constructed by master-builders from Debur after the ravages of the *kurjali* bandits; again the characteristic decorated kiosk and balcony create a light, lyrical ensemble. On impulse I brushed snow from a deciduous leaf and found it still strong, supple, bright maroon, surprised by the earliest snow for many winters.

The Doganov House (1815) is attributed to Plovdiv builders: its massive main door is on the south façade, and its two wings connect through party-walls. They date probably from 1843-4, when the carvings and frescoes are dated. The two-storey Gozbarov House (1856) has a twin staircase in the entrance niche, and differs from the rest of Koprivshtitsa's houses, as do the two Hajidonchov houses, of which the earlier probably antedates the bandit-incursions, and in its restored form (1840) enjoyed murals of great exuberance, including Christ on the ceiling and Cosmas and Damian under the iconostasis. The later Hajidonchov home, seemingly added for the needs of a growing family, also dates from 1840, and the paintings in the north-eastern room are especially noteworthy. A kiosk in the garden is again frescoed.

Dimcho Debelyanov's house-museum (1830) by the Peyovska fountain commemorates the poet and revolutionary, just as the statue of his mother in the garden commemorates the loss of Bulgarian women: 'in calm silence she waits for her child to come back'. The three larger rooms upstairs were set out as a museum in 1957 after the home had suffered forty years of neglect, and weeds had strangled the courtyard. Melancholy suffused the quiet place, the only sound that of creaking boards: outside a lullaby of snow-flakes. His father died when the boy was very young. A precocious poet, he studied in his native place, Ihtiman, and Sofia, anticipating his own early death in these lines:

> My heart does not regret
> the orphan's life that is my plight,
> for perhaps I shall have comfort yet
> in death, the triumph of my fight.

Here is the Italian translation of his songs, *La leggenda della regina traviata ed altri canti* (Rome, 1942), and here too the infants' swinging cradle.

The Dragilska House (1860) now accommodates the Dyado Liben Inn, where you can take lunch and dinner in a carefully-preserved atmosphere of the past. After a break, I wandered to the Sv. Nikola, also called the 'New Church' locally, though it dates from the 1840s, its marble flagstones having come from the coast of the Sea of Marmara. The life of Sv. Spiridion is told in ten medallions. Contemporary with the church is the Morovenov fountain, left of the entrance. Saunter a while in the Toroman quarter, with its old wooden houses, twisty alleys, bridges over the Kyosovo-Dereh river; and in the Selishteto quarter called the 'Hill' locally (Mogilata) which is believed to stand on the site where the first groves were felled for the timber to make the village's first houses.

A painter from Plovdiv invited me to look at the Bazev House, occupied nowadays by the Artists' Union. Six pine-columns support the gracious verandah (1830s), and wings added later do not diminish the harmony of the ensemble: a low cellar, a ground floor, and the upper floor with its splendid verandah. The Tako Dorosiyev House-Museum (1840) is devoted to the life and activities of this member of the Central Committee of the Bulgarian Communist Party, whose subversive activities led to his suicide in 1925, and there are photographs of the revolutionary movement in Sredna Gora, as well as weapons and uniforms. The Georgi Benkovski House-Museum (1831) again should be visited for the picturesque interior, even by those uninterested in the subject, who became a rebel commander, and must take the responsibility for designing and making the rebel uniforms in a striking white almost guaranteed to stand out on hills, roads and glades. Benkovski himself almost predictably died in ambush.

Etropole
To my lasting regret I never saw Glozhenski Monastery, near Glozhene village, in the vicinity of Teteven, nor a dozen other monasteries of similar individuality, such that to miss each one is a deprivation. We should never forget the concealed role of Bulgarian monasteries in the life of the people, in education, scholarship, the continuity of oral and literary traditions, and a burgeoning nationalism. Rila Monastery planned and manned fifty-two cell schools throughout the country, furthering literacy and fostering Christianity while Islam remained predominant. In the 16th-17th centuries, the principal centre of scholarship north of the Balkan Range was Varovitets, the Monastery of the Holy Trinity, 5 km from the village of Etropole. To reach Etropole, take a right turn on the road from Koprivshtitsa to Sofia at Srednogorie and continue 27 km on the road towards Pravets. The honoured names of Basil of Sofia, Daniel of Etropole, Rafail, Deacon Yoan and the grammarian Boicho should resound in the memory, for they were the scribes who copied important manuscripts and wrote new books for the furtherance of knowledge, their language, and their faith. Such manuscripts may now be seen in the National Library and in the Central Ecclesiastical Museum Library in Sofia. The monastery, founded in the 12th century, was torn down many times by Ottoman raiders and as many times replaced. The current walls and cells date from 1833, and the current church from 1858, when

master-builder Ivan Boyanin from Bratsigovo (near Peshtera) designed and built the new cruciform church with a nave and two aisles and a central dome on an octagonal drum. Reaching the monastery is half the enjoyment, as it suddenly comes into view on the wooded northern slopes of Mount Cherni Vruh.

There is a good hotel in Etropole, a town much more relaxing than the purpose-built tourist compound at Pravets, with a large motel, even larger hotel, and an entertainment area with supermarkets and car-repair facilities. For this is the new Bulgaria, with its A2 international highway bypassing towns like any Italian *autostrada* rather than wandering through them like a traditional Balkan carriageway. One can stop off at Pravets for the birth-place museum of Todor Zhivkov, delineating the life and exploits of the statesman born on 7 September 1911 into a poor family. He worked as a printer at the State Printing House in Sofia, and in 1932 joined the underground Communist Party. He formed and fought with the Chavdar Partisan Brigade during World War II and in 1948-9 chaired the Sofia City People's Council, in 1950 achieving the position of Secretary to the Central Committee of the Bulgarian Communist Party. The ideological handbook he wrote entitled *Bulgaria along the Road to an Advanced Socialist Society* (Sofia, 1971), has the following anonymous lines in the introduction: 'As a Party and state leader, Todor Zhivkov elaborated major theoretical and practical issues of Bulgaria's socio-economic development: the character of its socialist revolution, trends and rates of its socialist industrialization, consolidation and perspectives of the co-operative system in the countryside.'

As the closest and friendliest ally of the U.S.S.R., Todor Zhivkov has maintained good relations with each successive leader in the Kremlin, and this relaxed attitude between the two governments makes travel in Bulgaria as easy and risk-free as anywhere in the world.

2: SOFIA

*National History Museum — Lenin Square — Mosques — Hali —
Synagogue and Jewish Museum — Dimitrov Mausoleum — National
Art Gallery — Bulevard Ruski — Alexander Nevski Memorial
Cathedral and Icon Museum —Sveta Sofia —Art Galleries —Literary
Museums — National Opera — Sveti Sedmochislenitsi — Theatres —
Railway Station — University — National Palace of Culture —
Vitosha*

The present Bulgarian capital spreads at the foot of Mount Vitosha
in the southern plain, almost entirely surrounded by mountains.
Within half an hour's drive in any direction you will come to rivers
(such as the Iskur), forests (near Kostinbrod), ravines, lakes (like
Pancharevo) and mountains.

The Slavs called it literally the centre: 'Sredets', for Sofia, later to
be christened the city of 'Wisdom', lies roughly equidistant between the Adriatic and the Black Sea, Belgrade, Tirana, Istanbul
and Athens. The city's climate is temperate and continental, with
skiing on nearby Vitosha in the winter, and warm summers. The
best seasons to visit Sofia in my opinion are spring and autumn, but
the most concentrated months for music, ballet, opera and drama
are in winter. Whenever you arrive, ask at your hotel (or buy for a
few stotinki at any street kiosk)*Edna Sedmitsa v Sofia (One Week in
Sofia)*, the programme guide. The text is in Bulgarian, but if you
can make out Cyrillic characters the chances are that you can iden-
tify composers or playwrights known to you: a hotel information
desk can always help, in any case.

I should recommend five days in Sofia, not least because of varied evening events, at prices so low that you will hardly credit them.
The first day could start with a half-day city tour and continue with
the National Historical Museum, ending at an opera or a concert.
The second day could be spent exploring Vitosha and places not
covered by your city tour: the churches and galleries and museums,
and the Lyudmila Zhivkova National Palace of Culture, with a play

Map of Sofia

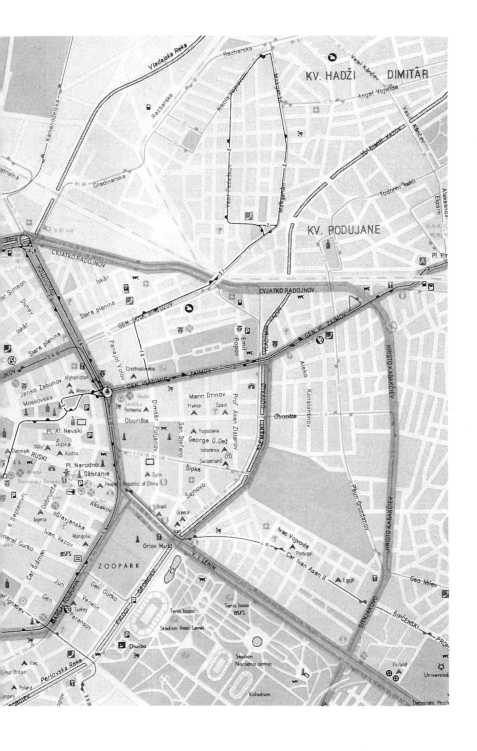

or ballet at seven p.m. The other three days might include the remaining sights covered in the following chapter, renewing acquaintance with the National Opera at 58 Bul. Dondukov or the National Theatre at 5 Ul. Vasil Levski. Operetta can be seen at the Stefan Makedonski Music Theatre, 4 Bul. Volgograd.

In the middle of the 19th century, Sofia slumbered in the prolonged siesta of the Ottoman Empire, which lasted here for nigh on five centuries, with a population of barely twenty thousand and thirty mosques, their minarets making the little town something like an outpost of Edirne. Then the Russians, with their Bulgarian allies, swept through the country, and Sofia began, with wide new streets and three-storey houses and offices, to look like an outpost of Austria, with a Battenberg on the throne. In 1879 the Sofia of Prince Alexander Battenberg covered only one square mile, but today's sprawling city, its suburbs rushing ever outward like some tidal wave, has extended far beyond the city conceived in 1935 by the Dresden town-planner Alfred Mussmann. The 1950s flamboyant style is represented by the seventeen-storey 'Home of the Soviets'. The Bulgarian Communist Party headquarters looks something like Moscow University.

In the 1990s Sofia is a European capital splitting at the seams with new arrivals from the countryside, more than a million people in a city revamped since World War II with monumental Soviet blocks of the 1950s sorting oddly with beautiful churches like the tiny half-buried Sveta Petka Samarjiiska almost invisible between the elegant lines of the Banya Bashi Mosque on Bulevard Dimitrov and the ecumenically balancing magnificence of Sveta Nedelya in the roundabout of Ploshtad Lenin. Lenin's statue stiffly observes a steady procession of trams, the life-blood of Sofiote traffic, and beyond them the Balkan Sheraton Hotel next to the massive supermarket acronymically known as TsUM: Tsentralen Universalen Magazin. This name reminds you irresistibly of the close linguistic ties with Russian which, with the emotional bonds of political and military allegiance, make it natural for Russian to persist as the first foreign language taught in schools, and the principal language of Bulgarian scientific and technological education. There are Russian-language bookshops, but Bulgarian bookshops usually include a wide selection of Russian titles too. Some Russian dishes emerge on the menu, but basic fare remains Turkish, with kebabs, kawarma, kyofteta (grilled meat balls) and the stew known as gyuvech.

My Balkan flight from London had, according to the pilot, flown at 950 kph at an altitude of 11,000 metres, statements I was in no position to confirm or deny, though I did note that we had taken only 2 hours 40 minutes to cover the distance from London, over-flying Brussels, Frankfurt, Linz and Budapest. I took the airport bus to the Hotel Pliska, owned by the airline, and dined there, overlooking a food store (*hranitelni stoki*) and the busy dual car-riageway named for Lenin, on veal soup, shopska salad, pork and potatoes, with Coca Cola.

National History Museum
Next morning, after a buffet breakfast at the Pliska, I took a tram to Lenin Square for the National History Museum on Bulevard Vit-osha. The neo-classical Palace of Justice (1926) may not be an ideal setting for a display of ancient Bulgarian art and artefacts, but this is the most important single collection for an understanding of the country's archaeology, and demands half a day from even the bris-kest visitor. The central hall opens with a fanfare: the 9th-century

National History Museum. Thracian phiale from Rogozen (4th century B.C.)

71

icon of S. Theodore from Preslav on painted and glazed ceramic tiles, brilliantly restored. Objects from more than 170 graves in Varna's Chalcolithic Necropolis of about 4,000 B.C. whet our appetite for Varna's own museum. Finds come from Durankulak, near Tolbuhin and Roman mosaics from Ivailovgrad, near Kurjali. A bronze head of Gordian III represents the best objects from Nicopolis ad Istrum. The Thracian gold treasure from Vulchitrun, discovered in 1949, dates from the late Bronze Age. A wreath from Vratsa which 'sings' in a draught because of the thinness of its gold-leaf is lodged in the National Bank: this is a copy. Copies of Pliska columns reused in Turnovo stand near the sumptuous Panagyurishte gold treasure. The internationally-exhibited Rogozen hoard found near Vratsa in 1985 is possibly connected with a 4th-century B.C. silver treasure found at Barovo on the way to Ruse. A silver-gilt breastplate comes from Mezek (south-east Bulgaria), with a corridor tomb and false-vault in the same tradition as the Kazanluk Tomb we have already seen. Madara's pagan sanctuaries preceded the first Christian churches; here too is an appliqué with gryphon from Preslav, and ivory carving from Turnovo. An episcopal throne from Rila Monastery dates from the 14th century and a newly-exhibited bronze cross bears the name of Sevast Borislav (12th-13th centuries). Two lively peacocks in red schist (10th-11th centuries) come from Stara Zagora.

Having been dazzled by these highlights, we are ready for the systematic sequence, beginning with prehistory. My eye was taken by small ritual altars (6500-4500 B.C.) from Hotnitsa near Vratsa. The Copper Age (4th-3rd millennia) was succeeded by the Bronze Age (3200-1200) but it is with the Iron Age Thracians that we collide full tilt with landscapes such as burial mounds and treasures such as golden bowls or cups: The Thracian Serdi in this region gave their name to Serdica, one of Sofia's many previous appellations. Thracians exported corn, wax, timber, wool and hides to Greece in exchange for olive oil, silks and other fabrics. Serdica was inhabited by the Thracian Odrysae in the second half of the 5th century B.C.: their jewellery and pottery were excavated during the building of the Balkan Sheraton in the very heart of the city. In the 4th century B.C. Philip II of Macedon pillaged Serdica on his way from an expedition against the Scythians but the town revived as a Roman settlement in the 1st century A.D. and was granted the honorific Ulpia by Trajan (98-117) as a full *municipium*. The first city walls of bricks on great stone blocks are dated by inscription to the time of Marcus Aurelius (161-180). In the time of Aurelian (270-5) Serdica Ulpia achieved the status of capital of Inner Dacia, and was girt with a higher city wall about twelve metres tall, defended by equidistant round towers, surrounding the area of present-day central Sofia in a rectangle whose shape was broken by a diagonal that ran sharply southwest from present-day Dimitrov (northern gate) down to the western gate in the area Tsanov-Washington-Boboshevo, then due south to a round tower, due east across Vitosha between Positano and Alabin past the southern gate to just west of Lege. The eastern gate (now accessible with its pentagonal tower to visitors after excavations below the House of the Party) stood at the beginning of modern Dondukov. Serdica Ulpia squared off at the north roughly parallel to modern Ul. Exarch Iosif. Its original walls were razed in 447 by Attila's Huns but the Byzantine Emperor Justinian (527-65) restored the city walls once more (after an earlier reconstruction in alternating stone and brick) with a second brick wall.

The bouleuterion or city council building of Serdica in the form of an amphitheatre has been found below the northwest corner of the Balkan Sheraton Hotel, whose courtyard reveals, beside the round church of Sveti Georgi, remains of a pagan temple, and thirty metres of a Roman road.

The National History Museum's Hall of the 1st and 2nd Bulgarian states emphasises the Glagolitic alphabet created by Cyril and Methodius, then modified by Kliment of Ohrid and others, the latest orthographic change dating to the 1940s. Historic manuscripts and inscriptions on stone and brick evoke a distant past, when writing belonged to the priesthood and to few others. Here is an 11th-century MS from Rila, and Priest Dobreisho's Gospels, with his illumination of John the Evangelist (13th century).

The origins of the Bulgars is next shown, from the area of the modern Chuvash Autonomous Republic in the U.S.S.R., to the last pagan ruler, Khan Omurtag and the first Christian ruler, his son Boris. We are introduced to the successive capitals: Pliska (681-893), Preslav (893-927) and Ohrid on the modern Albanian-Yugoslav border, up to 1014.

On the first floor, the Ottoman period is represented by coins and weapons, and the rise of new towns: Kotel, Zheravna, Pazarjik. The goldsmith George achieved canonisation as the New S. George of Sofia when he was burned at the stake in 1511 in front of the church of Sveta Sofia because he refused to renounce Christianity. The New S. Nicholas of Sofia was stoned to death. Religious art from Turnovo of the 16th-17th centuries testifies to the persistence of Orthodox faith: an icon of S. George and the Dragon, murals from Arbanasi, icons from Bachkovo, a life-size S. Nicholas (1607) from Nesebur, arts of the book and icons from Etropole Monastery, including Four Gospels of the 16th century with a splendid Celtic-style interweaving pattern opposite a portrait of S. Luke. One of the best icons is a 17th-century S. Demetrius from Sofia. One room is devoted to Rila Monastery, with a MS of 1483 and the Iconostasis of S. Luke (1779). Restored Samokov-school icons accompany self-portraits of Zahari Zograf (1840-2) and Dimitur Dobrovich (1875-80).

I found my concentration dipping after a couple of hours in the National History Museum, and at Mehana Koprivshtitsa (3 Bulevard Vitosha) close by lunched off kawarma and pancakes. Remember that the museum is closed on Mondays.

Lenin Square

Sooner or later you will want to change money, and the place to do it (for the best official rate; but of course conditions may change) is Tsentralen Universalen Magazin, the Central Universal Department-ment Store, open from 8 a.m. to 8 p.m. on Lenin Square, and teeming with everyday Bulgarian life. I exchanged £100 for 440 leva whereas the best rate in my hotel was 293 leva. I didn't have my passport with me, but the helpful lady behind the grille accepted my details off a previous exchange of currency slip. Impressions are relative, but compared with Romania or Albania TsUM showed that the Bulgarians had a good deal of money to spend; prices were low enough for them to feel that they were able to buy whatever consumer goods were provided without the benefit of hard currency; and the range of goods on offer was wide enough for everyone to get enough to eat and to be decently dressed. On the ground floor pottery and flowers were on sale; large wooden bowls cost from 25 to 33 leva; a practical shoulder-bag like mine fetched 24 leva, and embroidered blouses could be bought for 25-38 leva. A woman's cardigan was priced at 20, and a fur jacket relatively cheaply at 60 leva. Queues were short enough for me to buy a road map of Bulgaria for 1.50 leva by just handing over the cash, with no paperwork at all.

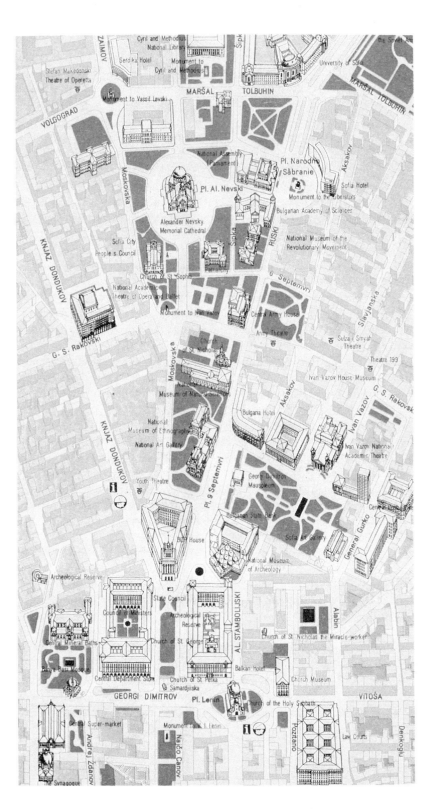

Most of the noise and queues seemed to be concentrated on the textile floors, where women were buying cloth to make up dresses and shirts on their sewing-machines at home. The queues remained good-natured, without pushing or shouting. The building, forming a group with the Balkan Sheraton and the Communist Party Head-quarters, was designed by P. Zlatev and finished in 1955 in the monumental style.

Just as Moscow's Red Square relinquishes its communist hard line at the fantastic curves and colours of S. Basil's Church, so Sofia's Lenin Square relaxes before the portals of Sveta Nedelya, calm amid the endless traffic flow along Bulevard Dimitrov, Bulevard Stamboliiski, and Bulevard Vitosha, formerly named after Stalin. A vast Roman praetorium underlay this great church, but this gave way to a cluster of small churches and family chapels, among them the Church of the Blessed King Stephen Urosh II Milutin of Serbia (1272-1321) also dedicated to the Holy Sabbath. The old wooden and stone church was devastated in 1856, but rebuilt seven years later. Pomerantsev, the Russian architect, was responsible for the church we see nowadays, which is why it looks like any other Russian church of that generation. After an assassination attempt on Tsar Boris and his courtiers failed in 1925, the Church of the Holy Sabbath was restored in 1933-5. Trees protect the church from a little of the lead pollution from traffic constantly crashing past. Yellow trams clank round the corner, disturbing neurotic pigeons. The iconostasis by Professor Travintski and mur-als by Nikolai Rostovtsev (1971-3) carry one's gaze up to the high dome with a single nave, so different from the five-nave Alexander Nevski Memorial Church. A number of icons are by Stanislav Dos-pevski of Samokov, but these are overshadowed in quality by the immigrant Czech painter Jan Mrkvička's 'Last Supper'.

From Sveta Nedelya I crossed in front of the Balkan Sheraton towards an elusive hole in the ground occupied by an enchanting little church dedicated to Sv. Petka of the Saddlers, a wealthy guild. Sv. Petka is a saint from Epivados, on the Sea of Marmara, whose sanctuary was used here from the fourteenth century until 1948, throughout the whole of the Ottoman period. At the lowest level, Roman Serdica's fortress walls have been revealed; at a higher level, graves from a 12th-century necropolis have emerged, and the church itself was located above that, but deliberately set below the level of the Turkish town in tactical abasement before the Muslim

The Largo, with TsUM (left), the Communist Party HQ (right) and Sv. Petka Samarjiiska (partly underground)

powers-that-were. They required a simple exterior, but within imposed no restriction on artistic expression, with the result that the earlier frescoes (very recently redated, somewhat later than by traditional scholarship, to the 16th century) have decorative and expressive strength that we recognise in the art of all repressed communities. The decorator may have been a certain Pimen, a name jogging my memory of the opening scene of Mussorgsky's opera *Boris Godunov*, when the monkish chronicler Pimen takes a rest for a moment:

Some grave industrious monk
Shall profit by my pious, nameless labours;
And like myself, some night
He'll light his candle,
And shake the dust of ages from this ancient parchment,
And then transcribe my faithful chronicle:
The grandsons of the Orthodox believers
Shall read and learn our land's historic past.

On 1 June 1961 I heard the ringing tones of Boris Christoff, the greatest bass of his time, and a Bulgarian, sing the rôle of Boris on the stage at Covent Garden, and afterwards he signed my programme, both of us still overcome by the final scene, as Boris sinks dying in his chair with the words 'Bozhe! Smyert! Prosti menya!' (God! Death! Forgive me!) and points out his son to the assembled boyars: 'Vot! Vot vash Tsar! Prostitye... prostitye...' (There! There is your Tsar! Have mercy... have mercy...).

Pimen's murals resemble others on Crete and Mount Athos stylistically, and they have been restored to the same high level of excellence that we have seen across Bulgaria from Pliska by way of Turnovo. I stood still between the nave's barrel vault and the apse's half-vault in the half-dark, delighting in the unusual capitals. One feels almost in a rock church and yet overhead the pulsing traffic of central Sofia bustles like Piccadilly Circus. A life-size portrait of Sv. Ivan Rilski appears opposite the niche on the right of the apse. An icon by Zahari Krusha (1847) showing miracles of popular Sv. Petka, dedicatee of many churches, who was born to a wealthy family in the 11th century.

If you turn behind the Balkan Sheraton and into its courtyard you will be astonished to see a very beautiful church, dedicated to that most popular dragonslayer, George. Its rotunda is of the early 4th century, and thus the oldest preserved building in the capital open to view. Even so, Constantine's Christian rotunda stands on the ruins of a pagan temple (opposite the Fantasy Night Club, as it happens) and is surrounded by two narthexes: a third has been lost. It is thought that the hypocaust-like subterranean brick columns did not actually form part of a public bath system but ventilated the church and kept it level. During my stay, the interior of Sv. Georgi was open only two days a week, on account of restoration, but I managed to pass by one day when it was open. I located the earliest, 11th century, frescoes between and above the late 10th-century

The Rotunda of Sv. Georgi

windows. It is thought that the Christ Pantocrator on the dome may be of this first period. Above the arches I made out 12th-century frescoes, and the 14th-century evangelists, angels and prophets, the last additions before the church was transformed into the Gül Jami'a, or Rose Mosque, under Ottoman auspices, with a minaret on the southwestern side now unfortunately demolished. All that survives of that epoch is a fragment of decoration just above a window over the main door.

Mosques

Ottoman Sofia has not entirely vanished, as we can see from Mehmet Pasha's Great Mosque, or Büyük Jami'a, completed in 1494 which was converted into the National Archaeological Museum as long ago as 1879 and thus inevitably crowds into too little space too many objects in a manner reminiscent of the old Ethnographic Department of the British Museum before it moved to the Museum of Mankind. Büyük Jami'a has enough space for a small aeroplane below its nine domes, so that even its finest works are dwarfed by their surroundings, like a goldfish in a swimming-pool. This is a pity, for many objects are worth treasuring in the mind: there are no guidebooks, catalogues, postcards or captions in foreign languages. A hunter had pierced a tiny hole in a cave-bear's fang as ornament, grubbed out by an archaeologist 37,000 years later in the Samuilitsa Cave near Kunino, in the district round Vratsa. There are more than four hundred Neolithic burial mounds (6th-5th millennia B.C.) in Bulgaria, none more significant that Karanovo's, in Sliven region: a veritable Jericho that would have exercised a Kathleen Kenyon. Inscribed slabs of the 4th millennium from Karanovo have a form of writing antedating those of Crete and Mycenaean Greece. I recall a 16th-century icon of Doubting Thomas and a huge Demeter, being a Roman copy of a Greek original by Praxiteles. Works come from Nesebur (1704) and Devin-Marcianopolis (4th-5th centuries), a town named for the Emperor Trajan's sister Marciana. A fine 4th-century mosaic with birds and bees from the Church of Sveta Sofia takes the eye, as does a superb 2nd-century marble horse and rider from Brestnik near Plovdiv. The coin collection is outstanding, likewise a lapidarium displayed higgledy-piggledy outside like wreckage after the Day of Resurrection.

The underpass just outside the Great Mosque has been beautifully organised with finds from the Museum for the History of Sofia, preserving foundations of the fortress wall that guarded Sofia from the 2nd century to the 14th. The mosque familiarly known as Banya Bashi, because it was erected next to the baths, faces Sveta Nedelya and the slopes of Vitosha with all the jauntiness of a master-architect's zeal to spread the faith as far into heathen Europe as the heathens would allow. The mosque, with its arcade of four columns, three graceful entry domes and large central dome, dates from 1576. Four workmen nodded to me as I walked around their wooden boards supported on high scaffolding. To the right of the mihrab with a honeycomb squinch the name of Allah was inscribed in gold on a black circle; with Muhammad's name on the left, then came Abu Bakr, Uthman, Hasan, Husain, Ali and Umar. The wooden minbar was inscribed on the arch at the foot of the steps *bismillahi ar-Rahman ar-Rahim*, 'in the Name of Allah the Compassionate and Merciful'. The ablutions area remained open and had clearly been used of late. Rush mats had been rolled up in niches. A recent wooden gallery hung above the entrance door, and below, a tiled platform had been raised above the floor at each side of the door. The great dome shed light on me as it had done on Muslims for more than four centuries. The mosque is contemporary with the baths next door which were superseded by a grander neo-Renaissance monument designed by Petko Momchilov and completed in 1913. I liked the leisurely atmosphere of the marble-columned mineral baths, whose waters at 46°C are used to treat digestive and nervous disorders.

Hali
The National Revival-style covered market known as Hali (1909-11) was designed by Torbov and in its ornate splendour housewives incongruously haul shopping baskets laden with beer and mineral water, sugar, and non-alcoholic soft drinks, milk, biscuits, frozen meat joints and chicken, eggs, tinned fish and mayonnaise, queueing at twenty tills. Internally, it has been reconstructed on the open-plan method giving more light and space. There seemed to be few shortages during my visit, though the clothes upstairs were dull, predictable and often badly cut.

Synagogue and Jewish Museum

On the corner of Exarch Iosif Street I found Sofia's enormous synagogue, with a wide gallery and green dome. Evidence of slow reconstruction lay everywhere in thick dust: scaffolding, groundsheets, buckets. The only functioning synagogue in Bulgaria holds its services not here, but in a little room with a grey wall-hanging from the defunct synagogue of Vidin, and another hanging presented by Dr S.D. Lessner of Nagasaki. Sofia synagogue was designed by the Viennese architect Grünanger, the same responsible for the former Royal Palace opposite the Dimitrov Mausoleum, and opened in 1909 after four years' work. Since most of Bulgarian Jews are Sephardic, Grünanger chose as his model the Sephardic synagogue in Vienna, destroyed during World War II. About twenty to forty Jews congregate on Friday evenings and Saturday mornings throughout the year, but numbers swell to a hundred or so on major religious festivals. Before World War II there were 50,000 Jews in Bulgaria, and now there are about 5,000 of whom more than 3,000 live in Sofia. The rest of the Jews chose to emigrate to Israel after the state was formed, having been saved from Nazi death camps by the actions of the Bulgarian Communist Party, workers and intellectuals. The story of the Jews in Bulgaria is documented in the exhibition 'The Saving of the Bulgarian Jews' at 50 Bul. Stamboliiski, on Ploshtad Vuzrazhdane (closed on Saturdays). Here you can discover how a Jewish community and synagogue of the 2nd century have been identified at Trajan's town of Oescus near Gigen. Massive immigration occurred after the expulsion of the Jews from Spain in 1492, strengthening Jewish groups in Vidin, Sofia, Nicopolis, and Pleven, as well as in Ohrid, Thessaloniki and Edirne outside present Bulgarian frontiers. They suffered equal persecution under the Ottoman yoke, adhering passionately to Levski's stirring 'Rules for the Fighters for Bulgarian Liberation':

'..and the rule of Turkish masters shall be replaced by concord, fraternity and complete equality of all nationalities. Bulgarians, Turks, Jews and others shall be equal in faith, nationality, civil status, and every other respect, all being ruled by the same law to be approved by the majority vote of all nationalities.'

On 24 May 1943 thousands of Jews demonstrated in the streets of Sofia against deportation orders served on them by the pro-Axis

Government of King Boris III, which would have led to their destruction at Nazi concentration camps. The Government did not execute the deportation order, giving the Jews three days to reach the Danube ports, but over the next months Jews left the cities for the countryside, rejoicing in the arrival of the Soviet Army and Bulgarian partisans at the end of the War, on 9 September 1944. Though the exhibition is captioned solely in Bulgarian, an excellent English-language book is available: *Saving the Jews in Bulgaria, 1941-44* (Sofia, 1977), reproducing many of the photographs and documents on Ploshtad Vuzrazhdane.

Dimitrov Mausoleum

Strolling back from the square along Bulevard Stamboliiski and across Ploshtad Lenin, I turned round the back of Büyük Jami'a to Ploshtad 9 Septemvri, with the cool classical Dimitrov Mausoleum, guarded day and night. Stamboliiski and Dimitrov were two energetic politicians who made a great mark on the course of life and affairs in Bulgaria. Alexander Stamboliiski, whose monument is silhouetted against the National Opera, became Premier during the short-lived government of the Agrarian Party (1919-23), asserting peasant power long before the Communists seized power, but the influential Internal Macedonian Revolutionary Organisation which fought against the Turks with the cry 'Liberty for Macedonia or Death' saw Stamboliiski as a traitor to the cause and murdered him, after he had dug his own grave, in 1923. Dimitrov (1882-1949) led the Communist Party after World War II, before the Chervenkov years and the beginnings of de-Stalinisation, 1950-6. East of the white stone mausoleum you can find the tomb of Dimitrov's close associate and successor, Vasil Kolarov. Facing the Dimitrov Mausoleum, the former Royal Palace has been reorganised as the National Ethnographic Museum (17 halls, closed on Mondays and Tuesdays), which I was not able to see; and the National Art Gallery (closed on Tuesdays).

National Art Gallery

The former Palace was used by the Queen after the death of King Boris in 1943, and subsequently by the Council of Ministers. I learned that a catalogue was 'available' but 'not on sale' and 'not for consultation' which is a great shame, if you like illustrated records of galleries you have visited, but no great loss if you dislike socialist realism as an aesthetic. Yet there is much more to see than mere propaganda, especially in the first rooms, covering the National Revival, beginning with a self-portrait by Dimitur Dobrovich (1816-1905), a friend of Garibaldi; and others by Zahari Zograf of Samokov (1810-53) and Nikolai Pavlovich (1835-94), founder of the Bulgarian Academy of Fine Arts. I enjoyed the domestic scale of a 'Portrait of His Wife' (1875) by Hristo Tsokev (1847-83), and his equally delicate 'Angelina Bruchkova' (1874). Stanislav Dospevski (Zahari's nephew) was another gifted portraitist: here are the essence of his father Dimitur Zograf, Smaragda Samokovleva, and Ekaterina Hajigyurova. The murals of Sveta Nedelya are recalled by seeing Dospevski's work; some of the icons and murals in the Alexander Nevski Memorial Cathedral are by Anton Mitov (1862-1930), whose self-portrait quite properly conceals more than it says: suggestion of half-held beliefs, propagation of half-truths insisting on compromise as a basic human need. The Czech Jan Mrkvička (1856-1938) worked so long in Bulgaria that he is claimed as a native son, like El Greco in Spain. His celebrated 'Rachenitsa' depicts an endurance dance in a village pub, but the subtler 'Virgin' from the Rhodopes trails longer in my memory. The first significant woman artist in Bulgaria, Elena Karamihailova, is represented by a portrait of her sister. Nikola Petrov (1881-1916) has a view of Chepino, in the Rhodopes. Artists began to study and travel abroad after Liberation in 1878, and Sofia's 'Orlov Most' (Eagles' Bridge), to which I had taken the no. 4 tram from Hotel Pliska, was painted by Petrov in 1910, nine years after the introduction of the first tram. Stefan Ivanov (1875-1951) has a striking image of the poetess Dora Gabe. Your eye might be taken by 'In the Field' by Hristo Stanchev (1870-1950) or 'Icebergs on the Danube near Silistra' by Atanas Mihov (1879-1974). The Danube doesn't ice over completely any more. The most monumental yet plastic of earlier painters was Ivan Nenov, born in 1902, whose portraits of women and girls in the 1930s and 1940s set him apart from simplistic academicians. 'A Girl' (1935) occupies a massive area with a graceful economy of colour and line more commonly connected with a sculptor in bronze. Zlatyu Boyajiev, paralysed at 40, has a vibrant 'Winter in Plovdiv' near Tsanko Lavrenov's 'Old Plovdiv'. I was left unmoved by a 'Self-Portrait' of the over-rated Vladimir Dimitrov (1882-1960) but not by Dechko Uzunov's 'Self-Portrait at 84' (in 1983) and a sympathetic 'Portrait of the Actor N.A. Sarafov' (1932).

Bulevard Ruski

Specialists will head for the Natural History Museum at 1 Bulevard Ruski (closed Mondays, Tuesdays, and weekend mornings) with worldwide and Bulgarian sections ranging from the history of the earth to half a million species of insect.

Bulevard Ruski has a concert agency (no.3) where you can pick up tickets for the Bulgaria Concert Hall at 1 Ul. Aksakov or the Slaveikov Concert Hall on Pl. Slaveikov; the Hungarian and Polish Cultural Centres, where I enjoyed splendid temporary exhibitions of ceramics from Pecs and paintings by Jerzy Duda Gracz respectively; and the charming little Russian church of S. Nicholas (1913-4), designed by Preobrazhenski. The Russian artists who worked on Alexander Nevski Memorial Cathedral came to adorn this active church, more intimate yet fully in the Russian tradition, with icons (such as a Christ Pantocrator) copied from those in Kiev, typical murals and a familiar Russian iconostasis. The church belonged to the Russian Patriarchate up to 1953, but now services are in Church Slavonic, as in the rest of Bulgaria.

The Museum of the Revolutionary Movement at 14 Bul. Ruski is captioned only in Bulgarian, so those intending to travel widely in Bulgaria (where there are many similar museums) might prefer to miss this out. Like the Museum of Revolutionary Vigilance at 5 Ul. Lavele it is really for domestic consumption.

Bulevard Ruski opens out into Ploshtad Narodno Subranie (National Assembly Square), in which the neo-classical National Assembly (1884-1928) faces the Liberators' Monument, a work by Arnaldo Zocchi (1862-1940) whose Garibaldi Monument is not the most pleasant sight in Bologna. If you stay at the Grand Hotel Sofia as I have, extremely convenient as to location, you will see the back of Tsar Alexander II waving the declaration of war against Turkey above Russian troops, with bronzes around his pedestal commemorating the Battle of Stara Zagora, 1877; the Treaty of San Stefano, 1878; and the Assembly of Turnovo, 1879.

Alexander Nevski Memorial Cathedral and Icon Museum

Beyond all this grandeur, the Bulgarian Academy of Sciences can be seen, hardly interfering with the golden-domed, green-domed

Al. Nevski Memorial Cathedral (centre) and Bulgarian Academy of Sciences (left) from the Grand Hotel Sofia

pomp of the Alexander Nevski Memorial Cathedral (1904-12), which now overlies a part of Serdica's millennial necropolis, at the modern capital's highest level. The 13th-century prince of Novgorod was Tsar Alexander II's patron saint because he saved Russia from invading Swedish armies in 1240. The memorial cathedral is not a functioning church but, like that other Russian-inspired church near Shipka Pass, pays tribute to the two hundred thousand Russians who fell during the liberation of Bulgaria in 1877-8. The choir, specialising in liturgical music, has produced first-rate but very cheap gramophone records normally on sale from the ladies with the candles, just inside the narthex. Of the twelve bells, the smallest weighs 10 kg and the largest 12 tons: this latter tolls only on Sunday mornings. The five-aisled structure is reminiscent of all the great Russian cathedrals, with the emphasis on huge spaces, divine power and majesty, through the medium of arches, vaults and a complex of domes, taking its cue from Byzantine structures such as Hagia Sophia in Istanbul. The dome rises to a height of forty-six metres, and we feel our human frailty and insignificance without further prompting. It is not permitted to walk round during morning services, which finish well before noon, so the best time to visit is after lunch, when summer light intrudes, streaking the icons and murals with shafts of sudden radiance.

Matters of status and precedence were dealt with tactfully. For example, the central iconostasis is Russian; those lateral to it are Bulgarian (on the south, the patron saint being King Boris I) and Slavic (on the north, the patron saints being Cyril and Methodius). Thirty-two Russian artists worked on the frescoes in the centre and thirteen Bulgarian artists under Anton Mitov worked elsewhere. Ferdinand never used the throne he ordered: it was used by Boris. The Bishop's throne behind was part of Pomerantsev's original plan. Subjects of the murals include 'Christ in the Temple' (grids in the wall have been incorporated into the pattern as seats) painted in 1924; Boris, who introduced Christianity to Bulgaria in 865; and Vladimir, who introduced it to Russia in 980. It is not fair to comment critically on the artistic standard of Kisselev's 'Nativity of Christ', 'Baptism' and 'Last Judgment' because these works were required to be compatible with a building directed more to national fervour than to mainstream religious painting, which has evolved elsewhere through Sutherland, Chagall and Stanley Spencer, for example. Bulgaria's isolation from modernism in art has paralleled that of Russia, for much the same good historical reasons, and we must accept the Nevski Cathedral for what it is, not for what it might have been.

Below the anachronistic temple to the fallen, however, pay tribute to a truly engaging and illuminating gallery: the Icon Museum in the crypt, accessible from a door beside the main entrance to the church. We have seen how Orthodox Christianity arrived here from Byzantium before any other Slav country, and we know that many icons were produced in ceramic form at Preslav, but icon painting on wood developed during the second Bulgarian State (1187-1396), when Veliko Turnovo, the capital, became the centre of religious painting. A major work of this period was the Christ Pantocrator with Apostles, a double-sided icon (with the Virgin Eleusa) from Nesebur; an attendant told me it was officially 'under conservation' but in fact it has not been seen for many years; another is the icon from Poganovo Monastery dated about 1395 and showing the Virgin with S. John the Theologian on one side, and on the other the Vision of Ezekiel and Habakkuk in Palaeologan style: dramatic,

Icon Museum. Deiesis (1577)

refined, attenuated, with drapery as eloquent as a homily. Magnificent works, worthy to set beside those of Andrei Rublyev or masterpieces in the Byzantine Museum in Athens, include a 13th-century mosaic Virgin Hodigitria, a Virgin Phaneromeni of 1541 from Sozopol, a Christ Pantocrator of 1607 from Nesebur, and 16th-17th altar doors from Veliko Turnovo which mark the 2nd phase of icon-painting, that of Turkish dominion, such as a glowing, effeminate S. George (16th century) from Plovdiv and a remarkable Deiesis (1577) of unknown provenance. The decadence of icon painting dates from the 19th century, when whole families no matter how untalented tried their hand at a craft by now recognised as nationalistically necessary to bolster National Revival. The Turks abhorred images of living creatures in the image of Allah, so what could be more praiseworthily subversive than to mass-produce Christian icons? As usual, however, except in the case of a prolific genius like Picasso, more does not generally mean better, and it does not take a connoisseur to prefer S. Theodore Tiron and S. Theodore Stratilates (1614) from Dobursko village, for instance, to Zahari Zograf's S. Menas and S. Onufrius (1845) from Dolnobeshovishki Monastery, east of Vratsa.

Sveta Sofia

The Nevski Cathedral is isolated in its square, like the head of S. John the Baptist held aloft on the platter by the triumphant Salome; but near at hand in a modest garden is a less obtrusive church, with a much longer history. Hagia Sophia it would be called in Greek: the Holy Wisdom, or in Bulgarian Sveta Sofia, the church which in the 14th century gave the city its name and still appears on its coat of arms. We know of a 4th-century church on the site from apse and floor mosaics now kept in Büyük Jami'a: it served as the cemetery church for the surrounding necropolis of Serdica. A second church fell to the Huns, and mosaics from this church have been preserved too. The present church rose on 6th-century foundations laid during the reign of Justinian, as a domed cruciform basilica with a central nave and two aisles. In the 16th century the Turks converted Sveta Sofia into a mosque but, perturbed by 'bad omens' of earthquakes in 1818 (demolishing the minaret) and 1858, they abandoned it altogether. With S. George's it was one of the two largest churches in 16th-century Sofia, so its transformation into a mosque became inevitable. 'The bigger they come...' It was reconstructed in 1930, but today only the narthex is open for services. The perpetual flame honouring the Unknown Soldier illumines lines of Vazov: 'Bulgaria, for you he died...' and someone has framed a lock of Vasil Levski's hair and hung it in Sveta Sofia for all to see. Vazov's grave can be visited close by, below a weeping willow, as he requested. The south-western flank of Nevski Square ends in the dignified Palace of the Synod (1904-7), designed by Petko Momchilov.

Art Galleries

Among the best collections of art in Eastern Europe is the Zhivkova Foundation Gallery at Ulitsa 1/19 February, on Alexander Nevski Square, in the former State Printing House designed by the Viennese architect Schwanberger at the end of the 19th century. Open since 1985, it is the home of the former collection of Kostadin Delchev, a dentist from Asenovgrad who has lived in France for more than sixty years, and his French wife Claudia, including works by Delacroix, Renoir, Maximilien Luce, Signac, Valadon, Matisse, Rouault's 'Le Boucher' of 1903, Villon, Vlaminck, Derain, Dunoyer de Segonzac, the Vidin-born Julius Pinkas known in Paris as Jules Pascin, Lanskoy, Clave, Atlan, Jansem and Buffet.

Beyond the Delchev Collection there is a wide range of objects from Goa (polychrome wood figures of Christ and S. Christopher), Africa, and Japan. I was astonished to find a Giovanni Rossi (d. 1549), son of that northern Italian Antonio Rossi who became Titian's first master and has a 'Virgin and Child' in the Venice Academy. A Henry Moore 'Helmet-head No.6' (1975) was presented by the artist, and another eminent bronze is Rodin's 'Woman with a Crab' of 1886. The collection continues to grow, often by donations, but problems with hard currency make it impracticable to bid for major works at international auctions.

If you want to see more of Bulgarian art, the City Art Gallery at 1 Ul. Gurko (closed at weekends) specialises in works of the 20th century, with a graphics room at the top showing Lyuben Dimanov and Ruman Skorchev, for example. National Revival art, which we have already sampled in the National Art Gallery, can also be seen here, with interesting paintings by Ivan Angelov, Anton Mitov, Jan Mrkvička, and Jaroslav Vesin. Vasil Barakov has a landscape, 'Chepelare', and David Perez a vivid 'Still Life', with mushrooms. It is worth exploring the halls for works by Elena Karamihailova, Ivan Nenov, Dechko Uzunov, Sirak Skitnik, Bronka Gyurova, Ivan Bukadinov and Vanko Urumov, though sculpture does not reach the same high standard.

The Art Gallery of the Union of Bulgarian Artists at 6 Ul. Shipka (open every day) buzzes with creativity. 'Imagination is the will of things', Wallace Stevens notes in his 'Colloquy with a Polish Aunt', and here is the youngest (dare one say the best?) generation of Bulgarian artists working in many media: Margarita Dobcheva's 'Alternative' in textiles, the ingenious use of stone in vertical plaques by Alexander Mandrajiev and Penka Boyanova, superb wallhangings by Mirela Doneva and Danelina Koseva. By contrast the temporary exhibitions by established artists showed a drought of inspiration. Svetlin Rusev's portraits and landscapes have gradually reduced to a stark palette of white, grey, black, with the occasional startling crimson blaze. Can this be the master whose expressive, sturdy and bold blocks of colour irradiate 'An Old Fishing Town' (1966)? Naiden Petkov's recent works struck a false note of simple optimism without technical or imaginative depth. On the first floor, the 'National Exhibition of Young Artists' produced a bevy of striking posters, sensitive restoration (showing historic icons before and after, including an iconostasis at Kyustendil), dresses, pullovers, jewellery, glass, ceramics and signs. By far the most enjoyable exhibits in my Lewis Carrollian opinion were the silly umbrellas by Kerstin Vilana Yaneva of Stefanovo (Lovech oblast), with their extraordinary, eye-catching motifs such as a cat or a mouse. Some western entrepreneur should contact Yaneva quickly... The shop of the Union of Bulgarian Artists, where you can acquire national dolls, jewellery, objects in wood and leather, ceramics and wrought iron, can be found at 6 Bul. Ruski near the Mineral Souvenir shop at no. 10; paintings, sculptures and graphics are on sale at the Union Shop at 147 Ul. Rakovski. For crystalware, try Quartz at 8 Bul. Vitosha or 35 Bul. Nansen. The best gramophone record shop and bookstore I found in Sofia are close together in the shopping precinct below the Zhivkova National Palace of Culture. Other exhibition halls can be found at 125 and 133 Ul. Rakovski.

Literary Museums
Just as literary pilgrims to England head first for Stratford on Avon, so those visiting Bulgaria should make time for the House-Museum of the national poet Ivan Vazov, at 10 Ul. Ivan Vazov, open at eccentric hours, but definitely closed from Saturday afternoon until Tuesday noon. Photographs, books, quotations try to evoke the spirit of a man of letters and action: here he is at Kalofer (1865-6), at Sopot (1870), his home at Berkovitsa (1879-80), at Odessa in 1888 (he lived by coincidence at Sofia St there, now no. 32 Korolenko St). A bedroom with a single bed and simple washbasin is made claustrophobic by heavy curtains and a tall glazed ceramic stove like a stolid intruder always looking over your shoulder. Heavy drapes seem to half-fill the private library, with Vazov's sofa, rocking-chair and early telephone, and Vazov always retained immense affection for the 'desk', in fact just a plain deal table topped with baize. His friends urged him to buy a more 'suitable' desk, partly because one of the legs was shorter than the others and needed to be propped up with wads of paper. 'No', replied Vazov, 'what matters is *what* a man writes, not the piece of furniture *where* he writes'. The bookshelves are fitted with editions of his works, such as *Pod Igoto*, but I found an English-language *Russian Manual*

and Vapereau's *Dictionnaire des Contemporains*. Wallpaper printed red-on-cream, another stove and more heavy drapes clutter the sitting-room. His mother's bedroom's walls are decked with sepia photos, as is the dining-room, back downstairs, where he died. The birch is surrounded, in the little garden outside, by sad cypress. Vazov's house foundations were laid in March 1895 and by that September he, his brother Nikola and his mother had moved in, next door to the family of Vula, his younger sister. The house was destroyed by an incendiary bomb on 30 March 1944, and reopened in its present restored form in 1950.

A nation's soul is not visible: it resides in the poetry, plays and great novels of its writers, so while on my way to the 'Sulza i Smyah' (Tears and Laughter) Theatre at 127 Ul. Rakovski I wanted to find time to breathe in the atmosphere of two more museum-houses: Peyo Yavorov's at 136 Ul. Rakovski and Petko and Pencho Slaveikov's next door at 138. Like the other literary houses once inhabited by Hristo Smirnenski (116 U. Shekerjiiski) and by Nikola Vaptsarov (37 Ul. Kanchev), the opening-times are 12-7 on Tuesdays and Wednesdays, 9-5 on Thursdays and Fridays, and 9-1 on Saturdays. Yavorov (1878-1914), a prominent poet and play-wright, spent the last years of his wife Laura's life here, in a late 19th-century house, before she committed suicide in a fit of jealous torment. Born Kracholov, Peyo withdrew into himself after losing faith in socialism and the possibilities of the proletariat, and having struggled for Macedonia, though not a Macedonian himself. Here is the map of Macedonia he himself used, 1899-1903, with pistols and rifles. His study broods with the burden of self-murder like an indelible shadow. Laura, daughter of the party leader Petko Karavelov, had committed suicide earlier. 'I'm coming after you', he wrote but merely lost his sight: the second time he shot himself he also took poison to make doubly sure. The desk, bookshelves, candlesticks breathe the name of a man imbued with Russian symbolism, French symbolism, who could entitle a 1907 volume of poems *Insomnia and Intuitions* and penned dramas in the penumbra of Chekhov such as *At the Foot of Mount Vitosha* (1911) and *When the Thunder Rolls* (1912). The guest-room where literary friends came to visit is opposite the original bedroom of Laura and Peyo. Here are souvenirs of Peyo's mistress Mina Todorova, his muse while they lived in France for a full year, who inspired his best love poems, such as 'Two Beautiful Eyes'. Furniture from the sitting-room opposite the study comes from the house Yavorov lived in after Laura's death.

In Tryavna we have already seen the home of Bulgaria's great intellectual and poet Petko Slaveikov, born in 1827 the son of Racho Kazanjiyata of Veliko Turnovo. Though Racho was a domineering personality, Petko rebuked him with words which have resounded down the decades since then: 'Na zhivot mi si gospoda, no na volyata ne mi si', a melodious aphorism that might be translated 'You are the master of my life, but not of my will'. In 1879 Petko and his son Pencho came to Sofia and their lives here are illustrated in a room left of the entrance. Pencho collaborated with Yavorov in publishing collections of Bulgarian folksongs, and translated German poets in addition to *Romeo and Juliet* and *The Taming of the Shrew*. The original house on the site was destroyed, but many of the contents survived, and other memorabilia have been brought. Here is Petko's library, quill pen, snuff-box, a watch showing European and Bulgarian time, neatly exemplifying the distance separating Sofia from the vortex of European life. In Pencho's room I pored over photos of his father and his sister Penka, and the residue of his once excellent library: some two thousand books in nine languages: Euripides, Goethe, Heine, Nietzsche, Verlaine. Another room is devoted to Pencho's companion Marya Belcheva, widow of a Minister of Finance during the Stamboliiski government who was assassinated when Marya was only 23. A confidante of Ferdinand's mother, Clementine, Marya lived with Pencho from the age of 35 to the end of his life, closing his eyes at Brunate on Lake Como in 1912, when he was 46. Her room displays a glass lamp from Venice: how fragile is life compared with glass!

Slaveikov rejected Vazov's realism, seizing as models the balladic spirit of German literature, and Nietzsche's passionate invocation of human possibilities in an age ruled by religion and obscurantism. He transcended national boundaries in clarity of Russian tragic intensity. Never wholly emerging from his father's giant shadow (one thinks of Witkiewicz in Poland and his son Witkacy; or Gosse's sado-masochistic *Father and Son*), Pencho nevertheless worked out his destiny in part during the Leipzig years (1892-8), flashes of originality in his nature poetry, and above all in the magazine *Misul* (Thought') produced jointly for seventeen years with Yavorov, Krustev, and Todorov. If one is looking for the

Dionysiac in poetry, one prefers Kiril Hristov (1875-1944), but the Apollonian poet of *Song of Blood* will always merit attention. Pencho wrote autobiographically of 'Ivo Dolya': 'Disappointment clutched at the poet's heart with its bony fingers many a time, and year by year it gripped him more strongly until finally it became absolute master as if by official title deed'.

National Opera

From the Slaveikovs' House I hurried to the National Opera where at 7 p.m. I was due to attend not the advertised programme but a hastily-rearranged Verdi *Requiem* dedicated to the distinguished baritone Nikola Smochevski who had died a few days previously. Ruslan Raichev conducted a reverently heartrending performance with the National Opera Orchestra and Chorus, and outstanding soloists: Stefka Evstatieva, Hristina Angelakova, Kaludi Kaludov and Stefan Elenkov. A Roman Catholic masterpiece was being sung (with such beauty that the work had indeed recently been recorded by similar forces) in a Communist country where members of the chorus would appear in an Orthodox service. Stereotypes of 'grim', 'monolithic' Bulgaria quickly drop away when one is involved in day-to-day life.

For instance, one day I was kindly invited by a parent to visit the mixed Victor Hugo School on Mladost Housing Estate and there I waited outside a classroom, watching vigorous, bouncy youngsters in the ten grades (6-16) from six years of age to sixteen changing classes at the end of a period. No uniforms impeded their individuality: quite the reverse, each youngster seemed to wear different clothes and even different kinds of bags, satchels, and backpacks. Sneakers, plimsolls and shoes seemed equally varied. Girls wore jeans, some choosing earrings, but the keynote was lack of inhibition. Form rooms had also been organised into subject rooms, so 2A doubled as the history room, and 2D as the Russian room. Everyone has to study one western language, the choice being English, French or German. Mladost Estate is by no means the oldest of the high-rise housing estates in Sofia: the oldest is named for Lenin and the second is called Iztok, 'East'.

Sveti Sedmochislenitsi

If you stay at the Park Hotel Moskva or the Pliska it is a pleasant walk to Freedom Park (Park na Svobodata), where you can see young people enjoying themselves, 'trying it on' with milder versions of Western hair styles and trends in clothes: jeans and slogan-bearing T-shirts. I walked down Ulitsa Tsankov with the Druzhba ice-hockey stadium on my right and, across the Perlovska river by way of Friendship Bridge (Most na Druzhba) to Ul. Graf Ignatiev. Where it meets Ul. Tsar Shishman rises the emphatic, underrated Church of SS. Sedmochislenitsi, which means the Holy Apostles, in this context, but literally refers to the 'number' (*chislen*) 'seven' (*sedmo*): Cyril and Methodius, with their disciples Kliment of Ohrid, Naum, Gorazd, Sava, and Angelairi. Originally a mosque, called black from the colour of its granite, it dates from 1528, and was ordered by Sultan Sulaiman the Magnificent, antedating the Banya Bashi Mosque by nearly half a century. Finding the mosque abandoned in 1878, the Russian liberators used it to store weapons. The energetic Russian architect A.N. Pomerantsev, also responsible for the Nevski Cathedral, was entrusted with the overall design for a new Orthodox Church under the day-to-day control of the Bulgarian architects Yordan Milanov and Petko Momchilov. Many of the icons were painted by Stefan Ivanov and Anton Mitov, but I felt overwhelming relief at the sensitivity which persuaded the Bulgarians freed from the Ottoman yoke to preserve the Black Mosque's awe-inspiring interior. Little has changed structurally, except for the porch and two wide side doors of 1901-3.

Ulitsa Rakovski

I always take the opportunity to meander along Ulitsa Rakovski, the Boul' Saint-Mich' of Sofia, with patisseries (*sladkarnitsa* is the sign you will find outside) and cafés such as the Havana, the Opera, and the Prague. I like the Hungarian cuisine at the Budapest (145 Ul. Rakovski), where dark-eyed beauties glanced around mysteriously, their assignations kept or missed: how should we know what they are thinking? I was seated in the rush-hour at a table with three women, one silent and two suddenly given to bursts of rapid cigarette-filled passion. *Die schweigsame Frau* in a tight black cardigan kept fingering the gold necklace that hung recklessly round her sallow neck, as if daring her to let it go. I matched her silent games with my letter-changing pastime: gold - good - food - fool, gold - gild - wild - wold - wood - wool - fool, gold bold - fold - food - fool. A fool and her gold are soon parted, but not for long.

Theatres

I ran, late because of a waitress's extraordinary delay, to the Ivan Vazov National Theatre for a stunning performance of Molière's *Don Juan*, played to a 30% capacity audience with Stefan Danailov in the leading part. The proscenium arch stage is traditional, and this is the showpiece for the best classical drama in the capital. Nothing but the neo-classical exterior of 1904 by the Viennese architects Felmer and Helmer survived the fire of 1923; in its present form the theatre dates from 1929, to the design of the German architect Dülfer. Acting styles and costumes, sets and poise: all except the language combined to evoke Molière's vision of Spain through cynical 18th-century French eyes, and nobody should miss a chance – anywhere – to see contemporary Bulgarian acting. The interval also made a dramatic impact, excited teenagers sipping Schweppes Bitter Lemon and munching Borovets chocolate wafers from the buffet, while serious citizens queued quietly for cigarettes, chocolate, and open salami sandwiches. The repertory on the main

Ivan Vazov National Theatre, with fountains

96

stage at the National Theatre included Tennessee Williams' *Cat on a Hot Tin Roof*, Maeterlinck's *Blue Bird*, *Hamlet*, Ibsen's *Peer Gynt*, and plays by Radichkov, Kovačevič, Vezhinov, Haitov, Minkov, Vazov, Shatrov and Tsanev. The smaller stage offered pieces by Peter Shaffer, James Saunders, Dudarev, Strashimirov, Anastasov and Galin.

If you arrive early for a show on a summer evening, sit down beside the pool and watch the passers-by. There strides a purposeful civil servant, with a slim brown document-case, decorous in a matching suit. Yonder two shy teenagers are courting with the earnestness of those who have paddled, but never swum. Over there a woman of forty in a dark grey dress and a navy handbag stands with her feet apart the prescribed distance, balancing her glance between absorption and absentmindedness. A war veteran on the theatre steps delves deep into a newspaper's words for double meanings, triple insinuations. A flighty girl in a yellow dress trips ostentatiously beside the pool so that Heaven is allowed to glimpse her legs in the reflection.

I thought in my ignorance that the National Army Theatre at 98 Ul. Rakovski would devote its persistent labours to strident battle scenes of men in uniform shooting each other and writhing on the floor in exactly the best sightlines. But the Cold War is thawing out, and interspersed with plays by Stanislav Stratiev and Konstantin Iliev the theatre puts on Beckett's *Waiting for Godot*, and especially Brecht's *Herr Puntila und sein Knecht Matti* with such pungent pugilistic gusto and wit that I wondered how much the director owed to the authentic tradition of the Berliner Ensemble. Brecht's *Entfremdungseffekt* drapes naturally on Bulgarian actors' shoulders, and this is by any standards an epoch-making production.

At the Stefan Makedonski Music Theatre I saw a captivating *La Belle Hélène* by Offenbach greatly superior to the contemporary Sadler's Wells production in London.

The Drama Theatre repertory at 28a Bul. Zaimov during my stay in Sofia included Erdman's controversial *The Suicide*, Georg Büchner's *Woyzeck*, and works by Valeri Petrov and I. Radoev. The Youth Theatre at 10 Ul. Narodno Subranie offered Friedrich Dürrenmatt's *King John*, a version of *Alice in Wonderland*, and works by Cocteau and Dario Fo.

Railway Station

The simplest way to judge a nation's character is by behaviour at railway stations, from messy cacophony at Bologna to smooth efficiency at Wiesbaden. In Greek trains, bread and olives are produced as soon as one chugs out of the station. At Bombay several million bodies seem to converge on one seat, which was in any case already occupied. Sofia Central Station is a place to sit and wait for passengers. A fat man in a raincoat bearing a transistor radio listened intently to Engelbert Humperdinck's 'Please release me, let me go' as he walked deliberately past. A woman of thirty quickly flattened her hair, charmingly, needlessly, to draw attention to its raven's silk. The underground concourse pulsated with private enterprise from popcorn vendors to trinket-stalls. Umbrellas were being laid out; cheap watches on another stand. Ice-cream and flowers, newspapers and magazines. Indicator boards showed arrivals due and delays due to wintry weather: Moscow at 15.20, 200 minutes; Svoge at 17.12, 60 minutes; Pleven at 17.30, 50 minutes; Varna at 17.40, 50 minutes; Kyustendil at 17.42, 60 minutes, Plovdiv at 18.03, on time (?); Vidin/Lom at 20.05, 50 minutes. Women intensely private strode past. A little farmer with an ill-fitting suit glanced about him apprehensively: they don't have underground concourses in the Rhodope mountains. Two boys played tag round columns. A dramatically sullen beauty in a maroon coat fashioned her Marlene Dietrich impression from slightly lifted eyebrows. Two old women, plainly sisters, bumped each other in yet another vain attempt to become Siamese twins. Would one be seeing the other off, away from confidence, warm tea and gossip, to a husband forever strange and barely tolerated?

Back in my room on the fifteenth floor of the Novotel Evropa, I peered down through mist at the snowy railway lines converging on the Central Station. In the streets below tiny matchstick figures unwittingly shaped themselves into an L.S. Lowry painting, each figure a steeple of personality on the wide church roof of earth. I felt guilty about seeking analogies: one part of Sofia a kind of Salford; another (around Nevski Square) a kind of Kiev.

University

The University is, as in any other land, a good place to meet young people, and 'students' can be of virtually any age of course in a country where education is taken very seriously, and enjoys ever-increasing investment, especially at vocational and training levels. Sofia University named for Kliment of Ohrid graces the corner of Bul. Tolbuhin and Bul. Ruski with a neo-Baroque façade oddly anachronistic in 1925-34, designed by the French architect Briançon and the Bulgarians Lazarov and Milanov. The donors of the land and cash, the brothers Evlogi and Hristo Georgiev, are honoured with statues flanking the staircase. In fact, the University as an institution dates from 1888, when four full-time and three part-time lecturers taught a Higher Course in Education to forty-three students. The University currently teaches forty subjects in fourteen faculties, with around twenty thousand students being taught by 11 academicians, 135 professors, 340 readers and 760 assistant professors. No fees are charged for tuition, sports or cultural activities, libraries or any other facility.

National Palace of Culture
Possibly the most futuristic of Sofia's buildings is the octagonal National Palace of Culture (1981) on the ample Ploshtad Baba Nedelya terminating the southern end of Bulevard Vitosha with a metro station and a landscaped pedestrian precinct, tourist office, booking centre, a restaurant and cafeteria, a first-rate shopping arcade, discotheque, night club and bowling alley. I phoned the administrative office for a guided tour, and Vesela Stambuliiska offered a cordial welcome, comparing the palace to London's new Barbican Centre, combining an exhibition centre with halls for concerts, conferences and congresses. Low-raked seating in red plush provides excellent sightlines for an apron stage suited to visiting companies such as La Scala, the Bolshoi, the London Symphony and the Vienna Philharmonic. The N.D.K. (Naroden Dvorets na Kulturata) hosted the 23rd General Congress of Unesco in 1985: I felt nostalgic for the super-dynamic Divinova, my Bulgarian personnel manager at Unesco's Paris HQ in the 1970s. The main building has eight floors above ground and three below, with a capacity in its twelve halls ranging from 100 up to 3880. During my visit a Bulgar-Japanese Trade Conference was in progress. The Great Hall is used for major film occasions such as the Bulgarian première of Bernardo Bertolucci's *The Last Emperor*, costing 2.50 leva a ticket. Prices rise to 10 leva for the best seats at the New Year Music Festival, to hear Ghiuselev, Freni, Gedda and other great stars. The designer of the N.D.K., named for the enterprising

National Palace of Culture , with Vitosha in the background

Lyudmila Zhivkova, deceased daughter of the Leader, Todor Zhivkov, was Alexander Barov, also responsible for the Grand Hotel Sofia and Varna's festival complex. The works of art in the N.D.K. might be categorised as nationalist-rhetorical from the foyer's bronze of the city of Sofia shown as a young woman with flowing golden hair, her arms outstretched in stiff welcome, by Dimitur Boikov, to the tapestry by Marin Varbanov jumbling up copies of selected Bulgarian works of art in clashing juxtaposition. Technical brilliance with lighting, acoustics and equipment has regrettably not been matched by artistic excellence: instead we have ceramic tiles by Vanko Urumov, a sub-Blakean mural of 'The Ascent of Bulgarian Culture' by Dechko Uzunov, and a sub-Rivera view of 'Man and Peace', colours and composition discordant, by Yoan Leviev. Hristo Stefanov's mural 'Fire' manages to incorporate 43 historical figures and six symbols, including 'Mother', as though trying to cram as many disparate martyrs into one space as humanly possible. Why settle, the planners must have concluded in committee, for any fewer? The result is less satisfactory than those ole solutions to pictorial hyper-activity: 'truth to material, or leave it blank'. I wonder what they think, those old women in black who remember the square with its old barracks and ramshackle open-air market in days gone by?

Vitosha

The best hotel in Sofia at present is generally thought to be the Vitosha New Otani at 100 Bul. Anton Ivanov, south of the city centre on the way up to Vitosha. The other five-star hotel is the Balkan Sheraton, central as the inner bull on a darts board. The four-star Novotel Evropa I found very convenient too, for the Central Railway Station, and the three-star Grand Sofia for churches and theatres. The four-star Rodina is situated at 8 Bul. Totleben.

If you choose to spend a lot of time up the granite and syenite massif of Vitosha, the three-star Hemus is very comfortable, at 31 Bul. Traikov. From here it is a quick drive up into Vitosha National Park. Fine hotels in Vitosha itself, all very close to each other, are the three-star Prostor, and the two-star Shtastlivetsa and Moreni, where I enjoyed the best lunch I recall in Sofia on a new verandah looking north over the snow-covered city. An Australian woman with banana hands tourniqueted by rings asked the waiter what 'gupekmop' meant? The hospitable waiter politely answered that he had no idea. 'Gupekmop madam?'. 'Yep,' she growled. 'It's on the door on the way in.' 'Ah,', I smiled at her. 'The Bulgarian 'd' looks like our 'g' and the Bulgarian 'i' like our 'u'. If you put the letters all together, I rather believe you'll come up with 'direktor', meaning 'director'. 'Crazy language,' sniffed the moving marquee, and I grinned encouragingly at the waiter. As if waiting at table wasn't bad enough to start with...

To the skiing fraternity, Vitosha means the centre of Aleko reached by chairlift from Dragalevtsi or by chairlift from Simeonovo. Incidentally, the new location of Sofia Zoo is on the way from the centre to Simeonovo. It was a grave disappointment to the good folk of Sofia that their city was recently overlooked for the Winter Olympics. Vitosha is ideal, with the support if necessary of Pamporovo and Borovets, because it offers all grades from elementary runs to world championship difficulty, costs are very low in Bulgaria, the views are stunning, and the organisation would be impeccable. Aleko Ski Centre caters to 35,000 visitors a day on average, and ski schools train groups of no more than fifteen each at

Map of the Environs of Sofia, showing Boyana (left centre)

every level. You could also ski around Mount Kupena, and below the peaks of Ushite or Selimitsa.

To non-skiers, Vitosha means Boyana. After the Borovo housing estate, you cross the ring road enclosing the city area of 18,000 hectares and suddenly enter pure mountain air, suburbs giving way to private villas. The sign says 'Boyansko Hanche', a restaurant serving national dishes with a folklore show. Boyana church itself appears unimpressive at first glance, but it once formed part of a massive fortified aristocratic complex, with court, kitchens, residences and stables. A ruined tower on Maiden's Rock (Momina Skala) witnesses the power of the boyar, and archaeologists have found waterpipes and walls of houses and the outer stronghold. Boyana Church was enlarged in the 1250s by Sebastocrator Kaloyan, portrayed in carefully-restored frescoes with his wife Dessislava, (not to be confused with Princess Maria Dessislava, the 14th-century heroine of Parashkev Hajiev's opera). The first tiny church, of the early 11th century, comprised a small cruciform space with a dome. Kaloyan added a rectangular lower storey as a narthex and crypt, and an upper storey as the 13th-century church. The third period of the Church of S. Nicholas and the Holy Martyr Panteleimon represents the sturdy National Revival style in the mid-19th century, with mortar, stone and wooden beams to cushion the shock of earthquakes. Great frescoes of 1259 depict 240 figures on 89 scenes, with absorbing details of realism, such as the costume and accessories of Bulgarian feudal life at the time, for instance in the arched 'The Last Supper', with a typical check napkin on a table laden with food recognisable from a Boyana table today: bread, garlic and radishes. The pictorial naturalism of the portraits announces like a fanfare the beginning of a long tradition. Who could forget the steady gaze of bearded Kaloyan as donor, holding a model of the church, his mild and gentle consort, King Konstantin Asen and his queen Irina? In the southern room, a grizzled warrior saint stands with a firm spear aslant across his golden halo. In the western room, watch how the sea boils and whirls below a ship carrying S. Nicholas of Myra; how gracefully the chubby-faced boy Jesus faces that animated throng of disputants in the Temple; how majestically in her regal robes Queen Helena (finder of the True Cross) transfixes your attention. In the eastern room the manly figure of S. Eustratius gives heart: we who look as earthly as he, understates the hagiographer, can by virtue

Boyana Church. 'The Harrowing of Hell', a fresco of 1259

and heroism achieve equal sanctity. How different is the Cimabue-like Crucifixion, Christ's twisted body white against a background dark with grief! How transcendently moving is the Harrowing of Hell, beyond space, beyond time, beyond words! Ethereal, Jesus absorbs concentrated stares from men and women of every age and every estate. A rare image of Christ Euergetes blesses us with a calm joy more commonly found in a Buddhist mudra. Whether you prefer the sixteen scenes from the Life of S. Nicholas or the sensitive individuality of contemporary portraits, Boyana is a treasury of 13th-century art fully equal to the glories of Turnovo.

During my visit, there was a marvellous display of 11th-century and later MSS from the private library of Professor Ivan Duichev (1907-86), whose villa in Boyana houses the library and a new research centre for Slavic and Byzantine Art. Superlative Greek Gospels (1125) were distinguished by miniatures of Mark, Luke and John. Bulgaria's manuscript tradition persisted into the 19th century, despite the spread of printing, because of restrictions and censorship of the press, but the quality of illumination and calligraphy had fallen.

Boyana is the site of film studios producing five to seven new movies every year. I drove up to Zlatni Mostove for the view, but you could take the cabin lift if you preferred, arriving beside Hotel Kopitoto.

If you take the chairlift down from Vitosha's Hotel Moreni you arrive at Vodenicharski Mehani, an excellent restaurant close to Dragalevski Monastery, also of course accessible by car. Now an active nunnery, with six resident nuns, Dragalevski seems remote from the world in its rustling beechwoods. High on this mountain known as 'the little Athos' for the scholarly reputation and piety of its many mediaeval monasteries, as early as the 14th century, Dragalevski enjoyed a charter from Tsar Ivan Shishman (1371-93): 'Our Most Gracious Majesty deigned to grant this finely-indited and all-embracing golden charter to the Monastery of the Most Pure Mother of God, which is upon Vitosha and was created, built and decorated by the Parent of Our Most Gracious Majesty the Late Tsar Ivan Alexander of blessed memory, and thus Our Most Gracious Majesty frees this monastery of ours together with all its goods and chattels' – Ivan Shishman in Jesus Christ Our Lord, Pious Tsar and Autocrat of all Bulgarians and Greeks'. The document, racing with serpentine wiggles, can be seen at the Zografski Monastery on Mount Athos.

The Ottomans did not perceive this wooded monastery as a threat, unlike churches in cities, and so after 1382 Dragalevski Monastery was allowed to hold services, to train whiterobed clergy (who are permitted to marry) and celibate blackrobed monks, and to worship the Christian God. It remained a centre for icon-painting, its scriptorium produced such famous books as Nikola's Four Gospels (1469) now in Hilendarski Monastery, Mount Athos; the so-called Dragalevski Four Gospels (1534) with a silver-plated cover (1648, by the Sofiote goldsmith Velko) on the wooden binding; and the celebrated Psaltery (1598) copied by the brothers Danail, Stoyan and Vladko, now in the Athos monastery of Iverski. The 14th-century church is frescoed with two cycles: the first and better (1476) in the porch, with portraits of Radoslav Mavur and his family, Sofiote donors; the second (early 17th century) in the nave, with works by the Sofiote painter Father Pimen Zografski. Saints and ascetics on the exterior northern wall recall the age of hesychasts.

The perennial connection between monasteries and liberation movements in Bulgaria is neatly illustrated here by the monk Gennadi's alliance with Vasil Levski, who made the holy man a courier for the revolutionary committee in Sofia. When the Turks captured Dimitur Obshti in 1872, menacing the rebels with collapse, Gennadi escaped to Serbia and joined Voivod Panayot Hitov. The secret committee in Sofia was reorganised in 1873 by Deacon Ignatius Rilski, who at the same time became abbot of Dragalevski. Liberation would not be long in coming. The building overshadowing the church is the official residence of the Patriarch of Sofia, with suites of guest-rooms. He is a member of the National Assembly.

In summer, you can climb to Cherni Vruh ('Black Peak') by way of the Aleko hut: this is the highest point of Mount Vitosha, with sublime views worthy of Turner across to the Rila Mountains, and below to the expanse of Sofia.

3: VIDIN AND THE NORTH

Iskur Gorge — Cherepishki Monastery — Vratsa — Mihailovgrad — Vidin — Magura Caves and Dimovo — Belogradchik — Chiprovski Monastery — Berkovitsa — Pleven — Lovech — Devetaki Cave and Letnitsa — Ivanovo Rock Churches and Cherven — Ruse — Sveshtari and Sreburna — Svishtov and Silistra — Tolbuhin

Iskur Gorge

An ideal introduction to Bulgarian landscapes is the short but dramatic railway ride from Sofia's vibrant, busy Central Railway Station along the Iskur Gorge, sixty-seven km from Novi Iskur to the village of Lyutibrod. By car you can stop off at the Monastery of Seven Altars (Sedemte Prestola) and at the Monastery of the Assumption (1390) near Cherepish, among others, or make detours to such monasteries as Gornobanski, Iliyenski and Kurilovski, or Kremikovski, Seslavski and Elenishki. It would indeed be perfectly possible to spend a month in Bulgaria, seeing at least two monasteries a day on average, and still not visit all the important sights with unforgettable views such as those from Glozhenski (an easy drive from Sofia) or Preobrazhenski (very close to Veliko Turnovo).

Iskur Gorge itself, towering above the road, the railway line, and the most important Bulgarian tributary of the Danube, winds through the Balkan Range, known in antiquity as Haemus and in Bulgarian as 'Stara Planina', the Old Mountain. Sofiotes have long delighted in these green, healthy surroundings; their private cottages and villas dot the hillsides around Lukovo and Rebrovo. Older trees and new pine saplings cover red and grey sandstone interspersed with white limestone and green shale strata, and in spring the scent of pines reminds you of the aroma near Athens, as your train glides into the hilly countryside. The next station, Thompson, honours a British army major who died close by alongside partisans of the Second Sofia Brigade fighting the Germans in 1944. After the holiday resort of Svoge and Bov station comes Lakatnik Station, some way west of Lakatnik village, with a restaurant that makes a pleasant break, especially if you decide to explore caves, their waterfalls and icy pools. Near the village of Eliseina a narrow road will bring you in 9 km to the Monastery of Seven Altars, originally known as the Osenovlakski Monastery of the Blessed Virgin and dating from the early 16th century at the latest, for we have a Gospels manuscript with a marginal note marked 1511. The monastery was devastated first in 1737, and again after being rebuilt by Stoyan of Troyan in 1770. The present church of 1815, restored in 1868, has a unique plan of seven chapels, with a heavy cylindrical dome above a wooden chandelier by master-carvers of Osenovlak. Look for the metal bar, called a *semantron*, sometimes used in Orthodox churches in place of a bell: it was forged in 1799 during the period of Bishop Sophronios of Vratsa. The open outer narthex is much later, with an inscription attributing the mural in the dome to Dimitri Alexov and Angelko Mitrev (1868).

Cherepishki Monastery
We emerge from the Iskur Gorge near the village of Lyutibrod, point of departure for the 14th-century Monastery of the Assumption huddled below steep rocks beside a bend in the river. Ravaged during the Austro-Ottoman wars in the late 16th and early 17th centuries, it was one of those monasteries revived by the scholar and icon-painter Pimen Zografski, said in a biography by his pupil Pamphilius to have 'travelled around the whole district of Sofia and built three hundred churches and fifteen monasteries'; Pimen died here at Cherepishki in 1610. It is said that many battles between Bulgarians and Ottoman occupation forces occurred in this area, and the monastery derives its name from the skulls (*cherep* in Bulgarian) which littered the territory, but church legends and numbers are subject to fluctuation according to the listener. My enjoyment of Cherepishki, like that of S. Catherine's on Sinai, or Meteora, is connected in some Bunyanesque way with difficulty of access. Part of the revelation is the journey itself, like the peregrinations of a Hindu *sadhu* or the Wandering Jew, Ahasuerus, whose legend persists throughout Central Europe. Between the railway junction town of Mezdra and the village of Roman you can find just another such isolated monastery, that of Turzhishki dedicated to Elijah and now called Strupetski. *Struya* means column, and seventy wooden columns gave me a strange, momentary feeling of

being back in a Japanese temple like the great Kiyomizudera over-looking Kyoto. Wild roses sparked, stabs of pure colour, through wilder briers. Sunlight striped the wooden verandahs, which were damaged by fire in 1972. The church murals of the 16th or 17th century include 'Christ on the Road to Calvary', sandalled amid blackbooted and helmeted Roman soldiers, and a hieratic 'Mocking of Christ' achieving a notable architectonic effect.

Near the village of Tsarevets, a cave-complex has been disco-vered with over a thousand recorded graffiti and deep carvings ranging in subject matter from warrior-hunters to snakes and deer, and in period from epochs before the invention of writing, through the era of runes, to Cyrillic inscriptions. Astronomers believe that some symbols may represent a long-forgotten system of measuring time in days, months and years. Another major cave system, named Ledenika after the Bulgarian *lednik* (glacier), is situated near Vratsa and has been illuminated for regular visits since 1961.

Vratsa

Vratsa (a form of Vratitsa, or 'small door') is documented as early as the eighth century A.D., but we know the Thracians inhabited the town in the 4th century B.C. from the tomb of a Thracian princess excavated at Mogila in 1965, decorated *à la manière de Tut Ankh Amun* with an exquisite mask, in her case of silver, with zoomorphic figures; on her breast appear two snakes with panther heads. The Archaeological Museum (opened in 1980) displays much else from the Bronze Age, when matriarchate gives way to patriarchate, and the Iron Age, when the Thracian tribe known as Tribales populated Vratsa according to Thucydides (IV, 101) and Diodorus Siculus (XV, 36). Votive plaques of the Thracian horseman-god abound, though many more can be seen in Varna. The Thracians centred their religion on this god-hero, who used a horse in peace and war, and may have been associated with ideas of kingship on earth. The Thracians apparently did not give this god a single name, unlike the wordy Greeks; he borrowed attributes from Asklepios and Apollo, Dionysus and Ares: altogether a slippery personality. Or he had a local name, not recognised by a neighbour-ing tribe. His function, however, was clear: he protected the tribe and each of its members from destruction, represented by a boar threatening the tree of life. We recall that Cretan Zeus was mangled by a boar, and Hercules achieved immortality by slaying the

Erymanthian boar, not in any pointless hunt, but because it was devastating the fields near Arcadia. He was consequently at once powerful god, worthy king, and courageous hero. Not only did the boars of antiquity ravage the crops that fed the Thracians: they threatened the roots of the northern tree of life, Yggdrasil itself, in Celtic and Gallic myth. The Thracian horseman-god not only protected this year's food supply, but guaranteed perennial life (in nature and in religion) as long as he was propitiated. Thus did Iranian Mithras defeat the dragon and Roman Mithras overcome the bull. The horseman-hero as a patriarch demanded a wife, and the great mother goddess, a figure derided by some scholars as a conglomerate of female deities without any independent existence, is seen by some Thracologists as an extension of the Eleusinian cult of Demeter and her daughter Persephone. Hierogamy played an essential part in oriental religions, the mother (Persephone, Cybele and Aphrodite) marrying her son (Dionysus, Attis, and Adonis), an idea from which the necessity and the guilt of Oedipus will infect Western drama up to Eugene O'Neill and beyond. Artemis herself, like her lover and counterpart the Thracian horseman, was a divinity of the hunt, of animals, and hence of life in general. Her most popular manifestation among the Thracians was Bendis, and Plato records a Thracian festival of Bendis at Piraeus, where a sow was sacrificed, her blood being poured on wheat to be sown, to ensure fertility. Thus the hero conquered forces inimical to life (the boar) and the goddess guaranteed life itself (through the boar's female counterpart, the sow).

Among the treasures from Mogila in Vratsa Archaeological Museum, look for the goblet decorated with chariot racing, a masterpiece in gold. In such company, I suppose the Gradeshnitsa terra cotta plates and jars of the fifth millennium B.C. seem plain and even primitive, yet I found their dignity and simplicity oddly reassuring.

At the Hemus Hotel close to the Museum I lunched off beef soup, pepper and tomato salad, veal and sautée potatoes, followed by Turkish coffee, unadventurous perhaps but swift, elegantly presented, and wholesome. A town of seventy-five thousand people, Vratsa earns a good living from cement factories, lead- and zinc-mining, silk and textiles. Bare economic facts like these conceal a deeply-held belief in the significance of the passing seasons, and Vratsa's Ethnographic Museum has been quartered in just this manner. Christmas is a season for simple fare: bread and apples, a time when *koledari* (bachelors) troop from house to house proffering wishes for health, wealth and the fertility of animals. On January 1, S. Basil's Day, a cockerel is cooked in the household, and it is the turn of boys to make their rounds with good wishes. S. Lazarus' day is the girls' turn. Spring festivities would strike us more familiarly: Easter eggs and buns. May 6, S. George's Day, has become a secular holiday, when shepherds place garlands over lambs' necks and boys push the girls of their choice on an improvised swing in the countryside. March 1 (opening the only month with a woman's name, *marta*) celebrates the month of women with gifts of red and while silk ribbons, presented as a symbol of good health to people, and tied round animals' necks and tree-branches. This ribbon is called a *martenitsa* and when a countrywoman sees the first returning stork she puts a *martenitsa* under a nearby stone; if after forty days she turns over the stone and finds worms, bad luck will ensue; if ants, good luck. Maize and wheat grow in the Vratsa region, and a fertility rite in their connection is the placing of a doll in the river to augur rain and a good harvest.

First fruits of summer (here wheat) are formed into a bunch and decorated with flowers. Costumes are those of Romanian immigrants from the western marches or Banat. Autumn and winter are times for weddings, after the harvest has been gathered and activities slow down in home and field. Veneta Belichovska has generously donated her trousseau to the museum so we can see its style and proportions. Women in the region usually marry, between 20 and 25 years of age, men who tend to be one or two years older. Marriages are often arranged between families even today.

Turkish women began silk-breeding in Vratsa at the end of the 18th century and the first factory in Bulgaria started here in 1896; a small factory still exists, using mainly synthetic fibres. Villagers still breed silkworms at home, selling cocoons to the experimental station, one cocoon rendering up to 2,000 metres of silk thread. At one time the villagers used twigs or straw to separate cocoons: now plastic racks achieve a more systematic result. Interestingly, silk-breeding is a compulsory subject at schools in the Vratsa area, a splendid introduction to private enterprise by incentive. The first floor of the Ethnographic Museum is devoted to the composer and musician Diko Iliev (1898-1984). Two 17th-century towers, square and squat, add historical breadth to the modern buildings of Vratsa's town centre. Both were used as fortresses in times of struggle: the Kurtashov, and the Meshchii, the latter having been more recently used as part of the Archaeological Museum.

I enjoyed a display from the Orazov phaeton factory which opened in 1883 and provided all of Bulgaria's fine carriages. In Ivan Zambin's house (Zambin was Bulgaria's first ambassador to Russia) the interior has been restored, with displays of work by Vratsa gold- and silversmiths of the National Revival period. As well as jewels and ecclesiastical articles you can see the craftsman's table, his tools and his melting pot.

Scaffolding surrounded the church near Ivan Zambin's house, and tiles had been grouped on the roof for imminent use, but all around the mountains seem to close in like wolves on a sheepfold, and I shivered involuntarily on taking the road north to Mihailovgrad.

Mihailovgrad
Once divided into a number of smaller administrative regions, Bulgaria has recently been divided into eight much larger *oblasts*, using the Russian term. The southern four, east to west, have their capitals at Burgas, Haskovo, Plovdiv and Sofia; the northern four at Varna, Razgrad, Lovech and Mihailovgrad. This reshuffle has ruffled feathers at Vidin, Pleven, and Veliko Turnovo, not to mention Stara Zagora, Tolbuhin and Ruse. And one can see how Vidin, for example, might begrudge capital status to Mihailovgrad, a modern industrial town without any character or architectural pre-eminence, and a small population. Formerly called Kutlovitsa and in 1891 Ferdinand, its modern name honours the uprising in September 1923 of Hristo Mihailov and his companions against the rightwing government of Alexander Tsankov, a professor of economics acting as a figurehead for the army and crown; the revolt, centred on Vratsa, Stara Zagora and Plovdiv, failed for a variety of reasons, including paucity of weapons and poor preparation, and (with Georgi Dimitrov and Vasil Kolarov in Russia at the time) the frustrated men of violence organised isolated events that culminated in the bombing of Sveta Nedelya in Sofia on 16 April 1925, when a hundred and twenty people died, though the main targets of the bombers (the King and his close associates) were unharmed.

The monument on the main square shoots three flames: one to

commemorate the town's tribulations in 1688, a second those of 1923 and a third the liberation of 1944. Mihailov's house-museum deals extensively with the rising: politics and a view of socialism as the single acceptable state ideology typify such monuments and museums throughout Bulgaria, and the visitor may ignore them, of course. But since they offer a genuine flavour of what the Politburo encourages Bulgarians to believe, it would be misleading to pass them by on the other side of the street, and when we arrive in Vidin, we can explore one such museum in exemplary detail. Or you can find Mihailovgrad's fortress, with remains of a necropolis, and sanctuary-temple to Apollo and Artemis, finds from which are displayed in the Archaeological Museum.

Mihailovgrad is however primarily an industrial town, with a succession of factories: Zavod General Ivan Mihailov, Zavod Mir and Zavod Montana, set in idyllic mountains contrasting with the rattle and clank of machinery. The road north to Lom enters the Danube Valley plain: crows settle on wheatfields, agriculture takes over as the principal activity, and strange metal squares piled up on both sides of the road at intervals I found to be racks for setting vertically on field-edges, come winter, to hold back snow drifts from exposed roads. Instead of veering to Lom, I turned left at Rasovo for Archar, with its large church. Danubian islands looked uninhabited, skirted in mists that shrouded Romania from view. A pied sky chivvied Earth onward like an impatient schoolgirl above her slowing hoop.

Vidin

At nightfall I came to Vidin, and saw the lights of Calafat, on the Romanian bank of the Danube, winking across the waters from my Room 605 in Hotel Rovno. I pulled out my copy of *Danube Stream* (1940) by Lovett Edwards, who called Vidin 'one of those marvellous cities of eastern fairy-tale which, secure behind their fortress walls, are decorated with spires and cupolas and minarets piled one upon another in a fantastic medley of creeds, ages and styles.' Baffled by the thought of piling a minaret on a cupola above a spire, which never happened in the most eastern of fairy-tales, I discovered that the original settlement was a Celtic fortress to which the Romans gave the name 'Dunonia' ('Dundee' and 'Dundalk' incorporate the same Celtic prefix for fortress) before renaming their new town Bononia. The same Roman name given to an Italian city

Vidin. City centre, with the Danube

later became 'Bologna'. The Roman defensive system along the
Danube was overrun and destroyed by invading Huns in 444, and
rebuilt by the Emperor Justinian in the following century, but in
626 rampaging Avars devastated those Byzantine fortifications.
Khan Tervel now constructed a city known as Bdin on the ruins.
This fell under the rule of Hungary early in the 14th century,
though Mihail Shishman regained it in 1323 for Bulgaria with the
support of the boyars, and was succeeded shortly after his death in
1330 by the long-lived Ivan Alexander, after whom Ivan Stratsimir
Shishman became Tsar from 1371 until 1388, when the Ottomans
reduced him to client status.

The Ottoman Sultan Murad I attacked in three well-defined
periods separated by periods of consolidation. In 1362-8 he conquered northern Thrace and eastern Rumelia as far as the Balkan
range. In 1371-5 he subjugated western Thrace and the Macedonian lowlands, with Sozopol and Burgas. In 1385-9 he took, again
without serious reverses, the Macedonian highlands, Serbia and the

rest of Bulgaria: Shumen and Turnovo in 1388, but it was not annexed outright till the reign of Bayazit I. Turnovo, Nicopolis-on-the-Danube and Shumen retained Turkish garrisons, and Ivan Stratsimir remained as a Turkish vassal in Vidin until his ill-fated alliance with Sigismund of Hungary and France ended with Bayazit's victory at Nicopolis in 1396, and the annexation of Vidin in 1398 at the latest.

Now see Vidin's great stone fortress, initiated in its present form in the 13th century to dominate the Danube, the roads and passes into Bulgaria, using the river for moating its trapezoidal walls. If you thought about missing Vidin because of its relatively great distance from the historic heartland, then Baba Vida Fortress, as it is affectionately known, will change your view even if the old city doesn't.

The great fortress was strengthened by the Austrians, when they captured Vidin in the 17th century, and an 'Austrian' tower is pointed out today. A fascinating rebel called Osman Pazvantoglu seceded from the Ottoman Empire and ruled Vidin as a feudal lord from 1792 to 1807, constructing a barracks and garrison near Baba Vida (now used as a museum), mosques, schools and libraries. The so-called Pazvantoglu Mosque (though he built many others) can be seen in the old city next to a small Quranic library. Interestingly, Pazvantoglu must have enjoyed good relations with revolutionary France, because evidence exists of his employing French engineers and architects on his newly-envisioned Kingdom of Vidin, seceding from the Empire ruled by the Ottomans. He did not destroy the church of Sv. Panteleimon, of the 12th century, restored in the 17th century, semi-subterranean like so many churches built during the long Ottoman dominion, with interesting murals. The nearby Sv. Petka, also single-naved, is of original 17th-century foundation, and the Turkish-period Old Post Office stands on the riverside of them, close to the Pazvantoglu mosque and library.

The last part of Baba Vida to be built was the highest storey, including nineteenth-century breastwork with embrasures for cannon, but all is in keeping with the mediaeval style of the first foundations, even to the legend. It is said that an ancient king died, bequeathing vast territories between the Carpathians and the Balkans to his three daughters: Vida, Kula ('Tower') and Gumza (the local red wine). The two younger sisters married, but Vida remained a spinster, and built herself this impregnable castle,

Vidin. Within Baba Vida fortress

immuring herself hermit-like in one of the towers. There is no truth whatsoever in the legend, but its existence may in itself seem significant to those trying to understand the Bulgarian personality. Access to the walled city was by a number of easily-defended gates, including Telegraph Gate near the Old Post Office (overlooking the Danube), and from south to north on the landward side the Istanbul Gate, Bazaar Gate, Janissaries Gate, and Florian Gate, and one section of the Vauban-style fortifications (on the northern side) is well preserved. The synagogue of 1894 (near the guide pavilion outside the entrance to Baba Vida) is no longer used.

The French-designed barracks have been converted into a splendid museum (captions only in Bulgarian) divided between the history of capitalism and the workers' revolutionary movement, and ethnography. Originally, its two storeys accommodated stables and stores beneath the living quarters above, and as well as room for a garrison, a mansion and school were protected within the walled city. These 'Cruciform Barracks' were reconstructed after World War II and converted to museum use after 1965. At Liberation in 1944, Vidin had a population of twenty thousand, according to the vivacious copper-haired Carmen guiding me around her museum. Blagoev the Communist ideologue lived in Vidin for three years as principal of the secondary school. On high heels, with perfectly-manicured fingers she pointed to pistols, daggers, bullets and boots, with intimate personal belongings of partisans killed in the Resistance movement. As the only visitor, my footsteps echoed eerily in the empty halls of the first floor, where I was shown placards extolling socialist construction: 100% of Bulgaria's synthetic fibres made in Vidin, 74% of the national output of car tyres, a factory for men's shirts for export, all the country's gypsum comes from this area. I remembered Georgi Djagarov's poem 'Century of Miracles':

> *Probably it will always escape them,*
> *The wealthy men of the West,*
> *What our people fought and died for,*
> *And would defend again,*
>
> *Or why hordes of our brothers and uncles*
> *Conquered fields and hills in days gone by,*
> *To build the Kremikovtsi factory,*
> *To dig for coal and ore...*

But the Kremikovtsi factory near Sofia is a notorious pollutant, and the Bulgarians were not alone in defending their lands from Hitler. However, the Cruciform Barracks Museum is intended chiefly for domestic consumption, and a one-sided view is perhaps only to be expected. I learnt also that Vidin has been a major wine-producing centre since Thracian times, popular especially for the full-bodied Gumza, related in type to Bordeaux. An ingenious manual seed-drill is displayed in the agricultural section, where emphasis is also laid on local animal husbandry, fishing and hunting. Old Vidin, like any Turkish town, once had streets devoted to separate trades: saddlers, tailors and potters, and at one time thirty-two goldsmiths rubbed shoulders, not far from blacksmiths and farriers. A traditional *soba* (bedroom) was sparsely but brightly furnished with a bed and a round table, low on the floor, with low stools. Formal town dresses from the turn of the century had been brought from Europe, probably from Vienna.

In the summer you can see open-air theatre in the castle as at Danish Elsinore, and there is a choice of cinemas. Instead of *The Mission*, with Jeremy Irons, I preferred Georgi Djagarov's *Prokurorut*, a Bulgarian film in black and white at the Druzhba Cinema, with a simple story-line of honour, betrayal, and recrimination, directed by Lyobim Charlanjiev and starring Georgi Georgiev-Gets, difficult to act because of flat characterisation and unsubtle plotting. Foreign films are shown first in Sofia, then in major towns, and finally in villages, where films are changed every other day, giving a rich fare for those not keen on the choice of television between the Bulgarian channel 1 and the Russian channel 2. At a souvenir shop nearby I saw a pair of jeans priced at 58 leva, roughly two weeks' minimum wage. At a kiosk I bought the local paper, *Vidinski Glas*, 'The Voice of Vidin' and read it at a corner café while eating a ham and gherkin sandwich and cold chips with a scattering of cheese, and a gassy apple drink widely available. I felt safe and relaxed, because this whole area of central Vidin just outside the old walled city had been converted into a pedestrian precinct, yet near the Konak you can pick up a bus from early morning to midnight. Everywhere is sparklingly clean, though unpleasant smells occasionally drift across the Danube from chemical factories in Calafat.

The Archaeological Museum in Vidin (closed on Mondays in common with most Bulgarian museums) displays artefacts from the Early Palaeolithic Mirizlivka, near Oreshets, Belogradchik to the Bronze Age hearth constructed from evidence at Magura Caves. A map shows the distribution of Thracian tribes over the Balkans, with the Getae north of the Istros, or Danube, and the northern Tribales, Serdi (around Sofia) and Moesi, with the southern Besi (around Plovdiv) and Odrysae, south of Burgas. A scattering of Roman coins indicates the incursions of the westerners, while a Heracles from Ratiaria near modern Archar dated to the 2nd century A.D. emphasises the identification of this Greco-Roman strong man with our Thracian horseman-hero. Neither was I astonished to find an image of 'Mithras Slaying the Bull' attributed to pagan Romans. The most significant finds from Ratiaria are sculptures, friezes and small bronzes, for by the end of the 3rd century Ratiaria has become capital of the new province of Dacia Ripensis. The upper floor deals with the mediaeval period, from eighth-century Bdin to the attack on Edirne (now in Turkey) by Samuil from Ohrid, to the times of Ivan Stratsimir and the conquest of Bulgaria by the Turks.

Magura Caves and Dimovo

I took the road from Vidin south to Dimovo, because I wanted to explore the magnificent Magura caves, near the village of Rabisha. They are open from about 8 a.m. to 7 p.m. daily, but guided tours are taken only when at least thirty people arrive. Of the 3,600 metres of cave-length, only 2,300 are visited by general tours lasting 90 minutes. You may be lucky enough to see the extraordinary palaeolithic paintings in guano, but these are normally shown only by prior appointment to specialists who need a special guide: their group is kept small to minimise risks of vandalism. The humidity is 90%, and people with asthma and high blood pressure experience such a great sense of well-being within the caves that a Bulgarian doctor to whom I spoke had in the past actually experimented with 25 beds in the caves for asthma patients, enjoying good results. Magura Caves were caused by sea erosion followed by river action, over fifteen million years ago, when the Balkan Peninsula lay at the bottom of the sea, and then broke the surface. We enter first the Triumphal Hall, the greatest in Magura's whole network. Fragments of pottery and stone tools have been picked up beside a Bronze Age hearth later used by Iron Age cave-dwellers, and a skeleton of a cave-bear indicated that not only human families found refuge here. The cave has been open only since 1961, but its fame attracts more than 100,000 visitors a year into its gigantic, echoing halls with stalactites and stalagmites. The Hall of the Roman Girl is named for a first-century B.C. skeleton found here in 1927, with a gold bracelet on one arm, surrounded by animal bones indicating that she may have died as part of a sacrifice. In the 'Hall of Destruction' partisans were trained in shooting; here they maintained a library that was literally 'underground'.

Bat-droppings, or guano, harvested in coastal caves elsewhere for fertiliser (the Quechua original is 'huanu') were used here at Magura for artistic expression: women, a man clashing with a beast, a deer, and a bear, the whole presenting a picture of men and women involved in a complex ritualistic society of hunters and gatherers so susceptible to danger that fertility rites seemed necessary for the very survival of their race. Such is the durability of guano, and its faculty for holding the surface of the cave wall together, that painted lines stand out in relief above eroded surfaces.

The human imagination has invested rock formations in the caves with familiar shapes: a fallen bear (no. 166 in the inventory) on its back with one paw raised, a turtle higher and to the left, a Russian muzhik on the right, a harp with strings and organ with pipes sounding percussively when pinged, 'Cyril and Methodius', a 'fallen pine tree', and a 'frozen poplar'. The most magically-lit scenes are 'Baghdad' high above a 'gipsy encampment' in the plain.

Dimovo nearby is a one-street village, with its main street known predictably as 'Georgi Dimitrov'. Its demagogic social realist sculpture, celebrating local partisans, may strike you as depressingly inartistic, but you can always listen to local folksongs on tape, and revel in magnificent wooden landscapes.

Belogradchik
Belogradchik (pop. 7,300) is literally a 'Little White Town', from the same Slavic roots that give you Beograd (Belgrade) in Serbo-Croat. I wanted to wander among the splendid fantasy of sandstone and limestone outcrops, pink or red depending on the sun, or buff or grey, providing secure refuge for eagles and other birds of prey. One rock in profile resembles a Schoolgirl; another a Nun, of whom scandalous tales are told; another a *haidut* called Velko. The area of Belogradchik Rocks is 3 km wide by 30 km long: the Maiden's Stone still shelters a few hardy pines; the Bee Stone is believed to harbour honey-bees; in Belogradchik Gorge you can make out with a little imagination the Sphinx, Adam and Eve petrified forever in this forested Garden of Eden, Bears, Cloisters, and the Horseman. The Belogradchik Anticline dates from Palaeozoic times and in the course of two hundred million years sun, wind and rain have eroded, modelled, and transformed these outcrops into fantastic architectural shapes: castles and obelisks, towers and palaces, bridges and classical columns. Towards the east, a wanderer can lose himself in the lovely valley of Skoroshin Dol, Dolni Krupez

and Karlovitsa. The little town of Belogradchik is dominated by its fortress, begun by the Romans in the 1st century A.D. and strengthened in the 5th to 8th centuries, but not completed in its present form until the Ottomans under Sultan Mehmet II decided to make it a stronghold to protect the road between Archar (Roman Ratiaria) and Niš, now in Yugoslavia, from 1805 to 1837. A Bulgarian rebellion against the occupying forces which broke out in 1850 was extirpated with ease, and in reprisal the church of Sv. Georgi Pobedonosez was demolished. Liberation came in 1878, when Russian troops were welcomed with traditional bread and salt. Of three levels and three gateways only the uppermost incorporates ancient structures. Once past the second gate, you can see the Dog Rock above the third gate, and on the right the Elephant Rock. From the highest level you can make out a variety of rock formations, and find man-hewn pools to store rainwater in time of siege. On a sunny day the panorama is breathtaking, and an hour is well spent sauntering round the summit to enjoy the spectacle of shadow and profile, mirage and contour. Jérome Adolphe Blanqui noted in his *Voyage en Bulgarie, 1841* (1843) that from the Alps to the Pyrenees he had seen nothing to compare with the wonders of Belogradchik.

The neat two-storey Town Museum has departments devoted to ethnography, with old pistols and jewellery, and a traditional fireplace with a low round table and familiar half-moon wooden stools; and to natural history, with an interesting display of local birds of prey.

I took lunch at the friendly Mislen Kamuk Restaurant, named 'Thinking Stone', so one tale has it, because when a girl reaches this particular stone on the darkening path, she has to think about continuing into the pathless undergrowth with her male escort, or returning home with him. Of such decisions are destinies born. A little way downhill stands the two-star Hotel Belogradchik Rocks. A group of four merry Bulgarian men were celebrating the birth of a son to the wife of one of them, and invited me to toast the infant, which I could not do (as a driver) without breaking the strict anti-alcohol laws applied to motorists. To avoid insulting my host I raised the glass to my lips, kept them closed and licked my lips appreciatively. The new father explained that he was happy not only for himself and his wife, but also on account of the 15,000 leva that he would be able to borrow from the state, at very low interest rates. The rate of population growth among ethnic Bulgarians is lower than that among ethnic Turks, and national policy is to transfer ethnic Turks by change of name to the single Bulgarian nation, to discourage the use of the Turkish language in ethnic Turkish communities, and to encourage a higher birthrate among ethnic Bulgarians. To this end, with the birth of a second child, 3,000 leva of the original loan need not be repaid at all, and with the birth of a third child a further 4,000 need not be repaid. Official state policy seems therefore to be that parents should have three children: in 1989 the population totals a little over nine million. A woman earns three years of maternity leave from work for each child, of which the first two years are paid and her job is kept open for her. There is some dismay in official circles, I learned, that between 12,000 and 13,000 children each year are born out of wedlock.

Chiprovski Monastery
My aim was to wander back to Sofia through Berkovitsa by way of the Chiprovski Zhelezhnishki monastery, isolated off the minor road touching Dolni Lom west of the main Mihailovgrad road. Chiprovtsi village itself, some 5 km to the southwest, has earned undying glory as the focus of the 1688 rising against the Ottomans. The Chiprovtsi Rising, led by Georgi Peyachevich and Ivan Stanislavov, may have failed to dislodge the Ottoman yoke, but it certainly acted as a spur to further disaffection. The Ottomans burned down Chiprovski monastery in retaliation, and the bones of the Bulgarian rebels are preserved in the rebuilt monastery tower. The monastery itself dates from the early eighteenth century, and the church we see today from 1829, protected as usual in a courtyard by fortress-style cell-walls, with a finely-carved iconostasis and icons by Hristo Enchev of Koprivshtitsa (1828-91). Sheep graze safely in the meadows beside a silvery river encircling the whitewashed monastery, with its red-tiled roof. Look for the silver 17th-century altar cross, with its charming symbols of the four evangelists in gracefully-worked circles, and the great silver-covered Bible presented in 1802 by the Russian Tsar Pavel Petrovich.

Berkovitsa
Berkovitsa (with 17,500 people) is the last town of any size before your return to Sofia. The small Hotel Mramor (Marble Hotel) gives you the chance of another night in the country if you prefer to

arrive in Sofia early next day. Inhabited since the 3rd millennium B.C., Berkovitsa is situated at the foot of the Petrohan Pass (the sign reads 'Petrohanski Prohod') and enjoys a healthy climate, at about 430 metres a.s.l. You could also sample, before retiring for the night, the celebrated raspberry wine ('malinovo vino') or strawberry wine ('yagodovo vino') from the State Wine Store. Berkovitsa makes a favourite training-ground for Bulgaria's notable teams of wrestlers and weightlifters. Early Christian basilicas and baths can be seen, and there is a clock tower (1762) which once overshadowed a mosque. The French consul in Ruse noted that the population in 1874 consisted of about 6,500 Muslims and 6,500 Christians. The local Ethnographic Museum is not very significant, but don't miss a Turkish house built in 1840 serving as another House-Museum of Ivan Vazov, where the national writer came to live in 1879-80, after the Liberation, following two years in Bucharest as a political exile. He chaired the district court, but expected to die of tuberculosis and the town of Berkovitsa can claim indirectly to have given the world *Under the Yoke*, for her climate so improved Vazov's condition that he survived turberculosis, further exile to Odessa, and many years as Minister of Education. He did not die until 1921, by which time his position as the Grand Old Man of Bulgarian literature had become established. The Church of the Virgin Mary (1835) was constructed three feet below ground, as the Turks insisted, so that it should be seen at a level lower than that of the mosque, and it has no dome that might compete with the minaret. The icons are said to be by Dimitur and Zahari Zograf. On the east of the town you can find the Church of Sv. Nikola (1871) with a contemporary school in the churchyard. Its iconostasis is by Stoyan Fandukov from Samokov.

When Ivan Shishman ruled from Vidin, Berkovitsa was a border town, its principal industry being the quarrying of local marble. Little villages nearby have gradually been abandoned as the young migrate to cities for employment in heavy industry, the government bureaucracy and service industries. As the old die, their homes are being sold for summer cottages to the newly (relatively) prosperous in the towns, who can buy a place for 3,000 leva (roughly US$ 1,800 or £1,000 at present rates) and spend their weekends in the countryside, bringing the older place up to modern standards of comfort and hygiene.

After the heights of Petrohan Pass, the highest point in the western Balkans, the wooded valleys and rolling hills to Buchin Pass and Kostinbrod repeat patterns of depopulation and enchanting solitude, where virgin meadows shelter hares, rabbits, foxes, and such a multitude of birds that an ornithologist might falter for superlatives.

Pleven

In a café I took a glass of the thick non-alcoholic brown fluid, boza, deriving from maize, and left Vratsa for the road to Pleven via Borovan and Knezha. Wide, flat fertile plains extend southward from the Danube, and the excellent road eastward has recently been upgraded. Knezha boasts a new Institute for Maize Research, concentrating on new high-yield varieties. After crossing the Iskur River, and leaving behind the village of Pelovo, I noticed little oil-derricks and nodding donkeys, but oil horizons discovered in 1963 are already virtually exhausted, though the second-largest oil refinery in the country is situated a little farther on at Dolni Dubnik, elevated to the status of a town in 1977. Pleven itself is a city of about a hundred thousand people, who busy themselves with industry, viticulture (occupying a third of the region's land area), and with cement production, as well as textiles, rubber and foodstuffs. Human habitation here in the Tuchenitsa valley can be traced back to the late 4th millennium B.C., and Thracian settlements have been identified on the outskirts, at Kailuka, site of a park with a two-star hotel of the same name. The Romans called the place Storgosia, and worshipped the Thracian goddess Germetida as Diana of the hunt. Cults of Mithras and Hercules were also known here, but Storgosia suffered devastation at the hands of the rampaging Huns in the fifth century, and enjoyed only a brief revival under Justinian in the sixth century before the invading Slavs began a new settlement and gave the town its new name, which first enters recorded history in 1266, when it received a charter from King Stefan V, the Hungarian ruler. Pleven flourished under the Turks: the Ottoman traveller Evliya Celebi estimated that in the 17th century, during his travels, there were roughly two thousand houses in Pleven, many with large gardens. It was a great area for sheep and cattle, with associated wool and leather industries, but terrible losses in human life and livestock occurred during the rebellion of Vidin's despot Osman Pazvantoglu against the Sublime Porte, and later Pleven became one of the bloodiest battlefields in the early nineteenth century. Plague decimated Pleven in 1836-7, survivors escaping to the mountains. But the extinction of the Janissaries in 1826 and their replacement by a standing army gradually led to increased prosperity and the Bulgarian Orthodox Church continued its propagation of the Bulgarian language (against Turkish), of Christianity (against Islam), and of nationalism (against the colonialism of the Sultan). By themselves, the Orthodox monks could not dislodge the ruling Turks from Bulgaria, and the armies of the Russians and Romanians, with their allies, lost over forty thousand men to Osman Pasha's army in the bloody Siege of Pleven in December 1877, commemorated in a hilltop Panorama of the Pleven Siege in the museum park of Skobelev. The panorama itself takes the form of a circular painted backcloth, with a realistic hilltop foreground populated with fighting men and the wounded in three dimensions. An introductory room presents six paintings: the Cruelty of the Turks, showing young Bulgarian boys being snatched from their families to be raised as Janissaries, fiercely Muslim in the service of the Sultan; the Bulgarian Rising of 1877, supported by such figures as Wilde, Darwin and Gladstone; the Petersburg Assembly urging war on the Turks, to liberate Bulgaria; Russians crossing the Danube at Svishtov; the Battle at Stara Zagora, when General Gurko's army liberated Veliko Turnovo and Stara Zagora; and Bulgaria's Thermopylae, where seven thousand Russian troops and six thousand Bulgarian irregulars fought forty thousand Turks.

The moment depicted in the circular panorama upstairs is the third assault on Pleven, on 11 September 1877; as you enter, the Turkish army is encamped nearby, with the Russian HQ on the green hills to the right. General Skobelev, on a white horse, asks for reinforcements but is refused. The Turks hold a second fortified hill on the south side. Of this instant in time Nemirovich-Danchenko wrote: 'The battle was raging all around when Skobelev suddenly cried out, "Forward, lads, forward!" and his words acted like a spark on gunpowder. "Forward! Forward! Forward!" yelled the men in a frenzy. The wounded continued to attack and the dying added their words of encouragement. Blood covered the soldiers' bayonets, hands and faces, there was blood everywhere ...' The team of Bulgarian and Russian artists have created a circular trompe l'oeil where gunsmoke mingles with cloud; there seems to be no join between the vertical canvas and horizontal earth redoubt. The fallen may never rise again, many of those attacking will never see nightfall, and the doctors and nurses may find their heroism rewarded with instant oblivion. A diorama downstairs shows the battle of 10 December 1877, and the surrender of Osman Pasha to Tsar Alexander II. The consequence of this victory was the speedy liberation of northern Bulgaria. Pleven's Historical Museum, opened in 1984, is situated in the great barracks (1884-8) near the city centre. If you have relatively little time for the prehistoric stone implements, then at least look out for copies of the late Bronze Age gold treasure of about the 13th century B.C. from Vulchitrun, especially a double-handled drinking cup or *kantharos*, simple in form but elegantly worked with neat horizontal grooves ending in a fishtail similar to that on a Thracian axe-sheath excavated near Razgrad; a triple vessel from Vulchitrun may have been used in a ceremonial of brotherhood or religious ritual; and a lid or conceivably a cymbal, with a bronze inlay giving it resonance. There is a Roman copy of an Apollo after an original by Praxiteles, and a mosaic from Ulpia Oescus (now Gigen) near the Danube, with a scene possibly from Menander's comedy *The Achaeans*. A hoard of coins from the time of Ivan Shishman recalls the last hours of the Second Bulgarian Kingdom, but the greater part of the museum is devoted to the Liberation of 1877 and the revival of Bulgaria under socialist construction. Indeed, as you wander around the streets of Pleven you are constantly reminded of little else, by rearing statues and insistent street-names.

Two art collections demand attention: one is the Icon Museum in the church of Sv. Nikola (1834), with collections from the masters of the Debur, Samokov and Tryavna Schools laying particular emphasis on Dimitur Hristo Zograf, brother of Zahari Zograf and father of Stanislav Dospevski, all of the Samokov School. The other collection, near the multi-coloured fountains that play in the main square every evening, is the Svetlin Rusev Gallery, in neo-Tuscan churchlike public baths of 1905, with pink and white horizontal stripes and neatly arched windows. Svetlin Rusev is an artist who collected icons, sculptures and paintings from Bulgaria and over-seas and presented them to Pleven, where they are open daily from two to seven. Seek out Nikola Petrov's 'Sofia in Winter' (1907), Nenko Balkanski's 'Self-Portrait' (1930), Sirak Skitnik's 'Construc-tion Landscape' (1932), Tsanko Lavrenov's 'Lamartine's House,

Pleven. City centre

Plovdiv' (1940), Kara Yordanov's 'Portrait of a Woman' (1938-40) and works by the artist known to Bulgarians as "the Master": Vladimir Dimitrov, including 'Landscape with Poplars'. Very few visitors dotted these ample halls, and I felt sorry for the lack of international influences on even 20th-century painters and sculptors in Bulgaria. There are no books on Impressionism, Expressionism, Surrealism or Post-Impressionism in the bookshops, and the Stalinist ideology of socialist realism has only recently begun to thaw. Artists can rarely afford to visit Paris or Munich and, if they do, on their return they find scant sympathy for trends deriving from Dubuffet or Joseph Beuys. Bulgaria entertains no great exhibitions like Late Picasso at the Tate or Dalí at the Pompidou Centre, so artists and artistic public alike have little chance of coming into contact with vigorous new artistic forms and ideas.

There was no performance at the Kirkov Theatre, so I passed the time before sleep in the pedestrian town centre, watching crowds of young people talking and smiling affably, with dignity, so unlike the punks and rockers of western cities. In parts, concrete spread with such insistence that greyness seemed to have spewed out from underground seams. A young leatherjacketed woman crossed the square, her heels tapping like a monotonous xylophone. Public telephones are never vandalised, streets are free of litter, and mugging is unheard of. I stayed at the two-star Hotel Rostov na Don (Pleven's Soviet twin city) on Ulitsa Alexeiev but it would be quieter at the two-star Kailuka; the most expensive is the three-star Hotel Pleven on Ploshtad Republika.

Lovech

Quick and uneventful is the 35-km drive to Lovech, new oblast capital on the river Osum, with its new three-star Hotel Lovech, which opened in 1987. The original Thracian settlement was transformed into a Roman fortress with the name of Melta, amplified in the sixth century with walls extended in succeeding centuries and recently restored. From Melta's walls your eye roams over the clusters of red-tiled one- and two-storey houses below, then across the road bridges and footbridges over the Osum to modern Lovech, with high-rise apartment blocks in the distance.

The first covered bridge over the Osum was built in 1848. The third, reconstructed in 1931, follows the design and proportions of Kolyo Ficheto's masterpiece of 1874, which burned down in 1925.

Lovech. Covered bridge

Nikola Ivanovich Fichev was born in Dryanovo in 1800 and at ten began apprenticeship with master-masons in Tryavna, then worked with the builders of Bratsigovo on churches, bridges and belfries. He was responsible, among other achievements, for the Church of Sv. Constantine and Helena at Veliko Turnovo, Sv. Nikola at Dryanovo, the Holy Trinity (Sv. Troitsa) at Svishtov, and the bridges over the Yantra at Byala and the Rossitsa at Sevlievo. At the time when he threw the wooden covered bridge over the Osum, Usta Kolyo was 74 years of age, and he may have been recollecting the Arno bridge at Florence.

Ficheto's bridge was intended for leather merchants, but today's unobtrusively-lit successor, fortified with iron and concrete, accommodates souvenir shops and patisseries, knitwear, pottery, jewellery, and a café where you can taste boza and baklava. The bridge opens into a square of Varosha, the old city dating to the 18th and 19th centuries, which has been so sensitively restored that only careful examination will prove that the red tiles are new, that timbers have been replaced, and that central heating and drains have been laid to make this picturesque quarter inhabitable by the more searching standards of our time. Two schoolgirls were munching a cheese pie, called banitsa, outside the Youth Centre (Mladezhki Dom) near Orbita's Hotel Varosha. A Whitesnake T-shirt adorned a slouching youth of about 16.

Varosha itself, with its cobbled streets, overhanging balconies (chardaks), and hidden courtyards, seems to doze in the lethargy of an Ottoman summer, but it is no pedestrian precinct, and solitary strollers spreadeagle their bodies against house-walls against the tide of cars bumping up and down the steep cobbles. These are all private houses, with carefully tended flowers and little vegetable plots behind wooden gates and high protective walls for privacy, and flat surfaces whitewashed to give an air of pristine freshness. Owners of these traditional homes are given the opportunity to exchange them for a new flat in a high-rise block, or to move out while they are being renovated, paying 30% towards the cost after they move back in. At Hisarska 4, a three-room home of one storey, I found the birthplace of the first Bulgarian cosmonaut, Georgi Ivanov, who entered space in 1979. I sauntered up Ulitsa Todor Katsarov towards the fortress of Melta, with the Vasil Levski Museum on the right, in the former house of Nikola Sirkov. Wherever he went, the 'Apostle of Liberty' found refuge in humble homes anonymous in towns and cities, or in isolated monasteries far from the Turkish authorities. He was captured, following treachery by the 'Judas' among the apostles, a priest called Krustyu, near the village Kukrina. Levski was wounded, seized, and brought to trial in Sofia, where the Turkish authorities executed him on 6 February 1873.

Above the Levski Museum I found the Church of the Dormition of the Virgin (1834) in its own long slumber, still, quiet and full of echoes. Old Varosha nestles for comfort between Hisarya's rocky heights and the Osum's sparkling waters. The castle takes full advantage of the natural heights and the main street of mediaeval Lovech still curves down from the castle gateway through the burgeoning cottages of Varosha, to the river bank. Southward rises the rock of Chilinska and the Balkan range: I hoped to find the time to visit the Thracian tumuli in Lovech region, where at least a hundred burials are known, ranging in date between the 3rd millennium and the 3rd century B.C., but with the best intentions I could not explore Lazar-Stanevo, where a warrior had been entombed simply, with four animals: a stag, an ox, a dog and a puppy; Doirentsi, where a Thracian military leader had been buried in four different places, one each for a part of his remains, and a remarkable coat of mail, otherwise unrecorded among the Thracians; and Smochan, where Bronze Age and Roman interments incorporated bronze vases, weapons, and elegant glass cups and bowls. On Ulitsa Hashnova, I found the modest birthplace of the revolutionary Gecho Nikolov Kokilev (1899-1938), who sought refuge in the Soviet Union. A tiny white and ginger kitten arched its back at me and spat, huddled against a wooden drainpipe in the cobbled alley. Old Turkish baths near the foot of the hill are no longer used. Close by two men were out in their narrow garden preparing quinces for jam. Back on the main square of Varosha, neat as a Swedish pastry-board, I found the exhibition gallery filled with a temporary exhibition of contemporary artists: the 'Halley's Cat' of Alexander Ivanov, and the inventive Plamen Penov's 'Ruchenitsa', with its sly reference to the classical painting on the same folk-dance theme by Jan Mrkvička (National Art Gallery, Sofia); a witty 'Diana and the Landscape Artist', 'I Don't Believe in Storms', and the touching 'She Loves Me' in which a balloonist hauls up to him the girl of his dreams. Canvases usually hint at foreign antecedents, such as Dyanko Kolov's Klee-like 'Blockaded City'.

Devetaki Cave and Letnitsa
Taking the road northeast from Lovech to Levski you take a right turn in 20 km to Devetaki, and there come to the *Devetashkata Peshtera*, the Cave of Devetaki, an immense cave which may well be the largest in Bulgaria opened to the public, with almost continuous habitation since the Palaeolithic. Its underground river provides an unending source of fresh water, and a series of lakes and waterfalls give it a constantly refreshing sound even in the drowsiest of hot summer days.

The next town is Letnitsa, scene of a sensational find: a bronze vase containing no fewer than 24 exquisite pieces of gilded silver appliqué of Thracian and Hellenistic inspiration, the subjects being mythological and religious. The Getae worshipped a divinity called Zalmoxis, named for the bearskin enveloping him from birth. A vigorous Getic horseman is seen transfixing a bear, with a defeated wolf at his feet. On another masterpiece, a woman is seen feeding a three-headed serpent from a bowl; on a third, a dragon takes the form of a serpent with three bodies and three lupine heads. The find is dated to the 4th century B.C. Herodotus writes that the Getae of Thrace shot arrows into the sky, aimed to pierce clouds to induce rain to fall; comparative mythology shows the same ritual in India and in Iran. In dry lands, the hero associated with rainfall can be assured of divine status and 'married' spiritually or physically to any bride he chooses, having brought to an end the three-headed dragon's overlordship of the locked waters. Fertility of the earth was thus closely allied to fertility among mankind.

Beyond Levski I joined Highway E 83 towards Ruse, bypassing Byala with Ficheto's bridge of 1865-7, restored after severe flooding. I gave a lift to a garrulous German-speaking engineer on his way to Ruse, and we discussed wages and taxes. We worked out that the minimum monthly salary (120 leva, subject to 5% income tax) was worth about US$75 or £40 sterling, and the average, subject to 10% income tax, was worth about US$140 or £75 sterling. He could borrow money from the banks to buy an apartment at only 2% interest. The biggest household expenditures are on food, electricity, water and clothes, most families brewing their own drinks. Flights of black crows thudded on broad fields like dark balls from a cannon, squawking and cawing in a riot of civil disobedience. My Bulgarian passenger sucked on a succession of boiled sweets called 'Sportist' and complained about schooling in Bulgaria. 'We don't have the hooliganism and vandalism that you have in the West', he admitted, 'but we don't have education in the sense of bringing out everyone's individual capabilities. Most children go to a nursery school or crèche, then do the compulsory grades one to eight, between the ages of six and fourteen. The system is good at conformity, discipline, basic literacy and numeracy, but it makes people too similar; 95% or so continue their schooling to the age of sixteen, with professional or vocational training, with a second and/or third stage taking them up to eighteen, when you can apply for universities, institutes or technical schools. Mature entry is available to universities and institutes, but if you fail entry you need a certificate of at least eight months' work experience to apply again.'

Ivanovo Rock Churches and Cherven
I dropped him off on the main road and enquired in Ivanovo vil-

lage, near the school, for the guide to Ivanovo's Valley of the Churches, a Unesco monument. We drove along a fertile plain opening into a canyon, the Rusenski Lom river sparkling in its depths, and rocks climbing high, rough, naked and bearing all the marks of having been worked by man since prehistory. The caretaker, Miro, explained that conservation was not yet underway, and so the rock monastery had to be locked up against intruders. We parked below the rock, and clambered up to view the cells and church founded here by Tsar Asen II (1218-41). The monastery was presented to Joachim, first patriarch of Turnovo, and placed under the Archangel Michael's protection. The only remnants of the church's decoration are fragments of S. Peter of Alexandria's vision, but we possess substantial fragments of the monastery's conventual church paintings, by one or more unknown Turnovo school artists, mostly of the twelfth to fourteenth centuries, with some retouching. The friezes are painted to look like curtains, and the qualities of realism and human pathos mark a new departure in mediaeval Bulgarian art: Judas betrays Christ, then hangs himself after the arrest. Muscles are clearly depicted, and robes effectively

Ivanovo. Hermit's cell near the rock churches

draped; we are surprised by the ubiquity of bodies nearly naked, a feature almost unknown in contemporary religious iconography. Look at the vigour and originality of the figures in the scene of Christ Washing the Disciples' Feet, an animated Last Supper, the grim figures of Caiaphas and Ananias, and a stunning Ascension. On the crags overlooking the valley I met Veselin Iliev, a journalist from *Otechestven Front* (the newspaper 'Fatherland Front') and we explored together the Chapel of Gospodev Dol, with mural portraits of three patron saints of domestic animals: Spiridion, Modestus, and Blaise. Spiridion the Cypriot sheep-farmer calls especially close to one's heart in Ivanovo's valley, where sheep wander and goat-bells fill the skies with their irregular tinkling. The 'Demolished' Church conserves enough of its ceiling murals to show that they represented the ten major religious festivals. Christ stands before an altar, receiving a model of the church from a nun-donor, but the style is decadent, and dated to the mid-14th century.

Noon sun irradiated this verdant valley with ecstatic gold, but trees protected us from its heat. The hectic rush of squirrels and occasional fox-droppings reminded me that men had never really colonised this Arcady, but Stone Age men had carved unobtrusive niches for their own protection, and hermits had abjured wealth and power for the blessings that solitude can bring. Another redoubt long abandoned, 13 km to the south, is Cherven (like 'Ruse' it means 'red'), built as a fortress town from the 6th century when Ruse was being attacked by waves of Germanic and Slavic invaders. The oldest of the surviving ruined churches of Cherven dates to the tenth century, but the whole area teems with lost memories as countless as the ravenous crows, and Cherven's isolation became complete when the Turks crushed and annihilated the fortress and its inhabitants, building up their own Ruse as Ruschuk, which would form part of the Ottoman chain of towns defending the Danube's southern bank from depredations by rivals from the north.

Ruse

On my way back to Ruse I stopped in Bazarovo to admire roses and cabbages being grown on the very pavements lining the main street. At Ruse I took early dinner at the Restaurant Leventa, a Turkish arms depôt begun in the 17th century and now overlooked by a soaring television tower. Here is your best panorama high above the golden-domed Pantheon and then the grey Danube, with the Romanian bank a faint blur. Try the apricot juice, for the local apricots near Silistra are as famous as Sliven's peaches. But anything in the Leventa is enjoyable, from rump steak and onions for 2.89 leva to pancake with honey and nuts for 1.03 leva. As usual, I paid 10 stotinki to use the toilet, placing the tiny coin in a plate set strategically between the Ladies' and Gents', and as usual felt a twinge of regret that facilities should be paid for, but then remembered that even a hundred clients a day would render 300 leva a month and if the average wage is only 220, the stout lady offering you a single sheet of toilet paper would be among the top earners...

Ruse is a splendid city of 185,000 people, which made me wonder why Brian Hall, in *Stealing from a Deep Place: Travels in Southeastern Europe* (1988), spent more than thirty pages merely describing how he wandered around looking for a mechanic to repair his ten-speed Japanese bicycle. Knowing Bulgarian ingenuity at firsthand, I was not astonished that he eventually found salvation with one Andrei at a sports stadium in Ruse.

You can stay at the three-star Hotel Riga (named for Ruse's Soviet twin city) or at the two-star Dunav, east of the House of the Soviets, the latter reminiscent of the Stalinist 1950s. Private accommodation is available through a bureau next to Balkan Airlines on Lenin Square. But if you want to discover Ruse's long and tortuous history, and its relationship with shabby Romanian Giurgiu on the opposite bank, with the Romans, Turks, and Russians, start in the National Museum of Transport not far from the busy port. For Ruse is the hub of rail communications with the Soviet Union and river communications with Western Europe. Ruse's Transport Museum is mounted in the railway station built by a British company in 1866, and old carriages and engines bring back to your imagination those heady days of the original Orient Express which connected Paris with Strasbourg, Munich, Linz, Budapest, Bucharest, Giurgiu, where passengers embarked on to a ferry boat for Ruse, then on by train to Varna, whence a Lloyds ship completed the journey to Istanbul. This route was replaced by the Vienna-Belgrade-Sofia-Istanbul link in 1888, but rail enthusiasts can still follow the route to Varna, passing through Vetovo, north of Razgrad, Hitrino for Shumen, Kaspichan for Pliska, and Provadia.

The earliest populations lived by fishing the Danube waters, but

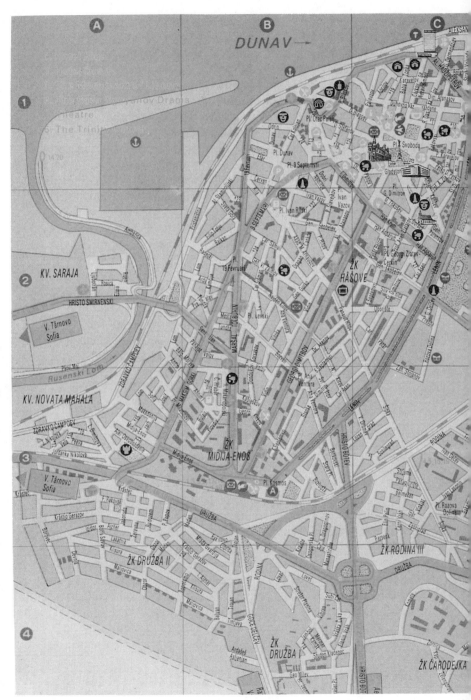

Map of Ruse

the Thracians were displaced by the Romans, who built here the port of Sexaginta Pristia, and of course Martial uses the number 'sixty' much as the Iranians use 'forty', to denote a vast number. You can still find fragments of the second-century Roman ramparts, which were further protected by a ditch. We have seen how mediaeval Ruse took refuge inland at Cherven, renowned as a 'city of bishops', which relied for secular prosperity on its ironworking. The Ottomans razed Cherven, then encouraged the 'raya', as they termed the Christian Bulgarians, back to the strategic harbour they called Ruschuk, where they formed a minority in the 17th century of about a thousand compared with fifteen thousand Turks. The Sublime Porte steadily enhanced Ruse's welfare with important fortifications and administrative buildings until, in the 18th century, Ruse became one corner of that fortified quadrilateral bounded at the other corners by Silistra, Varna and Shumen. Ruse's Ottoman governor Midhat Pasha provided the Ruse-Varna rail link (1864-6), and encouraged bilingual Turkish-Bulgarian printing, as well as textbooks in Bulgarian for new schools. While Varna looked to Russia as a model (in particular to Odessa

Ruse. Opera House

perhaps), Ruse looked to Western Europe, especially to Vienna and Paris. A wealthy new bourgeoisie built attractive houses, and public buildings reflected Viennese taste in music and opera, theatres and café society where art and literature take their rightful place at the centre of human life, instead of at the fringes, where the snapping dogs of religious and political controversy should be restrained. I admired the long span of the Friendship Bridge to Romania (1955). Other 20th-century additions to Ruse are less aesthetically pleasing: Simeon Zlatev's rhetorical Freedom Monument (1908) in Lenin Square, with bas-reliefs by the forgettable sculptor Arnaldo Zocchi; Yordan Kurchmarov's Monument to the Soviet Army (1949); and the gold-domed Pantheon, commemorating martyrs and heroes in an inflated histrionic style complete with eternal flame and tragic effigies. Some of the martyrs are family members of Baba Tonka, and you should see her house-museum, which is also the District History Museum, where Ul. Baba Tonka meets Bul. Stamboliiski. 'Granny' Tonka Obretenova, strongly influenced by Georgi Rakovski, allowed her home to be used as a meeting-place and arms cache for rebels. The historical section shows Ottoman Ruschuk, a town larger at the time than Sofia, with its mosques and gates, one of which survives west of the modern rail station.

At the end of Petkov, a pedestrian precinct encompasses Lenin Square, with the Dunav Hotel and City Council Building. Kino Prosveta, or 'Enlightenment Cinema', gives a clue to the type of film you are quite likely to see there. The Communist Party headquarters is shaped like a ship, and on the other side of Lenin Square rises in glory the truly splendid Opera House (1949), which has just been lavishly restored. In 1977, an earthquake centred in Romania cracked many of the buildings in Ruse, but there were no deaths. Khan Kubrat Square is more intimately European that the Soviet-style Lenin Square, and charming buildings dating from about 1897-1900 delight the eye in this once-residential area now given over to shops and offices. The City Theatre is a little later; the Art Gallery next door is also worth a visit. The oldest church was the Holy Trinity (Sveta Troitsa) of 1632, while Bulgaria still groaned under the Turkish yoke, constructed partly underground, and hidden by a ten-foot wall to avoid offending Muslim sensibilities. The new church on the site (1764) is more self-confident, with three aisles, and some exceptional icons. Archaeologically, the largest excavated zone is a Thracian necropolis of the late 3rd and early 2nd millennia B.C., first studied by Karel Skorpil (1905) when techniques were more primitive, and later in 1948: it lies not far from the sugar refinery. Some original Turkish baths are also to be seen in Ruse, a city that springs a surprise round every corner, from its row of flower-sellers near the opera house, and the central section of the Friendship Bridge, which can be raised at high tide, to the crowds enjoying Symphonic Music Days held every March. Anti-Turkish sentiment in Bulgaria has scarcely diminished though the Yoke was lifted more than a century ago. So I responded to friendly overtures in Bulgaria with my poor stock of Turkish jokes. In Ruse I told the tale of the admiral who was sent with a fleet to pay a goodwill visit to Malta, in the later days of the Ottoman Empire, when the Great Siege of 1656 had long been forgotten. The convoy returned to Constantinople some weeks afterwards and the admiral was asked how he found Malta. 'We didn't', he answered, 'it wasn't there'.

Sveshtari and Sreburna

Driving to Silistra from Ruse creates a dilemma, for the direct road offers views of the Danube along most of its length, while the inland route via Kubrat allows you the chance to visit (on any day but Monday) the Thracian tomb at Sveshtari (6 km from Isperih) discovered in 1982, a Hellenistic-age burial of a Thracian king remarkable both for its frescoes and its sculptural features in high relief. The mound covers a corridor leading to a triple-chambered tomb covered by a single semi-cylindrical vault. The king, who may have ruled over the Getae, was buried with his wife and five horses. Ten caryatids raise their arms above their heads as if to support the vault: they are related by the archaeologist Maria Chichikova to the Great Mother Goddess, guaranteeing eternal life to the deceased. The tomb is dated to the early 3rd century B.C. from Greek utensils and by analogy with the stylistically similar Ptolemeion of Samothrace and Didimeion at Miletus.

From Isperih I took the Silistra road as far as Dulovo, then headed north to the Danube, turning right past Sitovo for the nature reserve at Sreburna, like the Sveshtari Tomb a Unesco monument. Administered by the Institute of Zoology of the Bulgarian Academy of Sciences, it has been designated the Ecological Station of the Biosphere Reserve 'Sreburna' since 1977, and is best visited for birdlife from March to August, after which the pelicans leave. In 1863 Felix Kanitz referred to the lakeland here as 'the El Dorado of aquatic birds': and visitors can watch a hundred species of nesting birds from observation points. A sumptuous prospect faces the ornithologist: from *anas querquedula* to *egretta garzetta* and *anser albifrons*. Goshawks, kestrels, owls abound, as do kingfishers, cranes, hoopoe and many species of geese. The Natural History Museum within the national park displays stuffed birds and local mammals, including badger, deer, marten, fox and boar. Hopeful sparrows and magpies hop around in hope of instant stardom. If you cannot spare a lot of time in the reserve, its pools are visible from the main road to Silistra, a town of 55,000 people some 16 km to the east, where you can stay at the two-star Hotel Zlatna Dobruja.

Svishtov and Silistra

Driving the length of the Danube from Vidin, you will see both Silistra and Svishtov, the latter roughly halfway between Vidin and Silistra, near the Roman city of Novae, founded in the 1st century A.D. and fortified by Justinian as part of his defensive chain in the 6th century. Its mosques are closed, but two old churches remain intermittently open: S. Demetrius (1640) and SS. Peter and Paul (1644). The Holy Trinity (1867) is a work by Kolyo Ficheto. Silistra is much larger, as befits the regional outlet for the agricultural wealth of the Dobruja plain. Clearly of Thracian origin, Silistra became the Roman stronghold of Durostorum in the 2nd century A.D. When Bulgaria was incorporated into the Byzantine Empire between 1018 and 1186, one of its two administrative regions or *themes* were located at Silistra, the other being Skoplje (Turkish Üsküb), now in Yugoslavia. The Historical and Ethnographical Museum is to be found south of the town centre in a bastion of the Ottoman fortress which comprised one corner of the defensive zone also marked by Varna, Shumen and Ruse. But Silistra is of cardinal significance in the history of art for the discovery in 1942 of its fourth-century Late Roman tomb, in the last years before the Early Byzantine period: we can distinguish Greek elements, Roman elements, and a softer modelling technique. At the period of this tomb, Rome was waging frontier wars against the ravaging Goths, and we can find in the figures painted on the walls vigorous human types representative of the Empire's wavering stability in the face of barbarian depredations. The wealthy husband, shown full face, has short hair, large nose, full lips, and wears a long tunic and mantle, with sandals on his feet. His wife's face is unfortunately damaged, but her dress remains complete: a long-sleeved tunic, and a light-coloured scarf round her head halo-fashion. Rectangular panels on each side are charmingly filled with maidservants in long tunics and menservants in short tunics. Candelabra are painted on each side of the entrance as a pathetic, moving symbol of light to accompany wife and husband in their voyage to the afterlife. Hunting scenes depicted on the ceiling include a hunter spearing a boar, an image familiar throughout Thracian art and touchingly reverberant here. We can connect the master's long tunic and mantle (or *chlamys* to give it the original name) with the 4th-century mosaics at Piazza Armerina in Sicily, and the menservants' short tunics may remind you of costumes in the 4th-century catacombs of San Callisto in Rome. But it is fascinating, in the early years of the spread of Christianity in Thrace, to note the artist's delight in pagan themes: a leopard, birds and berries, ducks and flowers.

Then in 1968 another excavation brought to light a late-3rd century burial of a high military or administrative official accompanied by a chariot and grave goods, including two iron swords with wooden scabbards and a heavy gold ring bearing a gem portraying the Goddess Fortune, a golden fibula, and a coin showing the Emperor Probus (276-282). The chariot has four wheels, and the skeletons of four horses were discovered at its side. The body of the chariot is richly decorated with statuettes in bronze (a panther is notably vivid) and busts of Dionysus and satyrs. The weapons are of even higher artistic value, one ornamented with rubies and other precious stones; its gilded silver proves that it came from a first-class workshop.

The outskirts of Silistra intimidate: high-rise apartment blocks amorphous, anonymous, yet repeating themselves like great towering clones, off-white staining grey, peeling and flaking with sad sagging lines of washing giving away each family's secret underwear to public view. Singapore and Hong Kong, Manhattan and Tokyo have their good reasons for treating workers like battery hens, but Bulgaria still has ample space for the separate homes and gardens traditionally beloved.

Tolbuhin

I chose not the main road to Tolbuhin through Alfatar and Tervel, but the secondary route meandering beside the barbed wire of the border with Romania, where I made out silent, dim figures tending vineyards. Maize and ducks are my recollection of Voinovo village, and then a vast apricot plantation. We are in Dobruja, a flat, fertile agricultural plain extending from the region around Tolbuhin in the south to Constanţa on the Romanian Black Sea coast in the north. The Romans defended this territory by a Trajan's Wall in the form of a double rampart extending from Constanţa to the Danube. By the 1878 Treaty of Berlin, the Russians gave the territory then populated by Turks (in the main), Bulgarians, Tatars and Jews to Romania, annexing the territory of Bessarabia in its place, mostly inhabited by Romanians. It reverted to Bulgaria in 1940. The Turks called the town Hajiolu Pazarjik and its population in 1901 was 13,436 when the great annual fair of Panair (for horses and cattle) drew thousands of dealers from all over Eastern Europe every summer. The Bulgarians, when they changed its name after the 1877-8 liberation from the Turks, called it Dobrich after a local 14th-century boyar, then Tolbuhin after Field-Marshal Tolbukhin, whose 3rd Ukrainian Army liberated the zone from the Axis in 1944, but there is still a large minority of ethnic Turks.

Freedom Square is now a pedestrian precinct, and the main four-star Hotel Bulgaria can be reached by car only from the rear. I soon became lost, for helpful pedestrians quite understandably directed me towards the hotel's front, all too inaccessible by car. I bought a pizza from a wayside stall, weaving between buses and cars, trolleybuses and taxis, then parked on a side-street and prospected on foot. It was nearly time for the theatre, so I locked my car and bought a ticket at the Drama Theatre named for Yordan Yovkov. My proverbial good luck held: the play was to be Yordan Yovkov's own comedy, rarely seen in the West, called *The Millionaire* (1930), first performed in this town (though not in this theatre, which is brand-new) in 1931, and now directed by Georgi Popov, in vigorous performances by a gifted cast, with authentic costumes and sets of the period. The play satirises bourgeois greed, when it is rumoured that the local veterinary surgeon has suddenly acquired immense wealth. Nikola Maslarski has invited a fundraising committee to sponsor a musical celebration, but suddenly there is no need. For young Hristo Kondov has come into 3 million leva; the pillars of the community and their sycophants, secretly, private, and in cahoots first with one ally and then with another, plan to become part-owners of the fortune. There is a clear similarity with Gogol's *The Inspector-General* in the gentle analysis of small-town *mores*, while Dobrich was becoming a centre for textiles, handicrafts, the food industry and the repair and maintenance of agricultural machinery. The audience, mainly young people for whom Yovkov is a standard author, made spontaneous remarks and enjoyed jokes among themselves which would not be tolerated in a German or Austrian theatre, but added to the festive spirit of the comedy. Every one of us, after all, knew how it would end, and even if you do not understand Bulgarian I can strongly recommend a night in a Bulgarian theatre, with opulent seating, a foyer exhibition (here devoted to the poetess Dora Gabe), excellent production, and superb acting. There was no buffet, and programmes were reportedly sold out, but when I begged an usherette for one as a souvenir, the theatre manager rushed out and found one for me before curtain up with infinite courtesy, refusing to accept payment for it.

Next morning, awoken by cooing pigeons in the square below and Black Sea gulls screaming in the sky above, I prolonged the pleasure of Yovkov's play by visiting the Yovkov Museum at Ul. General Gurko 1 (off Ul. Nar. Republika). Born in Zheravna, Yovkov (1880-1937) finished secondary school in Sofia, studied law, then taught in primary schools of Dobruja, where he lived with peasant families and came to understand their lives and characteristics in much the same depth as did Elin Pelin (1877-1949). In Dobrich he stayed as a guest in Abaji Kolyo's home and married Kolyo's daughter Despina (inevitably a name bringing to mind the sly maid in Mozart's *Così fan tutte*). After World War I Yovkov worked in the Bulgarian Embassy in Bucharest and wrote several volumes of short stories, of which the best-known is *Legends of Stara Planina*, and novels, including *The Harvester*. Books from his library shown here include Caesar, Livy, Molière, Zola and Gogol. Yovkov's House-Museum can be found nearby, on the opposite side of Ul. Nar. Republika, on Lenin Boulevard, facing the Exhibition of the Revolutionary Struggle.

I preferred an hour in the District Art Gallery, founded in 1965, partly because here you can see how regional painters see Dobruja (Naiden Petkov, Todor Tsvetkov), and how more imaginative painters transcend their environment (Stoimen Stoilov, Mihalis Garudis). Among the distinguished works are those by Tsenko Boyajiev, Petur Chuklev, and Mariya Stolarova's portrait of Dora Gabe, a Whistlerian study in blue.

Off Freedom Square I discovered 'Old Dobrich' ethnographic complex, sensitively reincarnating many traditional workshops, including bookbinding, weaving, furs, woodcarving, goldsmithing, folk instruments, coppersmithing, knitting and embroidery. You are encouraged to see masters and apprentices at work, though regrettably the master-binder Racho died in 1985 and the quality has since deteriorated. Clients bring in books to be bound: it costs 2 leva for a small paperback; 3.50 for a hardback and only 9 leva for a leather binding, prices far below anything we pay in the West. A lady was knitting very fast to keep up with the demand ahead, during the winter. A tailor was making shirts for 40 leva each. Radoslav Kolev the coppersmith, perhaps ill-at-ease with hordes of schoolchildren invading his workshop, had mounted a sign in Bulgarian, 'If you don't know what you're doing, don't do it here': he learnt his craft from an old master and is passing it on to an apprentice, since Bulgaria has no formal school for coppersmiths. His brother Veselin, the blacksmith, makes ten knives, mainly for hunters, each month and they fetch anything between 100 and 130 leva each. The crafts shop sells the output of the specialists, including pullovers, sleeveless fur coats, embroidery and flutes, as well as books and records. I sampled boza and cakes at the pastry-shop, then examined the beautiful exhibition by the Guild of Masters of Folk Art, with gold by Misak Vanlian, Petur Lazarov's flutes, Yordanka Peicheva's lace, and embroidery by Nadezhda Hristova.

4: THE BLACK SEA COAST

*Obrochishte — Balchik — Kavarna and Kaliakra — Albena and Alaja
Monastery — Golden Sands — Varna — Sunny Beach — Nesebur —
Burgas — Sozopol and Southern Shores*

It was at the city of Konya in Anatolia that I first encountered
dervishes, albeit the ghosts of Veled Celebi and Abdul Halem
Celebi, haunting the Mevlevi-khane which had been unceremoni-
ously and abruptly converted into a museum after the dervish
orders had been abolished in 1925 during Atatürk's determined
policy to laicize his 'new Turkey'. Even in the 1990s hundreds of
ordinary Turks still approach the tomb of Mevlana Jelal ed-Din
Rumi with quiet devotion, for the refugee from Khorasan (with his
father Beha ed-Din) had become seven centuries after his death
probably the most celebrated Sufi mystic that the world has ever
known, making his 'dancing' order synonymous with the name
'dervish' though in fact there exist many kinds of dervish, both
monastic and lay, much like Dominican or Franciscan tertiaries.

Obrochishte
A dervish 'monastery' is called a *tekke*, and I was on my way to find
one of the large tekkes in the former region of European Turkey:
Obrochishte ('Sanctuary' in Bulgarian) found shortly before the
Tolbuhin road debouches into the resort of Albena. The heptagonal
16th-century *türbe* or tomb of Ak Azal Baba is approached by a
square antechamber also of limestone; it was closed during my visit
and a local farmer thought it was very seldom opened and couldn't
think who possessed a key. By contrast the great communal kitchen
or *magernitsa* is open to the winds, and could be imaginatively
restored as a historical museum of dervish lore, if only the
authorities could be prepared to reconcile themselves with Turkey
and the Turks, as Poland honours the Germanic knights at the
beautifully-restored castle of Malbork. We know what Obrochishte
was like in the 17th century from the description of the Turkish

Obrochishte. Arat Tekke. Türbe

traveller Evliya Celebi, who saw dervishes carving walking sticks
for sale to pilgrims; in the 18th century Felix Kanitz encountered
26 dervishes at Obrochishte; but now the dervishes are long dead,
and their memories difficult to rustleup, with only ruins to ponder,
and yellowing pages of earlier travellers to consult.

Balchik
In three kilometres the mood changes and one enters Balchik, with
glorious sea views north and south to attract Greek settlers among
the Thracian tribes in the 6th century B.C., when they called the
town Krunon ('Springs'). Five hundred years later it became

Dionysopolis, dedicated to the deity of wine and feasting. The Romans used it for a stronghold, but barbarian invasions made it impossible for the Romans to protect its eastern possessions and, like other cities of the Hexapolis on the Black Sea, Balchik fell into decline. The ruins of Dionysopolis can be seen today east of the town centre. A terrible tidal wave demolished the town in 544, so the citizens built a new mediaeval settlement high above the shore at 185 m. above sea level, with a great fortress (in the 'Horizont' quarter of the modern town) seized by the Bulgarians in the late seventh century and used as their own defence for four hundred years, when the town spread towards the shore line again. At this time the mediaeval fortress on 'Echo Hill' was built, five hundred metres southeast of the modern town centre. It fell into Turkish hands with the rest of the country and when the first Dobruja church, Sveti Nikola, was built here in 1845, the Turkish authorities, with the co-operation of the Greeks, managed to destroy it; it was not rebuilt until 1866, when it understandably came to embody Bulgarian nationalism in church and state. Its latest restoration was completed in 1982, when the Mutual School was also opened to the public.

From the cliffs above the town I gazed across at the white, red-streaked Cape called Kaliakra ('Beautiful Heights') in Greek, in whose cave it is said that Alexander's commander Lysimachos hid his treasure.

Balchik, named the Silver Riviera for its glittering cliffs and sands, throbs in summer sunshine with baking heat, dogs crouched with tongues lolling in patches of shade. Queen Marie of Romania spent her summers in a small but semi-regal palace overlooking the sea, with six terraces, one for each of her children, the sixth terrace being shortened at the cliff-edge as a touching in memoriam to the lad Mircea, who died of typhus when only two. A grand-daughter of Queen Victoria, Marie was born in England in 1875, wrote fiction and memoirs in English, and died in 1938 at Sinaia, while hoping to prevent a duel between her sons Nicholas and Carol, two years before Dobruja became Bulgarian again. The villa where she spent her summer hours from 1931 (some say with discreet para-mours) has become a rest-home run by the Union of Bulgarian Writers, Composers and Poets, but the public may visit the gardens, their white minaret, pillars from Alexander of Yugoslavia, a silver well, thrones, shrubs and flowers, waterfalls and limpid brooks. Marie wrote in her diary for October 1918, 'My forty-third birthday. I'm getting old, which is a pity, for I have still such a lot to do; a pity also because each year must inevitably take from me something of my good looks. My people always considered me pretty, and were proud of me, nôtre belle Reine. In a way it was considered one of my royal duties to please their eye, and yet it is the only duty for which I cannot be held responsible!' You can choose to stay in the Hotel Balchik on 9 Septemvri Square, with predominantly Eastern European visitors, or ask for a private room at the Balkantourist Office, 33 Ulitsa Georgi Dimitrov.

The Historical Museum on the same square includes rarities such as a Thracian racing chariot, buried with two horses to pull it and a racehorse at the back, bronze eagle-heads and bronze busts of Dionysus and two slaves. Marble sculptures include a torso of Dionysus and the god Pan. A mediaeval hall shows finds from the Second Bulgarian State and the National Revival period, with coins, arms and the interior of a local house, and elaborate local costumes, particularly interesting in an area where so many different influences commingled.

Kavarna and Kaliakra

Everyone has their favourite Black Sea town: Ahtopol or Michurin, near the Turkish border perhaps, or quiet Obzor halfway between Varna and Burgas; but there can be few settlements more attractive than Kavarna, 18 km east of Balchik on the major road E87, with a minor-road extension to Kaliakra. At the entrance to Kavarna looms the crag called the Candlestick, *Chirakman*, because it was used as a beacon to guide passing ships. The beach can be found in a little bay south of Kavarna, but the town itself is well worth a glance, with its neat historical museum, its modest churches devoted to the Virgin Mary and S. George, the friendly Hotel Dobrotitsa, and the hospitable, easy-going people. In the museum you can see how the Thracians colonised Bisoni, the Greeks took over in the fifth century B.C., and an earthquake four hundred years later toppled much of the ancient town into the sea, before the Roman conquest. The Bulgarians arrived in the seventh century, and the tug of warfare and international treaties moved borders back and forth, though Kavarna, with its luscious grapes and fat tomatoes, seems not to be familiar with strife.

Kaliakra has become a nature reserve: it is the only nesting-place in Bulgaria of the hooded cormorant, and you can sometimes see monk seals and dolphins cavorting in the waves. Exploring the caves of Kaliakra you will startle pink starlings and wild rock pigeons, Spanish wheatears and rock blackbirds. I remembered having seen in Sofia's National Museum the gold ingot shaped like a cowhide found in the sea off Kaliakra (literally the 'golden fleece' of the Argonauts?) which had been dated to 1400 or 1300 B.C. and contained 32% gold.

Albena and Alaja Monastery

Albena, named after a character created by Yordan Yovkov, is a resort of invigorating youth and energy, its vitality reflecting the new generation of post-Stalinist architects, who contrived after 1968 to swing the Black Sea coast into a new age, when Golden Sands (developed from 1956) had become a trifle old-fashioned. Young people from Eastern Europe still fill Albena's three camp-sites and dozens of hotels spread over a large and carefully-tended area near Baltata forest reserve, with its alder, ash, wild pear, white poplar, elm, wild cherry and willow, not to mention the protected fauna: wild cats, badgers, polecats, deer and wild boars. At the stepped three-star Hotel Karvuna I dined on chicken soup with noodles, *shopska* salad, veal with rice and potatoes, and crème caramel. Like most of Albena's hotels (except the four-star Dobruja) the Karvuna is open only between May and October. Excellent water sports facilities, volleyball, tennis, and even a riding-school can be found in Albena, as well as sauna in the three-star Hotel Kaliakra. The beach is seven km long. Parking presents no problem anywhere in the Black Sea resorts, even in the height of summer. If you think the beaches remain remarkably clean, the reason is that the City Councils organise cleaning by machine late every day. On package tours, beach fees are included in the hotel price; otherwise you pay 20 stotinki: a few coppers.

The next morning, after a stroll on the deserted beach (I thought unaccountably of the Seychelles, and strained my eyes towards the apparently illimitable sea), I drove off towards Alaja Monastery, signed off the coast road 'Skalen Manastir', which means Rock Monastery, a winding road wooded on both sides which makes a delightful hike uphill from Golden Sands if the heat allows (but the enclosure is locked on Mondays). Though not as spectacular as Ivanovo rock monastery near Ruse, Alaja ('multi-coloured' in

Turkish) may have been inhabited from prehistoric times, since these friable limestone cliffs provide a convenient refuge from the elements, wild beasts, from brigands, and ultimately from the world at large, for in the fourteenth century the quietist sect of hesychasts spread to these rocks. Gregory of Sinai introduced hesychasm to Mount Athos in the early fourteenth century, and Bulgarian hesychasts occupied these rock cells then, having been taught the practices at the Holy Mountain's Hilendar and Zographou monasteries. A certain Simeon had taught the oriental idea of contemplating one's navel in the eleventh century, and omphalopsychic practices, dismissed by Gibbon as 'the production of a

Alaja Monastery. Church and bell

distempered fancy, the creature of an empty stomach and an empty brain', caused an agonising schism in the Orthodox Church. 'When thou art alone in thy cell, shut thy door and seat thyself in a corner', urged Simeon. 'Turn thine eyes and thy thought towards the middle of thy belly, to the region of thy navel. At first, all will be comfortless and dark, but persevering by day and night thou wilt feel ineffable joy, and no sooner will the soul discover the place of the heart, than it shall be involved in mystic and ethereal light'.

Mural paintings, faded and damaged, have been dated to the 13th century, but their condition is so precarious that the chapel has been locked against visitors. Open to all are a range of hermit cells on two levels, connected on the outside by unromantic metal stairways, but they have long ago been looted by Turkish predators, and an earthquake destroyed the outer wall. Paths lead on a few hundred metres to grottoes even more lonely than their monastery, with its sociable kitchen. Unutterably melancholy, the deserted monastery has become even more remote and isolated from modern Bulgaria than the most inward-looked hesychast might have craved. Two women of cottage-loaf dimensions, uninterested in the monastery, were stuffing brown sacks with nettles that thrive below the sheer rock-face. I asked them what they were doing, and they responded without interrupting their rhythmic harvesting, 'Gathering nettles for soup'.

Golden Sands

Golden Sands (signs in Bulgarian are to Zlatni Pyasutsi) was begun as Bulgaria's first international resort in 1956, and its overwhelming success led to the expansion of nine hundred bungalows, more than twenty restaurants, and over eighty hotels. Mild winters and warm to hot summers guarantee permanent popularity for Golden Sands, which welcomes charter groups arriving at Varna International Airport from all over Europe. The biggest hotel, open the year round with indoor swimming pools, is the four-star International, but the town centre consists of a plaza with the Casino, the three-star Astoria Hotel, and the quay for ferryboats linking the resort with Balchik, Druzhba and Varna. This is however no Costa del Sol, even if Golden Sands counts as the most popular holiday magnet on the Bulgarian coast, for flower beds and woods are within easy strolling distance of the nightclubs and discos; in rural surroundings you can eat (with meal vouchers from your hotel) at restaurants evoking a wide gamut of atmosphere: a gipsy camp at Tsiganski Tabor; a Russian evening at the Troika; a forest setting at Mecha Polyana (Bear Glade); a shepherds' fireside at the Karakachanski Stan; and an authentic water-mill for open-air barbecues at the Vodenitsa, where I enjoyed delicious grilled chicken followed by pancakes.

Golden Sands, with its sailing, surfing, tennis and riding, is as suited to the young as nearby Druzhba is appropriate to the older generation: smaller, quieter, and possessing in the five-star Grand Varna Hotel the best accommodation on the coast, a venue for international conferences. Druzhba ('Friendship') has the advantage of lying only 10 km from the charming city of Varna, with its music festival from mid-June to mid-July. Eating out in Druzhba is particularly pleasurable at the Monastery Cave (Manastirska Izba) laid out in the former monastery of S. Constantine; and at the folkloristic Bulgarska Svatba (Bulgarian Wedding) with its rural atmosphere and evocative costumes. Just past here, also on the right-hand side of the entry from the main Varna-Albena highway, is the Balkantourist reception desk, where you may be able to locate a spare room in a hotel. But the forty-odd summer villas lying back from the pool and tennis courts are likely to be fully booked so, if you want to rent a home for self-catering in Druzhba, apply very early.

Varna

Varna astonished me. I expected a drab city of three hundred thousand people, with parking headaches, the racket of naval shipyards, a sleazy Portsmouth, a peeling Gateshead. But nothing about Varna is predictable, from its Dolphinarium and Aquarium in the Marine Gardens, to the Chalcolithic Necropolis excavated from 1972-83, its finds displayed in the Historical Museum; from the great Opera House on 9 Septemvri Square to the Roman thermal baths in old Varna near Ulitsa San Stefano. Many different races are represented in the Naval Academy, and it is common to see Africans and Asians in and out of uniform. At every season Varna offers bracing sea air, a great range of cultural opportunities (especially from mid-June to mid-July), and a feeling of cosmopolitan friendship and hospitality: visitors are expected and made welcome. Like Sofia, it has a Lyudmila Zhivkova festival building (near the Odessa Hotel), but whereas Sofia became a major city only recently, Varna,

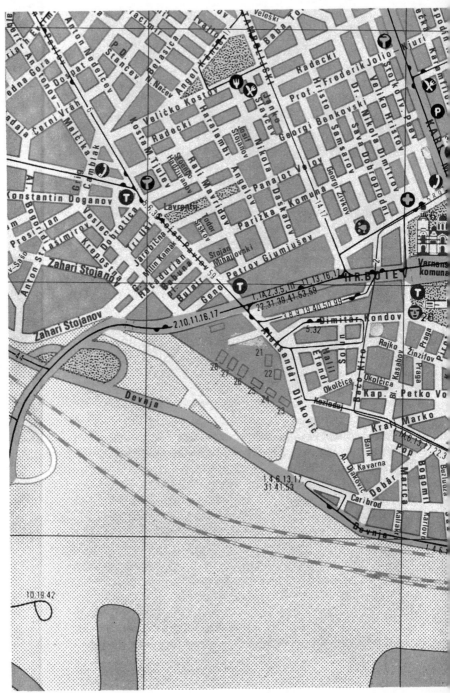

Map of Varna

the nation's third largest city, has dominated the Black Sea coast for five millennia, especially since the Greeks established the port of Odessos here in 585 B.C. A thriving Roman town, Varna fell to the Ottomans in 1391, and remained under Turkish control until 1878. It has subsequently developed textile, naval, and food industries, without losing sight of its gracious heritage as a resort of blue skies, green parks, and a sea virtually every colour but black. The best hotel is the three-star Cherno More, towering over Bul. Georgi Dimitrov's southern end, and the less formidable two-star Hotel Odessa. Even more central than these, and also open throughout the year, are the delightful one-star Hotels Republika and Musala, in facing period buildings close to 9 Septemvri Square and the pedestrianised district. Next door, at Ulitsa Musala 3, you can book private rooms both in Varna itself, and at neighbouring resorts. I parked near Hotel Musala and enjoyed the extraordinary frisson of contrast between the Buchvarov National Theatre in neo-baroque style (1931) and the City Council headquarters opposite. Varna's National Opera House opened in 1947 with *The Bartered Bride* by Smetana, and has recently been refurbished. Between Hotel Musala and the Odessos snack-bar the city authorities have preserved a Roman street and water-pipes, and on the corner of Lenin and Shipka you can find Roman foundations and a fragment of the fortress wall, with a second-century round tower. At 15 Bul. Cherveno Armeiiski are parts of Roman baths and walls. I couldn't enter the Church of S. Nicholas the Wonder-Worker (Sv. Nikola Chudotvorets) of 1866 on Lenin Bulevard, but even its domed exterior adds welcome shape and colour to the avenue. The main church of Varna is the enormous Cathedral of the Virgin built in homage to Russian style by the Bulgarian Gencho Kanev (1883-6), completed by the Russian architect Pomerantsev and decorated by Rostovtsev. Simple stained glass produces a subdued glow over the iconostasis combining classical and National Revival elements. Kliment and Naum appear in the north window and Cyril and Methodius in the south window. The three-naved, centre-domed sanctuary offers a serene grandeur, a generous sobriety and is the biggest working cathedral in the country (Sofia's Alexander Nevski is a *memorial* church).

Varna's best and most memorable secular buildings are those of the three decades succeeding 1878, though I recommend an hour in the ex-church of the Archangel Michael (1861) at 7 Ulitsa 27 Juli, near Exarch Yosif Square. It was intended as a school, but in 1865 the ground floor became a church, with a Bulgarian priest officiating in Old Slavonic. Now a Museum of the National Revival (closed Mondays, like most Varna museums), it has a typical classroom interior of the 1860s and a restored church interior, documents and photographs showing how Varna must have looked at the time. Like any architect, I see in any schoolboy's capital A a gable, and in every scrawled Z a cantilever.

On my way to the Ethnographic Museum at 22 Ulitsa Panagyurishte, I wandered along the revitalised Ulitsa Druzki, with its 19th-century houses converted into cafés, patisseries, restaurants (Stara Kushta, 1864), and the stylish Galera with its fragrant kebabs. To go to prison, find 5 Ulitsa 8 Noemvri, between the early and the later Roman baths. This is the Museum of the Revolutionary Movement, documenting one view of the history of Bulgaria between the Liberation and the present day, and it occupies three big rooms of the former prison.

Varna's Roman baths, partly excavated from 1959 to 1971, still to some extent underlie surrounding streets, but judging by the sectors revealed so far Odessos must have been a major Roman town when these great baths were constructed in the late 2nd century B.C., in the time of Septimius Severus, the Emperor born at York and responsible for the majesty of Leptis Magna, in Roman Libya. These baths were built by the confident for the arrogant, recalling in plan and grandeur the Baths of Diocletian in Rome (now a major archaeological museum) and assuming the existence of unlimited wealth including a supply of slaves to stoke the furnaces, once slave labour had built the baths and a palaestra still concealed under houses north of the excavated zone. An elaborate hypocaust stands revealed, and the latrine's floor and seats were all of marble. Shops and cafés once teemed with customers above the galleries where wood was stored to replenish the ravenous furnaces. Men and women clearly visited the baths on different days, a practice surviving in later public baths in Bulgaria. These vast baths fell into disuse in the early fourth century, while crisis spread throughout the Roman Empire, and some of its materials were reused in later public buildings, including the altogether more modest baths of the 4th century to be found just off 8 Noemvri and Cherveno Armeiiski.

Above the baths, hovering on their edge almost like a suicide on a

Varna. City scene, near main square

precipice, the church of S. Athanasius, rebuilt in 1838, was transformed in 1961 from its status as the Russian Church to an Icon
Museum, regrettably closed when I was there.

At 19 Ul. Khan Krum I found the most unobtrusive of churches
dedicated to the Virgin Mary, built below ground level in 1602 to
avoid offending the ruling Turks. Acacia branches dip over the
garden wall as though you were entering any gate, and then you
sidle guiltily through a small door into a quiet nave with a low
ceiling. The iconostasis takes your breath away for its brilliant
spiritual challenge in an era and a site inimical to Christian expres-

sion. A woman of sixty or seventy, wrinkled like a tortoise and moving as stiffly, whispered age-old prayers in her privacy, which I avoided disturbing by sudden noise or movement. She kissed an icon, and I followed her out in a circumspect procession of two.

Varna's richest treasure is neither the Art Gallery at 65 Lenin Bulevard, nor the Naval Museum at 2 Cherveno Armeiiski Bulevard, with its *Druzki* mine-carrier, famed for sinking the Turkish cruiser *Hamidieh* in 1912. It is the massive Museum of History and Art on Ulitsa Dimitur Blagoev, in the former neo-Renaissance Girls' School of 1898, opened as a museum in 1983. It deserves half a day, being open from 10-5 except on Mondays. Of the forty halls, perhaps those displaying superb gold ornaments, rivalling those of Colombia or Peru, have lent the most radiant lustre to the name of Varna, but the seven rooms devoted to prehistory possess the magic of distance. Flints date back from the beginning of the Black Sea Palaeolithic in 100,000 B.C. to its end about 10,000 B.C. The golden necropolis of Varna dates from the end of the local Neolithic and the early Bronze Age: the last quarter of the fourth millennium B.C. Ivan Ivanov announced in 1972 that he had encountered the oldest worked gold so far known. Many of the two hundred 'burials' gave up no skeletons, but some (no. 36, for instance) contained rich offerings in gold, sometimes weighing up to $1\frac{1}{2}$ kg. Ivan Marazov has suggested that the burials without a corpse may have been symbolic rites indicating that a monarch or chieftain had reached the end of his allotted span and could continue only if he 'died' with his royal diadems and accoutrements, following which he could again assume the robes of office. If this were the case, the same ruler might have been buried in fact in tomb no. 43, where equally opulent grave-goods were revealed. Archaeologists, supported by myth and literature, believe that the Neolithic cult of the Great Mother Goddess as progenitrix of all mankind is superseded here by a new patriarchal ritual equivalent to the Greek view that the smith Hephaistos (or in another reading the fire-stealer Prometheus) created males in his forge, until that moment when he created the first woman Pandora, who married Epimetheus and subsequently gave birth to the first family. The Varna tombs, possibly first symbolic then real burials, included female masks which parallel the myth. Marazov suggests that the enormous quantities of gold, some exquisitely fashioned such as a tiny Hermes in a shell on an earring, may not represent a hierarchy of wealthy aristocrats, but a royal treasure in which each piece honours in some way a god-priest-king of the Darius or Pharaonic mould.

Golden treasures from a variety of periods indicate that Varna possessed a great jewellery tradition, exemplified by a Thracian snake-head bracelet from Dolishte of the 6th century B.C. Greek ear-rings of the 4th century B.C. depict the Goddess of Victory with a bowl and cup. Roman gold rings come from the Odessos necropolis, Thracian tombs in the hinterland behind Varna, and from Marcianopolis, now called Devnya. If you go to Devnya, you will find a museum built over mosaics, as at Sandanski.

My eye was caught by great squat gravestones of Thracian chieftains of the 3rd millennium B.C., with a square staring head just jutting above a formless slab of rock. After colonists from Miletus had founded Odessos, amphorae arrived from Chios, Lesbos, and Thasos: here they are as vivid testimony to trade 2½ thousand years ago. Here too is a life-size marble Hercules from the second-century Roman Baths, with funeral steles of the same period, like one to 'Asklepiades, son of Apelles, Priest of the Great God of Odessos'. The 5th century A.D. is represented by a heavily-restored baptismal font from nearby Galata. The dark ages of barbarian invasions and anarchy produced little art of permanence: Varna offers only glazed pottery of the 12th to 14th centuries, when a walled fortress with a citadel rose between the modern streets Vaptsarov and San Stefano, on the other side of which were built the churches dedicated to SS. Athanasius, George and Theodore. Varna Museum exhibits fragmentary wall decorations from S. George, with glazed pottery mounted on the exterior wall in the manner of Chinese export porcelain dishes set into Balinese temples. After Varna (the name means 'limestone' in Bulgarian) had fallen to the Turks in 1389, it became a port in the Ottoman Empire, receiving ceramics from Turkey itself and ultimately also from China. The caretaker was reading her morning newspaper in a vain attempt to struggle into the present from the all-encompassing past that threatened to engulf her, to suffocate her like a child fallen into a thick drift of autumn leaves falling with her. She was trying to sharpen up her response to the day with thoughts blunted by old battles, rusty weapons, lost tribes.

An old man, slightly wavering on his legs, lacked one tooth, but in most other respects you would have taken him for a dependable shock-worker in a grainy 1950s film of factories and fields. Varna might seem on the outer edge of Bulgarian life, but the reality is different: it is the hub of Black Sea travel, with a new freeway to Burgas on way, and to Sofia another; Soviet passenger ships connect it with Yalta, Odessa, Piraeus for Athens, Istanbul, Larnaca and Naples; trains go to Sofia (but Balkan flights are preferable) via the Valley of the Roses or Pleven; hydrofoils call at all points south to Nesebur and Ahtopol; hydrobuses whisk you northward to Druzhba, Golden Sands, Balchik and Kavarna; buses are the best way of reaching almost anywhere nearby for value, views, and frequency, costing only 6 stotinki in the city, 10 to the airport, 15 to Druzhba and 30 to Golden Sands. At the bus station, you can take a number 14 or 24 to Devnya, known to the Romans as the Emperor Trajan's Marcianopolis (for the mosaics and museum) then a number 28 to the Stone Forest (Pobitite Kamuni), literally 'planted stones', which would seem to any von Däniken enthusiast to have been sown by extra-terrestrial gods arriving in a chariot from outer space. The reality is just as remarkable: Bulgarian geologists have explained that these hundreds of rearing columns up to five metres high and up to three metres in diameter began their immortal lives some fifty million years ago, when this area called Dikilitash lay under a shallow sea. Two strata chalk covered a sandstone stratum, and these strange formations were created almost like open-air stalactites.

Sunny Beach

From Varna I meandered along the highway south towards Burgas, woods above beaches on the left, and woods with scattered summer villas on the right, through Rudnik, Goritsa, Byala, Obzor and the lovely red-tiled hill village of Banya, arriving at the Balkantourist office in Sunny Beach, in Bulgarian 'Slunchev Bryag'. A little urchin reached through the window and touched the steering-wheel longingly, just as we all did at his age. The best hotels in Sunny Beach are three-star: Globus, Kuban, Burgas (all open year-round) and the Glarus, Pomorie and Saturn. I checked in at the Glarus with a group of tired but excited Polish tourists on an Orbis bus, and dined next to their table on an excellent veal cutlet 'in the Arabian style', with apricots, rice and potatoes, Russian salad, hot meat soup and apricots.

These are the finest sands in Bulgaria, and Sunny Beach is a safe

Sunny Beach

haven for those wanting to relax with sand, sun, sea and plenty of variety in restaurants and night life, such as discos, bars, and night clubs. Try the 'theme' restaurants such as Vyaturnata Melnitsa ('The Windmill'), Mehanata ('The Tavern'), Buchvata ('The Barrel') and Chuchurata ('The Fountain'). Sunny Beach is economical for charter groups, but I found it expensive for a lone traveller, and a small group would be better advised to book a villa. After an hour on the beach at dawn next day, I took a quick breakfast of scrambled eggs, China tea, white bread and honey (why is there never any wholemeal bread?) and slowly made off for the peninsula of Nesebur, three km to the southwest, through prosperous new Nesebur, then parked just outside the city walls, past an 18th-century windmill perched on the causeway like a sleeping sentry.

Nesebur
There is a kind of person for whom Zadar is the highest expression of the Dalmatian genius; if you are one such then Nesebur will attract you even more than Rila or Melnik, for here too is a penin-

sula that apparently the merest nudge would send sailing into the sea-dusk like a long low red and white craft. This, if you risk such a castaway existence, is the place to stay on the Black Sea. Oh, the Hotel Mesambria next to the New Metropolitan Church is comfortable enough, but here is your chance to mix with Bulgarians well accustomed to foreigners and their whims, and a call at the Balkantourist office (open till 5 p.m.) on Ul. Yana Lashkova (opposite the Cherno More Restaurant) will put you in touch with some of the hundred or so families in Nesebur who have restored and adapted historic premises to everyone's advantage. I luckily found the delightful home of Yordanka Atanasova at Rusalka 6. She would offer me wine, which I regretfully refused if driving, and huge home-grown black grapes, which I gladly accepted. A bespoke tailor, Mrs Atanasova runs a spotless and welcoming home of three storeys, including a basement where the family lives in summer: the coolest rooms in the house. Two guest families can live here independently as if in their own homes, with a kitchen on each floor, and a lounge terrace on each side; divans are pulled out as beds for children. We sat in a glassed-in balcony overlooking the ploughing

Nesebur. The curving bay from Ul. Rusalka 6

waves and I stroked a ginger cat, sipping coffee and admiring tomatoes so profuse and enormous that she cannot sell them all (everybody else grows tomatoes too) but provides them free of charge to her guests. I promised myself an hour before dark on the beach, part rock, part shingle, part golden sands, but first I wanted to explore the wonders of the silent museum-town, once crowded with forty Christian churches. A Thracian settlement called Melsabria or Menebria after a chieftain called Melsas or Mene was colonised by Dorian settlers from Megara and Chalcedon in 510 B.C., between the Ionian communities of Odessos (Varna) to the north and Apollonia (Sozopol) to the south. Monuments of the 4th and 3rd centuries B.C. include temples to Apollo, Demeter, Hecate, Asklepios, Dionysos, and the Egyptian gods Isis and Serapis. It is fourth-century B.C. Greek ramparts you first see when passing the windmill on the causeway. Fifth-century A.D. ramparts survive in part near the sea below S. John Aliturgetos, near the harbour; this is the period of the Old Metropolitan Church, centrally located along Ul. Shishmanidov, believed to be on the site of the Greek agora.

The Old Metropolitan Church and the shoreline basilica of the Virgin Eleusa (excavated in 1920 by Ivan Velkov) represent the first, Byzantine wave of church-building; the second group (such as Sv. Stefan on Ulitsa Ribarska, and S. John the Baptist), were erected in the 10th to 11th centuries; and the third and most hectic phase is attributable to the Second Bulgarian State in the 13th and 14th centuries, a major inspiration being Tsar Ivan Alexander (1331-71). From this period we have the Pantocrator, Sv. Paraskeva, Sv. Teodor, and an enlargement of the New Metropolitan from the old Sv. Stefan, the Archangels Michael and Gabriel, and the supreme achievement of the Nesebur Renaissance: S. John Aliturgetos, near the Turkish baths. The 17th-century Sveti Spas (Church of the Holy Saviour) is of slight interest apart from the recently-restored frescoes, as is the modern parish church; domestic architecture by contrast is of enormous interest, though nothing of this genre dates from before the early 19th century. Most houses were completed before the Liberation in 1878.

It was the earthquake of 1913 which demolished Aliturgetos' west wall, but the other three walls give a good idea of the original appearance of this dignified place of worship, contemporary with Sv. Sofia in the capital. Summer concerts held here in the open air are magical, other-worldly. I intuited that feverish activity characterizing the growth of Byzantine Mesemvria when the Eastern Roman Empire determined to establish Christianity as the new imperial doctrine and to fortify Black Sea towns against raids on church and state. The one preserved 5th-century gate, facing the isthmus, has exposed vertical grooves and jambs from which one easily visualises the original double door guarded by pentagonal towers. Once inside, one faced the Church of the Twelve Apostles (its southern aisle has been uncovered) on which a mosque was later erected; the Apostles' Church, like the Old Metropolitan, was a basilica with aisles separated by columns in the style of S. John Baptist of Studion in Constantinople. But the Old Metropolitan was restored in the 9th century, its original columns having given way to five pairs of pillars connected by brick arches. Bishops of Mesemvria were considered important enough to merit invitation to ecumenical councils: the first Nicaean of 325; the Constantinopolitan of 680; and the second Nicaean in 787. The seventh-century thermal baths between the Turkish baths and the most recent baths attest the high standing of Mesemvria, for even the small part of the complex so far uncovered reveals a monumentality associated with the basilicas. The Emperor Constantine IV Pogonatus (668-685) visited Mesemvria in 680; may have used local curative springs for pains in his legs noted in the chronicles of Theophanes and Patriarch Nicephoros; and may even be buried here in a rich grave discovered in 1947, with gold treasure now in Sofia's National Museum, except for one gold coin of Constans II in Nesebur Museum. The seashore basilica, close by a truncated windmill, has three aisles and three apses; it was restored during the Middle Ages, but erosion has gnawed away part of the centre aisle.

The New Metropolitan is another three-aisled basilica, but in the 16th century the nave was lengthened and in the 18th a new narthex was constructed. Glazing on the façade first used here became the norm on Nesebur's mediaeval churches. The frescoes within are particularly remarkable: one is of the 11th century (on the northernmost column at the entrance to the central apse) but the others are of 1599, and include a vigorous 'Christ Washing the Disciples Feet', the 'Forty Martyrs', and a 'Presentation of the Virgin in the Temple'. The overturning of paganism and triumph of Christianity in Nesebur is neatly symbolised by the use here of inverted temple columns with new Christian capitals.

The iconostasis doors of Sv. Stefan are contemporary with paintings in Bachkovo (1604) and show a seated Virgin before the Angel of the Annunciation, above four standing saints, of which the first three are identifiable as Cappadocian church fathers: Basil the Great, John Chrysostom, and Gregory the Theologian, all names known in Old Bulgarian texts from the ninth century. The fourth is probably S. Nicholas of Myra, miracle-worker and patron saint of children, fishermen and sailors whose wonders have been celebrated in Benjamin Britten's *Saint Nicolas* cantata of 1948.

S. John the Baptist possesses other frescoes including full-length portraits on the dome-walls and a fine portrait of the donor. But the

Nesebur. Behind the apse of S. John the Baptist, now a museum

church is now an archaeological museum. Do not miss the bronze of Dionysus and snub-nosed boon companion Silenus from the 4th century B.C. Christ Pantocrator close by is contemporary with the Boyana Church on Vitosha and the golden age of Turnovo. Those still unconvinced of the harmony and dignity of Byzantine art should give time and thought to Nesebur's Pantocrator, with its refined proportions, domes, multi-coloured decorations, narthex created over a vaulted crypt, square tower, brilliant brickwork with swastikas, those symbols of sun-worship that found their way here and into Hinduism.

The Pantocrator stands at the divide between two streets running the length of Nesebur: Lashkova leading to the Partisans' Museum (no. 33) and the Ethnographic Museum (no. 34), and Shishmanidov bringing you back to S. John the Baptist, the Holy Saviour, and the Church of the Archangels Michael and Gabriel, modelled on the Pantocrator but ruined, and locked against internal inspection during my visit. The use of complementary brick and stone effects is very striking here, as are the sparkling green plaques. Sv. Paraskeva too is visible only from without, but the ceramic and sculpted decorations will still strike you as original for the 14th century.

S. John Aliturgetos (the epithet means 'unconsecrated', particularly odd when applied to the architectural masterpiece in question) reaches new heights of ingenuity and sheer brilliance, not only in majesty of form and structure, but also in details such as variegated patterns of mussel shells, sun images, decorative plaques, the usual crosses and four-leafed clovers. Two pairs of marble columns divided the nave into three aisles and supported the fine dome. Symmetrical, carefully dressed limestone blocks create a dance of symmetry enlivened by the unexpected, like gargoyles gurning from a Gothic roof. Within, heraldic birds, lions and acanthus leaves are scattered like a lord's largesse before *hoi polloi*.

Having wandered back and forth across this mediaeval world in miniature (left undisturbed more tastefully than Mont Saint Michel itself), I enjoyed angles of light and shade on a hundred houses, built during the great days of shipbuilding, fishing and trade from the early nineteenth century, that is the National Revival, delightful balconies on the upper floors almost touching each other across shady cobbled streets. Kitchens and stores are usually situated on the ground floor; domestic rooms on the first floor, and courtyards flourish green and fresh behind stone walls. Woodcarved ceilings may not be as numerous as in Tryavna, but the Bogdanov, Lambrinov and Markov houses are splendid examples, and the Muskoyani House at Ul. Lashkova 34 has fine ceilings open to all, for the home serves as an Ethnographic Museum, on the first floor, the lower area being a store for fish and tackle. Small as the museum is, nobody should miss the chance of enjoying a Nesebur interior, with its weaving room, costumes, a fireplace in the living-room, jewellery, and a shepherd's cloak from Kozichino.

Burgas
The road to Burgas passes through Aheloi, where Tsar Simeon defeated Emperor Leo Phocas of Byzantium in 917, thus preserving the strongholds of Pliska and Preslav from a Byzantine army possibly a hundred thousand strong. Near Pomorie, salt-pans are visible: its salt was exported from ancient Greek Anchialos, inhabited by Greek settlers from Mesemvria. Signed off right of the main road is a Thracian brick tomb of the 3rd century B.C. inside earthworks.

Burgas itself looks like any big city, with the Izgrev suburb, then high-rise buildings, industrial areas for rolling-stock, engineering, cables, radiators. A Thracian settlement with Macedonian connections existing below present-day Burgas and suburbs is attested by recent finds of a bronze mask of Mercury, a necropolis, inscriptions, pottery, amphorae and coins dating to the time of Alexander the Great, but Thracian and Roman settlements have left little trace, and the town boasted a mere three thousand inhabitants as recently as 1878, when the Ottoman yoke came to an end. The new harbour of 1903-6 gave enormous impetus to the growth of Burgas, a name deriving from the Greek 'pyrgos', a fortress. Then the Sofia-Burgas rail-link of 1906 suddenly improved connections inland, and an anti-malarial institute helped reduce the incidence of the disease emanating from the town's three lakes. Balkantourist offer private lodgings: they can be reached at 1 Ul. G. Ganev or 2 Ul. Purvi Mai. Hotels are the two-star Primorets east of the railway station, and the three-star Bulgaria north of the railway station on Purvi Mai. If you have your own car, my advice is to stay in Nesebur or Sozopol, and visit Burgas by day and for evening concerts or plays. Burgas is not a tourist city, despite its attractive position on the Black Sea, and will be ideal for anyone just wanting to see how Bulgarians go about their everyday business. There are no distinguished churches for instance, for the town has no long history, and a quick glance in SS. Cyril and Methodius (1894-1905) will suffice. The Archaeological Museum at 21 Bul. Lenin is predictably sparse in materials, and more is to be gleaned from the Ethnographic Museum, set back from Ul. Slavianska at no. 69, in a delightful period of building. Downstairs you can find textiles, especially wool and silk, rugs and wall-hangings. At the head of the stairs a late-19th century shaman called *kukeri* has bells round its waist, a mock sword of wood, and a frightening mask, feathers in its hair, fur sleeves and trousers. Four upstairs rooms display a range of woven and embroidered textiles, including bags, napkins and table-cloths; and regional costumes, with some beautiful buckles.

The strangest museum in Burgas, and by far the most fascinating, is the District Art Gallery, filling three 'floors' of the former synagogue at 22 Ulitsa Vodenicharov. The lowest floor exhibits modern Bulgarian artists, whose best hope for the future seems to reside in the intimate world of graphics, rather than in the clichés of representational oils, in which socialist realism takes first place, second, third and fourth. The sculptures here are plain, prosaic and unimaginative, as though Degas, Rodin, Archipenko, Gabo, Hepworth and Giacometti had never lived. By contrast, Marinov's 'Composition with Tightrope Walker' is a vivid, poetic print, and de Chirico has clearly influenced Vanko Urumov. The middle floor is devoted to Burgas artists such as Georgi Baev, the Mondrian-inspired Georgi Yanakiev, the expressive colourist Nenko Tokmachiev, and the still-life specialist Lyubomir Kotsev. The highest floor, intruding artificially at angelic level below the synagogue's dome, is bizarrely devoted to the Christian icon. Seagulls screamed overhead in protest, flapping their wings which I glimpsed for an instant through one of four round portholes on the sky. The Burgas icons derive from the Nesebur area (mainly in the form of copies) and the Stranja district. Two 18th-century Virgin Hodigitria icons are parochial works based on Nesebur models, while a 17th-century crucifix must be based on an 11th-12th original, for Jesus is shown dead on the Cross, a convention stamped out as heretical thereafter. Many icons in this gallery depict the sea around Burgas, just as some 19th-century icons from Tryavna, Samokov or Rila can be identified by local landscape backgrounds. The Burgas collection has a number of icons representing S. Modestus with his flock of sheep, emphasising the rôle played by pastoralism in the Burgas hinterland. Hellenization is shown by Greek inscriptions and Biblical texts. The latest icon I found in Burgas was dated 1904, when Monet was painting his innovative *Waterloo Bridge at Sunset* (National Gallery, Washington) and I wondered how long it would be, in what hopeful period of *glasnost* or *perestroika*, before travelling exhibitions of the European avant-garde of the last hundred years could be shown in Bulgarian cities.

If you missed a fillet roast at the frigate *Lyulin* on the sands at Sunny Beach, there is another chance to dine on board a Black Sea vessel at the *Musalla*, an old motorized ship launched in 1912 to transport grain and timber now a restaurant called Starata Gemiya ('The Old Smack') beside the harbour breakwater in Burgas, where the house speciality is squid.

No programmes were scheduled for that evening at the Concert Hall on Ul. Slavianska, the Opera and Ballet Theatre on Ul. Kliment Ohridski, or at the Open-Air Theatre in the Marine Gardens. But the Adriana Budevska Theatre on Ul. Tsar Asen announced *The Last Supper of Deacon Levski*, a patriotic Communist drama by Stefan Tsanev, and I was eager to see whether Bulgarian agitprop theatre resembled the play I had seen in Berat, Albania. It did.

Though the theatrical tradition in Burgas goes back to 1883, its new drama theatre, designed by Boris Kamilarov, is a splendid new structure completed in 1983 with two stages, and a very strong company. The larger theatre was three-quarters full for Tsanev's new play, ideologically sound like the choice of operas in Sofia that season: Verdi's *Nabucco*, with Hebrew slaves to parallel Bulgarian servitude under the Ottoman yoke; or *La Traviata*, showing the decadence of Parisian society. The play portrays Levski as saint and martyr, reminding me that children had planted at Karlovo a forest in honour of the 'apostle' Levski. Hristo Simeonov played Levski to the life (we have many photographs) in a long grey overcoat with white shirt, grey trousers and black boots. In front of the darkened stage, chains were draped symbolically. Ten representatives of revolutionary committees he founded throughout the country included a monk and a nun, an intellectual (the poet Hristo Botev), and peasants from various regions denoted by their costume. Having been betrayed by a Bulgarian, Levski is led away to be hanged, though the gallows were on stage. Tsanev's style, passionate,

Burgas. Adriana Budevska Theatre (1983)

nationalistic, rhetorical, is in the main address to the audience, rather than to express conflict between the various characters in their own historical context. The volume is turned up, except for a few (much more effective) moments of meditation, and his failure to manipulate a large number of characters on stage means that many of the actors must stand woodenly, stolidly, while they have nothing to say, reducing tension. The conscious parallels of Levski with Christ and Krustyu with Judas may strike a Bulgarian audience as apposite and relevant: I found the relationship unconvincing, and the didacticism counter-productive. A theatre should not mimic a party congress.

At breakfast next morning I sat with two German businessmen. One observed: 'My teeth are gnashing with ache'. The other, also keen to practise English, confided in me that he had been bitten by a mosque: a swelling at the back of his hand looked painfully red. 'Don't you mean a mosquito?' 'Nay, nay, a mosquito is a *small* fly. This was a big one, a real mosque'. In the Corecom hard currency shop on the main concourse of Hotel Bulgaria I bought Cadbury's dairy milk chocolate, and admired Natalie's gold jewellery. She has a sign requesting customers not to clamour all at once so, as she was always busy, I regretfully left her counter and sauntered towards the busy harbour. I was hoping to find that Balkantourist would offer a trip to Bolshevik Island, but none was running that day to the island in Burgas bay where communists were jailed in the former monastery of S. Anastasia after the failure of the 1923 rising.

Sozopol and Southern Shores

So I drove south to Sozopol, the former Apollonia in Pontus founded by Greeks from Miletus in the 7th century B.C. An active fishing port, it is the Honfleur of the Black Sea Coast, refusing to be overrun by starry-eyed visitors who include discerning painters. A legend explains how the Ionian philosopher Anaximander chose this site from all others for his Milesian colonists, settling on the island now called S. Cyril, which was joined to the peninsula by a causeway in 1926. In the 5th century B.C., the Ionians moved their settlement to the peninsula of Susopolis, later known in Bulgarian as Sozopol. Bronze Age Thracian remains have been found below the Ionian town, but the Greeks quickly established full sway over the area, trading with inland Thracians for coal, metal ores and wood to guarantee their maritime supremacy against other fleets. Apollonia's emblems in the 5th century B.C. are revealed on silver and bronze coins: a Medusa head and on the other side an anchor, crab and the letter 'A' for Apollo, deity of Miletus and its colonies. The *boule* (Municipal Council) commissioned from the sculptor Kalamis known at Athens from 475 to 450 a huge bronze sculpture of Apollo, standing as Strabo asserts thirty cubits high, that is about 32 feet 6 inches high: over ten metres. When conquering the town for the second time in 31 A.D. (their first roving victories in Thrace occurred in the 1st century B.C.) the Romans destroyed it, removing the Kalamis Apollo to the Capitol, from which it has disappeared. Into Byzantine times, Susopolis failed to keep abreast of its own growing colony Anchialos (now Pomorie), and only as persistent fishermen kept alive their somnolent port century by century, through the time of the Ottoman yoke, and beyond. The Archaeological Museum possesses some of the loveliest of Greek ceramics in Bulgaria outside the National Museum in Sofia; the Maritime Museum in a disused church displays encrusted anchors. The whole winding, hilly peninsula town has remarkably

Sozopol. Wooden houses on stone foundations

homogeneous 19th century homes in the National Revival style, and I admired in particular those of Ghiaurov and Stefanov among the forty-five 'listed'. Was it a maple leaf that stirred on the cobbles, like an amputated hand, withered throughout a season of lost hope, disoriented in desiccated desperation: a wizened spinster among the noisy families of foliage?

The Church of the Holy Virgin in the town centre has decorations by artists from Debur: the bishop's throne, small altar, and the fine iconostasis. Because the popular harbourside restaurant called Perun was full, I took lunch in Balkantourist's Mehana Sozopol up on the hill. If you arrive by bus, you will alight near the harbour, which advertises sailings thrice daily to Nesebur and Varna between May and September. To secure a private room ask Balkantourist at 2 Ulitsa Cherveno Armeiiski. These southern shores of the Black Sea are less crowded than those of the north, with accommodation generally of a lower standard, so those willing to 'rough' it slightly more than usual will find Sozopol and the beach-resorts to the south delightfully secluded: in May or Sep-

Dyuni in summer

tember it is not unusual to find yourself alone on a beach. Apart from S. Cyril, Sozopol has two other islands: S. John, named for the ruined monastery formerly called after the Virgin, and S. Peter, a small reef.

South of Sozopol, you can sail (in season) to the mouth of the Ropotamos (Ro River), or drive across pleasant rolling landscapes to the beaches of Kavatsi (6 km) and Dyuni (another 3 km), the latter built by the Finns in 1987 to high specifications and used mainly by the Dutch, French and Germans. Its sandy beach sloping under a flawless, brimming sea is like Golden Sands, and immaculate villas in a young pine forest overlook the sea, tennis courts, swimming pool. The coastal village possesses a three-star hotel complex, also with a choice of restaurants. Dyuni offers its own shopping arcade, and for those with transport there is every opportunity to explore the rural Stranja, and the coastline to Primorsko (with its International Youth Centre), fishing-port of Michurin, and historic harbour of Ahtopol, just before the Turkish border.

5: PLOVDIV AND THE SOUTH-EAST

Kotel — Zheravna — Medven and Katunishte — Sliven — Stara Zagora — Haskovo — Plovdiv — Asenovgrad — Bachkovo Monastery — Smolyan — Pamporovo — Shiroka Luka

Breakfast at the Hotel Bulgaria in Burgas was scrambled eggs and chopped sausages, a banitsa (cheese pastry), honey and bread, tiny grapes, and three cups of boiling hot water into which I had dipped tea-dust from Shanghai. 'My cold', observed a Bulgarian business-man at the next table, practising his English, 'is improving in the wrong direction'. The receptionist stamped the morning's date as well as the previous night's on a slip of paper for me to keep with my passport as proof that I had spent the night in a recognised tourist bed, and wished me a safe drive to Sliven.

Kotel
The wide, flat fields, with low hills left and right seem to lead ever westward, and I was glad to leave behind me the ugly four- and five-storey apartment blocks of Ajtos for almost featureless fertile fields on the way to Karnobat and Venets. The sun was breaking through as I veered right at Lozenets, marked 'Kotel 39 km', with the difficult pass indicated 'otvoren', meaning open. My car climbed eagerly into forested hillsides radiant with autumn sun. I crossed the river Marash, passed through rural Avramov, and in a few minutes of a drive totally unspoilt by advertising, hoardings, billboards, I slowed up into the fresh air of mountainous Kotel, known as 'cauldron' from its permanently gushing hot springs. Momcho Draganov suggests that a town existed here at the begin-ning of the Bulgarian state, but the Czech traveller Jireček was told that immigrants had founded Kotel around 1545. Its apogee arrived in the 18th-19th centuries, like that of Koprivshtitsa, but Kotel was three-quarters destroyed by fire in 1894, so that only a few houses can be dated to the late 18th century and these have only one storey. Early in the 19th century it was the fashion to build asymmetrical

Kotel in spring. Wooden houses flanking a cobbled street

two-storey homes with an external wooden staircase and a verandah open on the façade. Rooms generally have wooden cupboards, a fireplace, a fixed wooden divan covered with rugs and cushions. The typical tiled roof extends far beyond the building. Homes of the later 19th century adopt the two-storey model, with a closed verandah, and one large hall occupying the whole width: these are the classical 'Kotel' homes, generally with stone or brick walling protecting a small garden. Streets are of cobbles, draining quickly and easily down natural slopes. Generously-overhanging eaves protect pedestrians from the elements all year round. I suppose the population today is about 8,000, compared with the one thousand of Zheravna. Its fortune consisted in its sheep, and the industry of its women who wove wool, to create the important carpet industry still active. Guilds of sheep-dealers could at one time count their flocks at 45,000 head, and their burgeoning wealth and importance, coupled with trade to distant Istanbul, Varna, and Dobrich, bred a national type with the resources financial and intellectual to carry forward the Bulgarian national revival with efficacious zeal. Bishop Sofroni of Vratsa, for example, advocated in his *Nedelnik* (1806, the first printed book in Bulgarian) the right of universal education, and that other native of Kotel, Georgi Rakovski (1821-67), pursued nationalistic aims by other means: that of armed revolution from abroad, though he died of tuberculosis in Bucharest before his dreams could be realised.

I parked near the eerie Rakovski Pantheon, in which a Bulgarian guide was telling her group of foreign visitors from the Black Sea, 'I give you information about the travelling of his bones'. His bones travelled back to Kotel in 1981, and their mausoleum is dark, dank, cold and more empty than any building has a right to be. Much more inviting is the Ethnographic Museum, beautifully displayed in the Radil Kyorpeyev House, topped by a periscope-like square brick chimney in the middle of the tiled roof. It was begun by master-builders from Tryavna in 1872, with charming built-on wooden cupboards carved in their scintillating manner. At the top of the stairs a guest-room welcomes you with long benches around two walls; a business-room is laid out as if the paterfamilias is due back at any moment, and a young girls' room has a trousseau neatly exposed to view. A bedroom has a low platform bed covering half the floor which reminded me of those low Rajput beds in Rajasthan from which a man might leap at a bare second's warning. A shelter in the courtyard is fitted with a furnace for a barbecue, and a bath for use in summer. In the women's room hangs a Jerusalem icon similar to one we have seen in Troyan Monastery. The upper floor has a charming verandah platform or 'kiosk' covered with a typically bright carpet in Kotel style beside the mansion's own weaving room. Here is the coarse serge men wear in these chilly mountains and exported in great quantity, and a medlar-tree (*mushmula* is how it sounds in Bulgarian). I found the stone Church of the Holy Trinity closed: a pity for it's another fine work by master Pavel Kolev from Tryavna. The Church of SS. Peter and Paul (1834) is by another Tryavna master, Dimitur Sergyuv. Kotel arts and crafts school is particularly noted for its carpets, and this folk-instrument school was the first of its kind in Bulgaria. You can attend courses at these schools by booking through an agency dealing with Balkantourist.

Zheravna

The two-star Hotel Kotel is comfortable enough, but the nearby village of Zheravna appealed to me so much more, with its tiny population, superb hilltop position, and intimate atmosphere evoking the National Revival. Rooms are available there at the Zlatna Oresha complex, eighteen two-storey walled homes not far from the village centre. Zheravna (related to the Bulgarian name for the crane, *zherav*) has conserved more than two hundred broad-eaved wooden houses. Stefan Stamov suggests that the high distinction of houses in Kotel, Medven and Katunishte has its origin in the architectural types of Zheravna. The earliest homes, of the 17th century, comprised only two rooms, with heavy boards, usually of locally-felled oak. The typical Zheravna houses, of the High Renaissance in the 18th century, consist of two storeys, with an open verandah and brackets supporting the overhanging first floor, and often ornate woodcarvings within. Towards the middle of the 19th century, the Late Renaissance offers a greater variety of styles, but the most popular was the closed house with one large hall and an internal staircase. Rusi Chorbaji's 18th-century home, with its own courtyard well, has been recently retiled, and its interior refurbished in period-style, with sliding wooden windows. Guests would sit with their backs against low cushions on raised platforms. Sava Filaretov's birthplace is now an ethnographic museum, and its rugs and carpets are as colourful as any in Zheravna, predominantly red. Chorbaji's shop, where he sold his *abbas* (rough serge garments) is now a modern bookshop, though Stamov's books on Zheravna were not available there.

Yordan Yovkov's birthplace, beautifully restored, shows the writer's humble origins: only one display area and the vestibule are open, but if you have seen the Yovkov Museum in Tolbuhin you will be here to enjoy the serene atmosphere rather than to learn more about the satirist. His house is numbered 225; it is no good looking for street names, for there are none. As usual, I explored the local church. Sveti Nikolai was built by Tryavna masters in

Zheravna. Red-tiled houses from the village limits

1833, frescoed in 1840, then painted in 1881 by Nedyo Fyodorovich of Zheravna. It remains active with an art collection in the gallery. The narthex has mounted icons, and gravestones dated 1783, 1787, 1846, 1862. From the gallery, you can enjoy the effect of a bright local carpet over the nave, and a dramatically shining iconostasis that looks as though it has been repainted in the last few days.

The art gallery (closed from 12 to 2 for the ladies to make lunch for their families at home) is laid out in the primary school of 1867. During my visit there was a special display of graphics, posters and sculptures by Burgas artists.

Medven and Katunishte
I took the road leading due south towards E773 and Stralja, but turned off left to the little village of Medven, founded from Butovo in or shortly after the 16th century. The new arrivals made their stout homes from secular oaks found on the spot, using simple planks, often with joints rather than nails, and preferring a single

storey. The Turks called Medven 'Papazköy', the priest's village. Sheep were the beginning and end of the village's economy, as at Zheravna and Kotel, and pastures became so overgrazed in the vicinity that shepherds would take their flocks to the Dobruja plain and to Karnobat. I wandered around the main street, the Sarekov House, the black ravine, the Zahari Stoyanov museum-house buildings and the Kara Georgi House, regretting the terrible losses by fire during the War of Liberation. Nowadays Medven possesses only three hundred houses with about eight hundred inhabitants. High Renaissance homes added a so-called *prust* or vestibule to the two-room pre-Renaissance plan, early in the 19th century. An external wooden staircase led to a large verandah and two rooms, the larger with a vestibule and the smaller giving access to the vestibule. Stores would be confined to the ground floor, and the upper floor would have thick wooden boards. If, as usual, the home is constructed on sloping terrain, the lower floor would have stone foundations. In the mid-19th century the closed house begins to predominate, with an internal staircase, and a reduced verandah-space, which now becomes an extra room. Paved courtyards effervesce with wild and cultivated flowers every springtime, and one can well understand the appeal of these hills and flowers to a people so passionately in tune with the heartbeat of nature.

I couldn't resist stopping, too, in the village of Katunishte, stepped alongside the left bank of the river Katunishka, with the Balkan massif towering along the other. The paths are paved with great stones worn smooth through the centuries. Posts and planks comprise the traditional Katunishte home, from the 17th century to the second half of the 19th. Vine-covered trellises give shade from the fierce heat of summer, and fine examples of dry-stone walling abound. Every house has its main room, a virtual reception salon, with a colonnaded mensofa and parapet, a hearth, cupboards exquisitely carved, and a brilliant use of red-orange-yellow carpets, cushions and rugs. Though no previous traveller I have read mentions Katunishte, I feel sure you will be delighted with the village in its secluded tranquillity, and never forget its great plank-doors, quaint cobblestones, and timeless river-ripple.

Sliven
But we are due in Sliven, for lunch at the Restaurant Deboya, once the town's caravanserai. The caravanserai was adapted for use as a

wool and cloth goods warehouse early in the 19th century, when it became known as the 'depôt', or *deboya*. After Liberation, its function changed to army workshop, divisional headquarters, and police station, before its demolition in 1973. The new restaurant, tavern and wine-cellar, designed by the Bulgarian Totev in 1973, forms part of the complex centred on a fine stone office-building of 1873, a masterpiece of Bulgarian Renaissance architecture. I liked the charming private homes with vine-covered gardens in Ulitsa Ablanovo, but Sliven's idea of progress is that dreary dogma of the high-rise apartment, necessary perhaps in Hong Kong or Singapore, where land cannot be found, but not in Balkan Bulgaria, so underpopulated that many jobs in Sofia cannot be filled at all. Hotel Sliven dominates the main square, with the sparkling new Kirov Theatre close by: it was showing Alexander Galin's *Retro* during my stay. Originally a Roman stronghold, the Confluence (which is what 'Slivane' means) was destroyed by the Turks for its opposition to their rule, and its revolutionary tradition persisted under Haji Dimitur, who fell in 1868 while leading insurgents. His house-museum is at 2 Ul. Asenova, and that of Panajot Hitov at 7 Ulitsa

Sliven. Drama Theatre next to Hotel Sliven

Cherno More. The District History Museum at 6 Bulevard Lenin (built as a house in 1895 by Kolyo Ganchev of Tryavna) has the usual selection of weapons, objects from a Thracian tomb at Kaloyanovo, and descriptions of local industries, beginning with silk, tanning, and wine, and continuing with textiles, a museum being devoted especially to local textiles in Dobri Zhelyazkov's textile factory of 1834. The Dobri Chintulov Museum, celebrating that poet, composer and educator, is located in the Church of the Holy Wisdom's courtyard.

The Blue Rocks above Sliven may be a dim version of Belogradchik, but I recommend the cable-car ride to the summit for its vast panorama of the plain in which Sliven snuggles for refuge from the cold *bora* winds. The Romans knew of the spa 12 km southeast of Sliven, but the baths you see nowadays are Turkish, and still used for gastro-intestinal cures.

Stara Zagora
Across the almost featureless Thracian plain I sped through Kamenovo and Nova Zagora to reach Stara Zagora before nightfall, to make sure of a seat at the theatre for Imre Kalman's *The Queen of Czardaş*. At 135,000, Old Zagora's population is the sixth largest in Bulgaria, and it has grown with each successive settlement, from Thracian Beroe in the 5th century B.C. to Augusta Trajana under the Romans, Vereia and Irinopolis under the Byzantines, Burue under the early Bulgarian States, and Eski Zaara (Old Fertile Land) under the Ottomans. 'Zad Gora' means 'across or behind the mountain', that is the Balkan Range, though *gora* means 'wood' or 'forest' in modern Bulgarian. Liberated by the Russians in 1877, it was stormed and devastated by the Turks, so that most of the town you see today is 'Old' in name only, and has been rebuilt in mechanical grid-fashion. But then the astonishment of Bulgaria plucks at your elbow and beckons you along the main thoroughfare (Georgi Dimitrov) to the crossroads Georgi Petrov (north) and Dimcho Staev (south). You take Petrov, then the second left will bring you, behind the new Regional Hospital, to a Neolithic settlement uncovered in 1969, and opened to the public with funds provided by Austria through Unesco, ten years later. A ground-floor display area shows stone, flint and bone tools unearthed in the mound occupied from the 6th millennium B.C. to the 2nd. Large terra cotta vases, bowls and pots painted in bold black lines and striking

designs contrast with incised lines from the 5th-4th millennia, and cult objects from the 6th-4th millennia, and copper axes from Gradva. The basement shelters two dwellings dated to the period known as Karanovo II, here Early Neolithic. The southern dwelling measures 6 x 5.2 metres and the northern dwelling of the same epoch 5.2 x 3 metres; both caught fire at once. The walls were of wattle and daub, and the double-eaved roof of thatch and reeds, the floor being plastered even with clay. A hearth provided heat for cooking and for warming the family, and a raised clay platform next to the oven would have been used for a bed, uncannily like the raised wooden platforms we have seen in the Balkan hills around Kotel. Stone querns near the oven have two millstones for grinding wheat and barley, remains of which have been identified. I shivered with recognition: my ancestors might have slept here seven thousand years ago, precisely here in these burnt-out shelters.

After refilling my tank (with petrol 1 lev for super and 80 stotinki for normal grade, and diesel at only 40 stotinki for a litre, it is clear why Bulgarians prefer cars that will run on diesel), I was keen to find the Roman city. Excavations have revealed the western gate, with the charmingly modest theatre recently opened for summer spectacles like the theatre in Plovdiv. Immediately behind the Roman theatre are thermal baths dated to the reign of Marcus Aurelius (161-3), and I found inscriptions not only in Latin, as expected, but in Bulgarian, for Khan Krum captured Stara Zagora, annexing the region to the first Bulgarian state in the early 9th century. I took a photo from Room 235 of the three-star Hotel Vereia on 11 Ulitsa Lenin across dignified town houses to the multi-storey Trades Union Secretariat, glinting cream with its slogan Slava na Truda (Glory to Labour) emblazoned in a grey wintry sky.

A quick wash and brush-up, and I ran to *The Queen of Czardaş*, Kalman's bitter-sweet operetta evoking for Zagora grannies the glamour of the Austro-Hungarian Empire much as Rochdale housewives will gaze open-mouthed at the expensive gowns of a Dallas super-bitch. How easily these singers slide into evening-dress and toss down what passes for champagne! The new Opera House opened in 1971, replacing the famous old auditorium of 1925 where Boris Christoff had first made his name, all those years before he had starred at Covent Garden as the best King Philip of his generation. The hero in *Boris* is not the Tsar himself, but the

Stara Zagora. Inscriptions in Latin and Bulgarian

Russian people: gullible, exploited, but slowly enduring like smoother rocks on ebb-high shores. A large army contingent in the stalls became gradually quieter as the three acts unfolded, but the audience generally made an intolerable racket, probably because the seats (under £1) were so cheap that people attend performances regularly. Many types attend who would not consider it if tickets were dearer: how I longed for a few minutes of good Teutonic silence! Escapist art has its place in every society, from the *kitsch* of Coronation Street to the Red Army male voice choir's stolid patriotism, and the Roman dedication to *panem et circenses* must never be taken for granted as an irrelevance. Semiotics has shown that each element in society has its own place, and its own signification. I looked for signs in the emptying streets around the Vereia Hotel on Lenin Bulevard. Here, a billboard in the window of a lottery shop proclaimed that on the 37th draw, one Ivan Genchev Ivanov of S. Kaloyanovets – with twelve correct results – had won 14,292 leva, a fabulous sum by Bulgarian standards but scarcely a fraction of the figures regularly paid out by football-pools companies in the U.K., or by the Spanish state lottery.

Back at the Vereia, the night-club had amplified the noisy singer and backing-group, to ensure that everyone received enough decibels to last them for the rest of the week. Couples danced like zombies, not looking at each other, in a style they must have thought similar to those of American youngsters of the same age, but without enthusiasm. It was, after all, something to do, proving that you were young. I fell into a pale sleep, as if a phantom had spread mist over torn gauze.

Next morning Stara Zagora, town of lime trees, woke to bright, brittle sunshine, and I walked carefully between the cracks in the paving-stones trying to give the appearance of not caring whether I stepped on a crack: the usual obsessive's sang-froid. The District History Museum was closed, and so I turned off Ulitsa Gurko into Ulitsa Geo Milev to find the Milev House-Museum. Geo Milev is the author of the poem 'September' which denounced the massacre of thousands following the unsuccessful September 1925 rising. His selected poems and prose poems have been translated by Ewald Osers as *The Road to Freedom* (Forest Books, 20 Forest View, Chingford, 1988). Tsankov's secret police murdered Milev in 1925, and this poet-martyr is poignantly immortalised in his modest home, where a new annexe commemorates other poets of this town of about 134,000 people: Ivan Hajihristov, Veselin Hanchev, Kiril Hristov and Nikolai Liliev. The District Art Gallery displays a variety of 19th and 20th-century paintings, none of outstanding quality. Its picturesque location below the southern slopes of Stara Planina makes Stara Zagora ideal for a botanical garden, and the Lenin Park provides this as well as a sports stadium, restaurant and open-air theatre.

The 15th-century Eski Jami'a, or Old Mosque, is one of the few reminders of five Ottoman centuries: it can be found where Ul. Blagoev meets Ul. Dimitrov, near the supermarket.

Haskovo

I bowled along sunny roads due south towards Haskovo, past the airport, through Budeshte of the mulberry-trees, where the silk industry is both domestic and industrial, and through Yastrebovo, where a warmly-clad shepherd reminded me of the weather-warning in Bulgarian winter days: 'sluntse no da ne si na vuntse': 'sunny, but still better not to go out'. Tobacco fields spread wide around Sredets, and cotton fields around Trakia. I was strongly tempted to roam from Haskovo to Uzunjovo, where Evliya Celebi gave news of the huge annual trade fair which disappeared in 1876, and to that other Turkish stronghold of Harmanli, comprising with Svilengrad the two major silkworm-breeding centres in the country.

But time, my bitterest antagonist, would impel me westward after a few hours in the former Muslim town of Haskovo, in recent decades overtaking Uzunjovo as the area's major town. Meanwhile I passed cotton fields surrounding Radievo of the traditional two-storey tiled houses, and crossed the Maritsa on the outskirts of industrial Dimitrovgrad (about 48,000 inhabitants), with open-worked lignite mines, chemical works, and the biggest cement works in the country. Pollution is a problem freely admitted, but not yet resolved. Outside the town I encountered the road-sign 'Beware Deer', and within ten minutes drew up in the main square of Haskovo, ignoring the customary battalion of high-rise apartment blocks menacing visitor and resident alike, like a besieging concrete army.

Founded by the Turks in the 14th century, Haskovo has a mosque (the Eski Jami'a, or Old Mosque) dating to 1395, within a couple of years of the Ottoman occupation, and it is greatly to the credit of the Bulgarian authorities that, though most of the mosques and other signs of Turkish occupation have disappeared, the Old Mosque is still preserved, and even active. I entered the courtyard at 11.30 that Friday morning, and found a dozen old men at their slow ablutions. Within, after removing my shoes, I sat cross-legged by a wall, facing the central mihrab. Thirty-five men, all of whom must have been over forty, sat fingering rosaries and reciting prayers to Allah. I received some suspicious stares, but an aged, stooped Muslim whispered in my ear, 'Where are you from?' and from my accent he could at once tell I was not a Bulgarian but a foreign visitor and relaxed. 'I have spent many years in North Africa and the Middle East,' I whispered. 'I come from England, and study Muslim societies'. The rough serge and corduroy clothes marked these Muslims as provincials, but distanced too by religion and by racial origin. 'You have mosques in England?' asked my interlocutor, wearing the distinctive dark blue beret of the Muslim, their only outward identification since the fez was barred by Kemal Atatürk. 'In the city of Birmingham alone,' I replied, 'we have sixty mosques, and as many as sixty thousand Muslims celebrate the end of Ramadan at London's Islamic Centre.' 'But you have Christians still?' 'Yes, we have Christians of many sects, but only 1.2 million regularly attend Church of England services, while 1.5 Muslims attend a mosque. At least 3,500 British people have converted to Islam.' 'But you have not yet?' 'No,' I replied, 'I have no religion, no politics, and indeed very few dogmas of any kind. When you travel around the world, sympathising with rich and poor, the clever and the stupid, it seems that every belief has as much chance of being wrong as right, and the more fervently you hold the belief, the more wrong you are likely to be. Not you,' I added hastily, 'it is I who am more likely to be wrong'. The dark blue of the gallery above mimicked sky; a minbar in the corner looked unobtrusive enough, and I felt that only the soaring minaret proclaimed the rigid aspirations of a faith locked by revelation into the seventh century of our era, the first of theirs. I left the mosque exhilarated by twenty minutes beyond time, as though I had stolen a flame from the gods. I found another minaret totally enclosed by later buildings, trapped and mute without a muaddin to witness that there is no god but God, and that Muhammad is His Prophet. Every district of Haskovo was occupied by Turks during the Ottoman period, except for one Bulgarian quarter situated around the churches of the Virgin Mary (1837) and the Archangels Michael and Gabriel (1861), the latter at 38 Ulitsa Tsar Osvoboditel, with an exceptionally fine carved altar. At 3 Ul. Petur Berkovski, the Church of SS. Cyril and Methodius displays church art of the National Revival. I always take the chance to glance round domestic interiors, and here in Haskovo you are invited to visit the Shishmanov House at 9 Ul. Bratya Minchev and the Paskalev House at 4 Ul. Yanko Sakuzov, both from National Revival times, showing respectively town handicrafts and town life. I was not impressed by the District Art Gallery at 1a Ul. Timok, but the fine new District History Museum on 9 September Square is essential for an understanding of Haskovo. As usual, it is closed on Mondays, but buzzes with excited schoolchildren on other days: it is a model museum, except for an understandable reluctance to present five Ottoman centuries in their relative chronological importance. The basement is devoted to prehistoric and protohistoric finds from both banks of the Maritsa, where 6th-5th millennia B.C. settlements have yielded domestic vessels and weapons of hunting and war. Bronze Age finds from Mihalich date from the 3rd millennium

B.C. (incidentally there is a rock church of the 10th century at Mihalich, and another at Matochina). Iron Age discoveries are connected with the life and wanderings of the Thracian tribes. During the Roman period, Thrace provided Rome with many of her sturdiest, fleetest horses for the cavalry, and it is no surprise to find the horseman-hunter-hero-god idolised in these Roman marches at a time when Philoppopolis has become a leading garrison-town. Haskovo was called 'Marsa' when the jewellery shown here was manufactured in the period of the first Bulgarian state. Note a hoard of silver coins from the Mezek tomb. The ground floor is devoted to ethnography, and local trades and industries: tobacco, cereals, cot-

Haskovo. Minaret surrounded by modern buildings

ton, and wine. In 1891 the tobacco production reached 200,000 kg in Haskovo district and over 150,000 in Harmanli. Women's buckles, glazed pottery, honey, hunting, fishing, and weaving all provided local employment and prosperity. An English traveller to Bulgaria (1665) is quoted as finding sesame and aniseed in the Haskovo district then: I asked a brisk gallery attendant if they are still grown. 'Yes, just the same,' he nodded. The first floor shows the National Revival period, which carries the same emotive pride as England's Victorian Age. Here are precious documents of Harmanli's past (the caravanserai in 1512), and Uzunjovo's: the fair in 1850, when merchants from Marseilles and Genoa, Moscow and Damascus, would trek to Uzunjovo to market their wares. In 1878 Haskovo was one of the last towns to be liberated, and the usual array of guns add that whiff of gunsmoke without which a Revival museum in Bulgaria seems incomplete. The museum, relaxed in a pedestrian precinct, faces the Oblast Building, with at the other two cardinal points the town theatre facing the Hotel Aida and a new clock tower.

Regretfully I left the atmospheric old town of Haskovo, bearing its latest stratum in the centre like a toupee on a bald head, and took the high road for Plovdiv, through Gorski Izvor, Filevo, Byala Reka, and flat, fertile fields towards Popovitsa, where peanuts were being laid out on the pavements by green-cardiganed grannies. Lettuces, spinach and spring onions were ripening in the Thracian plain, and in the greenhouses I saw cucumbers and tomatoes which would earn premium prices in city markets. In Plovdiv I was told that an enterprising family from the plain could earn an additional 10 to 20,000 leva a year from their vegetables. Sadovo, the next village, was given the first school of agriculture in 1892, 'sad' meaning an irrigated field. I could tell that nearly all the fields were irrigated by subterranean pipes, because of the poles every twenty metres, regular as rhythmic snoring. Apples were being picked by hand within full view of Plovdiv's dismaying high-rise apartments. A school had raised a slogan 'Glory to the Heroic Working Class' in the city named for King Philip of Macedon. This is Philippopolis.

Plovdiv
The National Archaeological Museum, on Ploshtad Suedinenie (Union Square), closed on Mondays, is the first port of call, for orientation to understand Bulgaria's second city. Its three halls deal

with prehistoric, Roman, and mediaeval times, beginning with a map of Thracian burial mounds, but in chronology the first evidence is of Old Stone Age settlements at Zlatovruh and Topchika cave in the Rhodopes, before 18,000 B.C. The local Mesolithic extended until 7,000, and the Neolithic until 5,000 B.C., when weaving, cereals, tools and female idols appear. I found, as usual in museums, not the sense of consecutive history sought by curators but a quirky, fabulous fragmentation at once banal and illuminating. Each step you take brings you to a spearhead of the Bronze Age (3rd-2nd millennia) or to clay utensils of the Iron Age (1200-481), when Homer and Herodotus begin to speak of the Thracians. I had turned away, bored by the platitudes of terra cotta, but then roused my spirits at the sight of red-figure and black-figure pottery imported from Greece. The Thracians believed like the Egyptians in an after-life, and like them buried women under mounds, with their mirrors and cosmetic jars. 'Pulpudeva' was the Thracian name (corrupted in Bulgarian to Puldin) until Philip conquered the town in 341 B.C. and named it Philippopolis. A copy of the Panagyurishte gold treasure discovered in 1949 can be seen here and in the place of discovery (roughly halfway between Sofia and Plovdiv), but the original is now in the National Museum in Sofia. Venedikov states that the nine vessels of the Panagyurishte drinking set were made at Lampsacus, on the Dardanelles, in Asia Minor and suggests a date around the beginning of the 3rd century B.C. The centre-piece is a phiale, ornamented curiously with concentric circles of acorns and heads of negroes, alternating with lotus blossoms and palmettes. The other vessels are all rhyta: three with an amazon's head in the body of the vessel, and four with animal heads finishing the base: a ram, two stags, and a goat, while the last is a fantastic amphora-rhyton more baroque in appearance than Hellenistic, its handles two centaurs, and its mouths in two negro heads. The vivid scene on the body of the vessel has been identified quite plausibly as the 'Seven Against Thebes', if one wanted to show by dreadful warning the perils of fratricide, for this vessel was intended to swear blood-brotherhood. We are at once in the barbaric Orient and in the sphere of Greek legend, as one enters the Mithraeum in Roman London: the wild cry of a savage beast pent up in laws it cannot comprehend.

Gems from the Roman period bring us down to the earth, but then we come across a chariot of the 2nd century sowing ideas of sudden death and destruction in your mind; and a bronze Latin plaque of 90 A.D. honouring the soldier Doles. In Gallery 4 we explore the destruction of Philippopolis by the Goths in 251 A.D., the new fortifications by Justinian, and the new Byzantine monastery church at Isperihovo (5th and 6th centuries) on the way to Peshtera. Slavs settle Thrace and Simeon undertakes the expansion of the Bulgarian empire to the Black Sea, the Adriatic and the Aegean, or 'White Sea'. We find the establishment of Bachkovo monastery, the fortress-church of Asenovgrad, coins of the 13th and 14th centuries, glazed pottery from Turnovo, and jewellery of the 1st and 2nd Bulgarian states.

Nearby stands the Imaret Mosque (1444-5), with a zig-zag design on its minaret. It is supposed to be dedicated to a new museum of sculpture, but the padlock on the gate looked as though it had not been touched for a long time, and as there was no sign of life I headed up the three hills which gave Plovdiv its Latin name of Trimontium, and is now a cherished architectural and historical reserve known as 'Old Plovdiv' where every street corner whispers in the wind and each houses rises on ancient bones: Thracians, Macedonians, Romans, Barbarians... to the modern Bulgarians. I suppose the major site of Old Plovdiv is the Roman Theatre, imaginatively if anachronistically used during my visit for *Carmina Burana*, Carl Orff's setting of mediaeval songs from Benediktbeuren. Classical plays are shown here during the summer and should not be missed, for the setting is much more intimate and acoustically effective than Verona's much-vaunted Arena. The theatre, constructed during the time of Marcus Aurelius in the second century, only reappeared to view in 1972 after a landslide, and now accommodates up to 3,500 spectators in a semi-circle of eleven tiers. The southern side of the theatre is closed off by Ionic columns of a façade decorated with statues in niches. Your view extends beyond Hotel Trimontium (of Stalinist grandiosity) to the foothills of the Rhodopes, and you can just make out the Church of Sveta Marina. Steps lead down to new Plovdiv from the Theatre, but you could spend several days in these winding, steep, astonishing streets with Byzantine fortress walls, extraordinary restaurants, and old houses restored for trades union use. I took lunch in the atmospheric Puldin Restaurant, each room designed in a different style, some incorporating ruins: it fits into the corner of Ul. Knyaz Tseretelev and Ul. Strumna and offers folk shows in the evening, as

Plovdiv. Roman Theatre in summer

do Trakiiski Stan (Ul. Puldin), Alafrangite (Ul. Nektariev), Kamenitsa (Ul. Vasil Kolarov) and Zlaten Elen (Ul. Patriarch Eftimi).

In the Mavridis House (1826) at 19 Ul. Knyaz Tseretelev Alphonse de Lamartine stayed as an invalid in 1933 while en route to the Orient. The house is more interesting for its interior than for the display. Facing 4 Ul. Knyaz Tseretelev is a terrace with a view over eastern Plovdiv and a cube-shaped prayer-hall for dervishes, and hence called Tekke Mevlevihane. Though not a museum, the 19th-century Tvorcheski Dom (Artists' Union Home) may be discreetly visited if the door stands open. Enchanting little tortoises push themselves around the garden like determined boulders, and a summer kiosk overlooks the street. Painted columns on two courtyard walls enchant the eye, and I found four cedar columns nostalgically reminiscent of the Lebanon of my youth. From Ul. Nektariev I wandered to the Hisar Gate and the Church of SS. Constantine and Helena, built on the site of a smaller church in 1832 and decorated in 1836 by Zahari Zograf. It was closed for restoration for a good ten years, but reopened in 1986. Close by on Ul. Gorki is the new Icon Gallery, dominated by a 16th-century Christ Pantocrator of the Plovdiv School, and contemporary paintings of the Virgin and Child and S. John the Baptist. I preferred the invigorating imagination of Veselin Todorov, who was showing recent paintings at 2 Ul. 4 January. Expressive abstraction provides his motive force, releasing the imagination and helping to shove Bulgarian art, however reluctantly, into the 20th century with 'Music on the Easel', 'Aggression of the Virus', 'The Empire of the Subconscious', 'Icarus 9121948' and 'The Child's Dream'. Outside, an organ-grinder cranked away monotonously to Todorov's 'Dance of the Microchip'. Opposite, I touched the 6th-century stone fortifications on which a new kindergarten was being built.

The Balabanov House at 57 Ul. Matanov displays paintings by modern artists and furniture from bourgeois Plovdiv homes; it was being used as a party venue for a prizegiving; homely bustle and a birthday cake added zest to the visit. Next door I explored the former home of the Armenian merchant Hindlian, built in 1820-6 for the trader with India whose first wife was Bulgarian: she was killed by a falling chandelier on her wedding day, and Hindlian's second wife, an Armenian, died of the plague. The furniture is authentically Plovdivian, but has come from many parts of the city. The Tryavna woodcarving is original, though the decoration is recent. Near the house itself is a storehouse with a painting of the wooden house over the doorway so that if the main home burns down it can be rebuilt from the design. Surrealistically, a car was learning how to walk on stilts outside the gate, but nobody

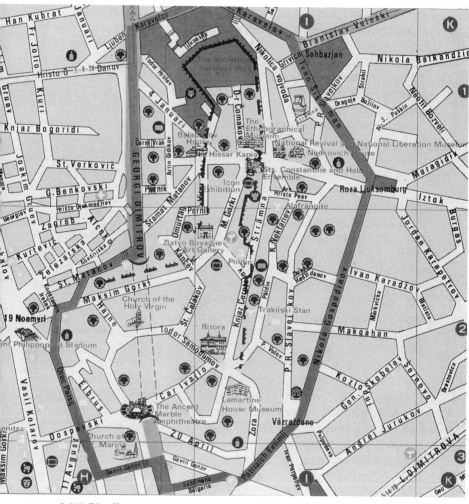

Map of Old Plovdiv

appeared to notice, so I politely looked the other way.

Back in the Balabanov House, I was struck by the great reception hall, in which the Mayor of Plovdiv receives guests; and on the upper floor by a Turkish-style kiosk raised above floor level in one corner.

The Ethnographical Museum at 2 Ul. Chomakov is arranged in

the Kuyumjioghlu House, built in 1847 for a Turkish merchant by a master-builder from the Rhodope mountains: one Haji Georgi. Chamber music is performed in the courtyard on summer evenings. At various times a home, a storehouse for local tobacco, and a girls' school, it opened as a major folk museum in 1962, to specialise in farming, crafts, textiles, music and folklore. The most striking painting is 'Bazaar in Plovdiv', by the Czech Jan Mrkvička (1856-1938), a genre scene in the style made popular also by the Bulgarians Anton Mitov (1862-1930) and Ivan Angelov (1864-1924), and another Czech called Jaroslav Vesin (1860-1915), all of whom worked and lived in Bulgaria. Mitov had studied in Florence and Angelov in Munich, so Bulgarian art was broadened in style and technique, aesthetics and subject-matter, from European trends. Mrkvička's scene shows a corner of the Friday Mosque and the twin minarets of the Imaret Mosque in the distance (right), the artist appearing in a rakish straw hat between the first two columns on the left. We see the evolution of hemp cultivation, honey, roses, rice, grapes, tobacco, and market-gardening. Here is a copper-boiler or *kazan* of the type which gave Kazanluk its name. In it distillers mixed three parts of roses to one of water for that precious attar which costs its weight in gold for the rose-petals alone.

Upstairs a wonderful carved ceiling in Tryavna style spreads above a delightful ballroom, with a bay window like a kiosk. I caught a whiff of glittering, perfumed, perfectly made-up ladies in the gowns brought from Vienna or Paris now shown in the central hall, before reverting to the ordinary but no less colourful tufted blankets of Rhodope mountain-dwellers in a family interior scattered with goathair rugs. In a bourgeois city interior everything had been imported but the carpet. A room has been reconstructed from Koprivshtitsa, with wooden benches on the walls. Costumes represent Pazarjik, Smolyan, and other towns in the Plovdiv region. A tambourine and other folk instruments, such as *gadulka* and the *kaval* can be found, not to mention the hurdy-gurdy, still being played nearby.

On the way to the Church of Sveta Nedelya you can explore two other magnificent houses of the National Revival: the Georgiadis House (1846-8) at 1 Ul. Tsanko Lavrenov and the Nedkovich House at number 3. In the former, again owing to Haji Georgi the self-taught master-builder, you can see a Museum of the National

Revival and the National Liberation Struggle. If you can tear your attention away from photographs and archives documenting the Ottoman yoke, and Bulgarian struggles to develop education, political freedom, and church autonomy, everything that characterises the best of National Revival domestic architecture can be enjoyed, from the symmetrical, elegant façade and the harmony of the ensemble to details of painting, carving and furniture. The Georgiadis House is closed on Tuesdays, the Kuyumjioghlu on Mondays, and the Nedkovich House on Saturdays and Sundays, so two are always open. The Nedkovich House dates from 1855-63, and enchants the passer-by with three elegant stone columns supporting arches within a strikingly harmonious façade; a riot of wondrous woodcarving in the ground-floor *hayet* or drawing-room has to be seen to be believed. Then you compare this with the elaborately-carved iconostasis in the Church of Sveta Nedelya hung with inferior icons, and you realise that wood must have been the natural medium for the Bulgarian craftsman since time immemorial.

On your way down Ulitsa Slaveikov, a turning to Ulitsa Peev brings you to Georgi Danchov's House (no. 4), an early 19th century home which had not yet been given the symmetrical plan later customary in Plovdiv.

Excavations can sometimes be seen in progress here on Nebet Tepe, occupied and fortified in the 5th century B.C. by the Odrysae, a Thracian tribe first mentioned by Herodotus. A secret tunnel led from this site to the river Maritsa.

One day I tried to find the Museum of the Revolutionary Movement, and climbed the quiet Ulitsa Angel Bukureshtliev to padlocked doors. Was it closed for good? A bearded face appeared at a window, gesticulating with open palms crossing each other, once forward, once backward. What could it mean? Was Lenin's seclusion being re-enacted? Eventually, the doors were opened to me. I was the only visitor, and an object of polite curiosity. From which country had I come? I nearly came clean and admitted to being trilingual: KGB, CIA, IRA: anything seems possible to a passionate reader of John Le Carré. Moustache-twirling revolutionaries frequented the Party Club, also known as the People's Home, here on Vasil Kolarov Hill, from 1905 to 1923. There is very little, however, of the first museum, founded in 1948, for in 1962 the exhibits were completely refurbished in reconstructed premises. The museum helps one (and in my case one was the operative word, for

Map of Plovdiv

there were no other visitors at the time) to examine the methods and history of the workers' revolutionary movement and the creation of the Commune of 1919 in Plovdiv district, Plovdiv being twinned with Leningrad, Kishinev, Poznań, Brno and Leipzig. Here are the familiar names and faces: Dimitur Blagoev, Vasil Kolarov, and others involved from Liberation up to the Armed National Anti-Fascist Uprising of 9 September 1944. To pursue these developments beyond 1944, you have to find 31 Ulitsa Ivan Vazov (also closed every Friday morning), which runs behind Hotel Trimontium: the museum stands on the left just before the junction with Ulitsa Vaptsarov. Here are the achievements of the State and Party, seen as indivisible, but nothing about the problems which Todor Zhivkov listed as endemic at the 1987 plenary session of the Bulgarian Communist Party's Central Committee.

I found spiritual solace in the State Art Gallery and such noble portraits as the unattributed 'Sophronius, Bishop of Vratsa' (1812) and Georgi Danchov's 'Haji Gyoka Pavlov', by the painter whose home we have seen at 4 Ulitsa Peev. Ivan Angelov's 'Woman in a Hayfield' exemplifies the rural realism tendency brought up to date by the 'Portrait of a Gipsy Girl' of Ts. Todorov (1877-1953). Nikola Tanev (1890-1962) has a portrait of the Patriarch Euthymius (Eftimi in Bulgarian) and Iliya Petrov (1903-75) one of Stoyan Ts. Daskalov. A portrait of a woman in red by Slavka Deneva bore recollections within it of a woman in red by another painter of shabby urban life: the Lancastrian L.S. Lowry.

In an antiquarian bookshop, one of very few I found in Bulgaria, I came across a Henry James paperback, *Come, All Ye Bold Miners* by A.L. Lloyd, and Shakespeare's Histories in Bulgarian.

Plovdiv Opera House (on Ul. Dimitrov) and Plovdiv Philharmònic (Central Square) were closed that evening, but three cinemas on Ulitsa Kolarov were open, showing Eastern European and American movies. At the N.O. Masalitinov Drama Theatre on Ulitsa Kolarov the month included plays by the South African Athol Fugard, the Italian Dario Fo, two plays by Stefan Tsanev, premières of plays by Konstantin Iliev and Ivan Radoev, and Stanislav Stratiev's *Sako ot velur*. The opera season, as well as guest performances by Sofia's National Opera, included Humperdinck's *Hänsel und Gretel*, the Cav and Pag double bill, Rossini's *L'Italiana in Algeri* which pokes fun at Muslims and Giordano's French revolutionary opera *Andrea Chenier* which denounces the French aristocracy. Another evening at the Republika cinema on Ulitsa Kolarov I saw a Czech documentary film on Sikkim (1984) preceding the Bulgarian film *Izlozhenie* (*Exposé*, 1988), which made up in correctness and dignity what it lacked in imagination.

Wandering around in front of Hotel Trimontium you can find marble paving-stones and colonnades from the Roman forum of the 3rd century, leading past the General Post Office along Kolarov (beyond Balkan Air and the House of Soviet Books) to an excavated sector of the Roman amphitheatre used once for chariot-racing and gladiatorial contest, but now a peaceful meeting-place for young people in the shadow of the illustrious Friday Mosque first established by order of Sultan Murad II (1359-85), and subsequently reconstructed in some parts. The proud, empty prayer hall with four columns reminded me of the smaller mosque in Samokov, but the domes covered in lead and slim minaret reminded me of my many years in Libya when the muaddin would call the faithful to prayer from the mosque in Tripoli's Shar'a Saidi and I would pad about the sandy roads behind the Saudi Arabian Embassy pursued like the Pied Piper but with a procession of cats, amusing local residents, rather than rats or brats. You might well find the Friday Mosque closed, for memories of the five Ottoman centuries remain distasteful to Bulgarians so relatively recently an independent nation. It would be a generous gesture to allow Muslim visitors (and Turks outnumber all other foreigners travelling in Bulgaria) the opportunity to visit mosques, and worship there. Instead, you might find yourself wistfully rereading the plaque on the west wall honouring five Communists executed here in 1919. I sat at an open-air café, remembering the poet Lucian's description of Trimontium as 'the most splendid, the largest and fairest town, whose beauty shines from afar'. The syenite hills have remained while civilizations have vanished leaving only wisps of tradition, altered by the next invaders to suit their own concepts. At no. 1 Ulitsa Karavelov the Turks had built public baths in the 16th century, and beyond the Maritsa are Park Hotel Leningrad and Novotel Plovdiv, accommodation for businessmen and industrialists visiting Plovdiv for spring and autumn trade fairs. You can see football matches at the Spartak or Lokomotiv stadia, straddling one each side of the railway line.

I visited the Common Grave Memorial Centre (1974), most familiarly known as the Pantheon, on Bulevard Malchika, a turning off

Plovdiv. Common Grave Memorial Centre, with a bride placing a bouquet on the grave

Ul. Yako Dorosiev. From the outside, the Common Grave seems to represent a collapsing bunker, light falling on great concrete slabs to make the interior alternately bright and dark. The grave is guarded by uniformed members of the League of Young Communists, and the custom is for a young bride to lay a bouquet on the grave as her first action after the wedding, accompanied by her groom. Above the entrance bold letters proclaim lines from Hristo Botev which I have translated, I hope correctly, as 'Whoever falls in the struggle for freedom will never die'. Lyubomir Dalchev's symbolic and naturalistic sculptures of debatable artistic merit stand round the walls in an endless circle, depicting a mother weeping on a child's grave ('The Ottoman Yoke'), Levski's conspiracy, the April Rising of 1873, 20 days of rebellion and the Turkish massacre after its failure, Shipka Pass and the Russo-Turkish War, Liberation from the Turks, Unification in 1885, struggles of the proletariat, the crushing of the Anti-Fascist Rebellion of 1923, cruelties of the fascists, helpers of the partisans, September 1944 with the slogan 'Freedom for the People and Death to the Fascists and

Monarchists', Meeting the Russians, Bulgarians help the Russians to liberate Hungry and Yugoslavia, Bulgaria on its way to socialist construction.

I drove from the Common Grave along Dorosiev and Friedrich Engels to the railway station, hoping to see the kind of erratic, endearingly eccentric or plain silly behaviour that one might see in Paris or Frankfurt. But nothing strange happened in this 1920s station, contemporary with those in Varna and Burgas, but charmingly old-world in comparison with the new Sofia station of 1972. A magazine stall on the platform was being surrounded, in a polite fashion, but there was no bookstall. Thirteen express trains a day leave for Sofia, and ten slow trains, the latter recommendable only if you *have* to stop en route. The best train is non-stop and takes only 1½ hours, but generally expresses take 2½ hours. Fares are extraordinarily low by Western standards, and the official *Sofia News* of 2 November 1988 reported poor safety standards, antiquated equipment, poor training, lax discipline, and low pay as factors responsible for problems on the rail network. A reservation costs only 20 stotinki at present, and the single fare (you cannot buy a return ticket) costs 4 leva to Sofia. First-class carriages take six people and second-class eight. A restaurant is available both on the station and on the train, and waiters sell food and drinks from trolleys passing through the train. Stalls on the platform sell rolls and cheese. Passengers seem generally unsmiling, withdrawn, private, disinclined to chat, much as on British Rail or on Finnish trains.

I felt lonely, isolated, and back at the Trimontium I lashed out into conversation with a friendly, fat, almost bald Bulgarian with odd tufts of hair in unexpected places such as the top of his head and both nostrils. We started to swap proverbs: 'Don't put off till tomorrow what you can do today', I ventured. He nodded: 'Good Bulgarian saying. Also, we have "a wolf may change his coat, but never his character"'. 'Right', I confirmed, 'a leopard doesn't change his spots.' 'We have wolfs, you have leopards', he nodded, 'now *kapka po kapka vir, vir po vir yazovir*'. 'I think I can manage that', I answered: 'drop by drop a puddle forms; puddle by puddle, a dam.' A waiter removed the empty bowls of chicken soup and brought us veal ragout. '*Ne pitui starilo a batilo*': 'don't ask somebody old, but somebody who has suffered'. And a warning: '*s tvoite kamuni po tvoita glava*': 'don't throw stones at your own head'.

Next morning, Sunday, I wanted to experience a Bulgarian Orthodox church service, and at 8 a.m. joined the congregation at Sveta Marina (1852-3), situated off Bulevard Dimitrov between Ulitsa Genov and Ulitsa Dospevski. The church has a magnificent carved iconostasis, pulpit and bishops' throne (both with animal heads at their feet) by craftsmen of the Debur school, and icons by Dospevski, including a memorable 'Nativity'. The basilica has three aisles divided by fourteen columns; its 19th-century belfry, much later than the church, was restored in 1953.

I stood, eyes closed to absorb mesmeric chanting, while a priest intoned the liturgy and the choir responded. Some of the church choir are members of the Plovdiv Opera. I had followed the ritual of buying candles, and placing them in metal crowns above a sand-bowl so that no flames could fall on the wooden floor. A high candelabrum is set to accept candles intended for prayers for the living, and a low candelabrum for the dead. Most of the worshippers stood alone, apart, old, in serviceable clothing; many came and went during the long celebration, favourite spots being near the heated stoves at left and right. Some chose to sit on the few chairs. Incense would swing in all directions. As the priest passed the bishop's throne I heard him praise the name of Tsar Alexander II, according to the Orthodox Church a saviour of the Bulgarian people. The choir would soar over the recitative, and a feeling of spontaneity would have to be rejected: though the texts bore no musical notation, every note must have been carefully memorised, as in opera, for the unison to rise like a solo. The priest sang in front of the door, a cross before him, as his black sleeves fell below his waist. What did Eliot say? 'Humankind cannot bear very much reality'? From time to time the woman selling candles in the narthex would emerge into the church to extinguish the dying candles. Faintly lit by four chandeliers, Sveta Marina nevertheless felt irrepressibly tenebrous: the antithesis of the great Cistercian churches as brilliantly illuminated as their manuscripts at Laon, Pontigny, Soissons, Alcobaça and Fountains. No, I still cannot answer Bergson's challenge to us materialists – what is it that separates or links nothing to something, inert matter to life, life to mind.

I followed one of the women out of Sveta Marina, a Philip Marlowe in unobtrusive pursuit of a dame, but she lured me no farther than an open-air Sunday market for fruit and vegetables on Pat-

Plovdiv. Open-air market

riarch Euthymius Street near the new museum. I splashed out on speckled apples as a white-jacketed housewife with a blue plastic bag negotiated for a jar of honey with a grey-haired woman wearing a dark brown overcoat.

During the week I had explored the so-called 'Artisans' Alley' at 1-5 Ulitsa Strumna, showing copper, embroidery, shoes and pokerwork in afternoons and evenings, but the Alley is closed at weekends so I strolled up Liberation Hill to the granite statue of a Soviet soldier locally known as 'Alyosha'. The Corecom hard currency shop in the Novotel was offering plimsolls for $34, a bra for $10 and a pullover for $22. The centenary Monument to Unification (Edinstvo) rises in rhetorical self-importance outside the new Museum of Unification, which opened in 1985, the centenary year. On a photograph of Plovdiv in 1885 I started counting the minarets but gave up at thirteen. A flag of the Cheta, or rebels, was draped in the hall, which – with high skylights and a grand piano – doubles as a concert hall. The building served as a library but was intended as the National Assembly of Eastern Rumelia, centred on Plovdiv, an assembly which never met as it was supposed to have done by the Treaty of Berlin (1878). The inhabitants of Plovdiv and King Alexander of Battenberg both favoured unification with the rest of Bulgaria, rather than remaining an Ottoman territory ruled by a Christian Governor-General. The Russians attempted to create a great Bulgaria by the Treaty of San Stefano, but by the Treaty of Berlin the great powers created a principality of Bulgaria under the suzerainty of the Sultan and an autonomous province in Plovdiv on 18 September 1885. Alexander of Battenberg, the German prince appointed by the Russian-inspired government organization, was the favourite nephew of the Tsar and always liable to suggestion and pressure. The Russians expressed themselves displeased with the union and Alexander felt he had to abdicate in deference to his uncle's disapproval, and was succeeded by Prince Ferdinand of Coburg, whose Prime Minister was Stambolov. At the time of the Istanbul Revolution of 1908, Prince Ferdinand declared independence for Bulgaria and on 3 October assumed the title of Tsar.

Asenovgrad
Driving to the Rhodope mountains from Plovdiv, it is a good idea to stop for a snack or lunch at the two-star Hotel Asenovets, unless a wedding is in full flow and all the waiters are run off their feet. The District History Museum at 25 Ulitsa Dimitrov has departments devoted to archaeology, the National Revival, and the history of capitalism and the workers' revolutionary movement. I personally didn't mind the long wait between courses, because it gave me a chance to watch the bride and groom formally greeting each guest and fixing a napkin to each one, receiving in return a gift of wrapped money. The band was so noisy that I found it difficult to concentrate on the tales of a hunter who assured me that his Rhodopes provided the best game in Bulgaria. I remembered lines from Ivailo Petrov's story 'The Stag' in his collection translated as *Before I Was Born* (Sofia, 1975): 'I had filled a few pages in my notebook, forming the habit of observing and guessing at people's lives. I've noticed that people are really frank in war, on a shoot, on the train, and in a hotel.'

A tomato and cucumber salad was followed by minestrone with white bread, pork and chips with a yellow pepper, and Turkish coffee. My new friend Doko clarified the term 'chorbaji', used to describe a rich man in old Bulgaria, a word used widely by Ivan

Vazov. Etymologically it means someone who gives soup, explained Doko: via the Turkish word *shorba*, from the Arabic root *sharaba*, to drink, which gives the English word 'sherbet'.

Asenovgrad, nowadays famous for a full-bodied wine, was known in the Middle Ages as Stanimaka, 'defence of the pass'. It was renamed to record Asen II's triumph against Byzantine hordes at Klokotnitsa in 1230, following which the Tsar rebuilt the fortress. A road leads up to it and the view would have appealed to Victorian painters of the beautiful and sublime, such as Loutherbourg or John Martin. The fortress itself is virtually gone: only one or two towers and shambles of walls remain, but the 13th-century Church of the Virgin of Petrich has been beautifully restored, crowing like the proudest cockerel from its perch above the Chepelarska Gorge. The lower storey was a crypt, and the upper storey the main church, with fine murals, a nearby reservoir to rely on in case of siege, and attached farm buildings. I could have stood aloft here all day, in the streaming sunlight, one foot on a jutting rock, remembering Byron in northern Greece and that other astonishing Englishman who passed through the Balkans: the gifted

Asenovgrad. Church near the fortress

landscape-painter Edward Lear. Romance can be found in the sight of a few mules once in a while, but the practical demands of hydro-electricity for Asenovgrad have dictated that the Asenovitsa or Chepelarska be tamed for human use. So too were the hills and woods at the foot of the mountains called Chervenata Stena and Momina Skala, where villagers sought spiritual protection from roving bandits by living close to Bachkovo monastery and physical protection by building their own stone houses like castles.

Bachkovo Monastery
Petrich Monastery, the Bulgarian form of Petritsoni as Bachkovo was originally known, was founded in 1083 by the Grand-Domestic of the West, that is the general of the Byzantine army in Europe, one Grigol Bakurianisdze from Georgia. From that period all we have is a cemetery-church with interior murals, one being that of Grigol himself. The general in the army of Alexis Comnenus (1081-1118) left with a monastery a typikon, or house rules, which governed daily routines and disciple. Like Troyan, Bachkovo's Monastery of the Assumption of the Virgin Mary is a stauropegial community, deriving its authority direct from the Patriarch in Jerusalem, and its revenue from lands, forests and farms bequeathed to it by Grigol, who died barely three years later in battle, and decreed a succession of Georgian abbots, a series which ended more than two centuries later. A second golden age of Bachkovo occurred during the reign of Asen II (1218-41), and the time of Euthymius here (probably 1394-1406) must have proved uplifting. Even during the Ottoman period, when the monastery suffered burning, looting and repeated damage and desecration, the determination of the people to restore its ancient grandeur in whatever manner possible ensured the rapid revival of its fortunes time and again. For instance, the refectory of 1601 is decorated not only with saints and martyrs but with philosophers, among them Aristotle and Socrates as a king in a red-robe, whose quest for truth despite all odds must have sparked a light of determination in the eyes of those prepared to look. Rather more peculiar, however, is the presence of Pericles, the comedian Aristophanes, Diogenes crowned, and the physician Galen.

Greek monks were not allowed at Bachkovo until the 17th century, because of the rivalry between Georgians and Greeks on Mount Athos.

Bachkovo Monastery

The kitchen has become a museum, with photos of the restoration and portraits of the Greek philosophers at Arbanasi recalled by Plato and Aristotle here. The murals of 1643 are by artists from Thessaloniki. The refectory, with its long marble table, was closed for ten years in the 1970s while overlying plaster was removed from the murals and the earlier paintings conserved. After the new refectory was erected, the authorities built the Church of the Assumption and All Saints chapel in the southwestern part of the grounds. Sv. Nikolai Church rose in 1834-40, since which time scarcely a decade has passed by without the creation of new buildings and the maintenance of the old. These days Sv. Nikolai is used for baptisms, remaining closed at other times: families come from afar to baptise their infants here, such is the reverence accorded to saint and milieu. 'The Last Judgment' by Zahari Zograf in the porch entrance of the church is only one of his many contributions to the decorations at Bachkovo: such as the panorama of Bachkovo on the refectory's northern wall, and the entrance of the Chapel of the Archangels which acts as the main church's narthex. In 'The Last Judgment', recognisable portraits of eminent contemporaries in Plovdiv appear in Hell, and a striking divergence from the Orthodox canon is the portrayal of sinners in the nude. Zahari from Samokov concluded Sv. Nikolai in 1840, but his pupils' hands are discernible in the weaker 'Procession of the Miraculous Icon' in the refectory.

Zograf's paintings at the entrance to the Archangels' Chapel include the 'Torture of the Rich Man' and 'Lazarus and Dives', in which citizens of Plovdiv are immortalised in contemporary clothes of around 1840. Just to the right, inside the main door, worshippers crowd round an icon of the Virgin and Child with a silver cover of 1311, though the painting is considerably earlier, and pious legend attributes to it miraculous properties. Nearby is the grave of Kiril (1901-71), the Patriarch before the present incumbent Maxim. On the dramatic National Revival iconostasis the most valuable icon is of SS. Peter and Paul, the third left from the centre. I spoke to one of the fifteen monks: yes, many surrounding orchards and fields belong to the monks, and enjoy mild winters even here in the mountains because the high surrounding rocks shelter them from bitter winds. He took me to the Church of the Holy Trinity (Sveta Troitsa), with mediaeval frescoes and portraits of the family of Tsar Ivan Alexander (1331-71). In the museum I recall with particular affection two gilt collection plates (one by the goldsmith Master Petur dated 1647) and a majestic 15th-century icon of three standing saints, each with a distinctive beard.

The drive up into the Rhodope mountains, into clear air and breathtaking vistas, brought me to the straggling village of Narechen, now called Narechenski Bani after the baths recommended for psychiatric disorders, diabetes and obesity. I filled with petrol and stopped for the view at the village called Hvoina, 'Juniper', a farming community. In a mountain like this, Ovid knw, Orpheus pursued Eurydice: each cavern looked likely to bring me to the Underworld, and only with great difficulty did I resist the temptation to leave the car at the resort of Chepelare with its Caving Museum and hike into mountain mists of primaeval myth. But I had a date at Pamporovo, a skiing resort beloved by thousands of British skiers, and wanted to see Smolyan before nightfall.

Smolyan

Modern Smolyan has all the amenities you expect in a town of forty thousand: the three-star Hotel Smolyan, the two-star Hotel Sokolitsa, a pedestrial shopping precinct, a planetarium, and a two-seat chair lift to Pamporovo. Mining and industry, tourism and stock-rearing are all important to Smolyan, the main administrative centre of the Rhodopes. But Smolyan is also the 'town of lakes', Ezerovo, as it was known to Slavs before the Turkish occupation, when its name was changed to Pashmakli. In modern times it was rechristened after the Slav tribe Smoleni or Smoli who once took command of these heights near the modern Greek border. It is to Bulgaria what Zakopane is to Poland, a thriving winter resort and population hub just north of a frontier. In 1960 the old villages of Raikovo (pop. 3,000) and Ustovo (pop. 2,000) were merged with neighbouring Smolyan village to form a new urban agglomeration which winds for several kilometres through attractive yet unexpected valleys and gorges, spreading out in new Smolyan to a wide plaza almost within howling distance of Rhodope wolves and jackals. Brown bears are sometimes found in these forests, and I glimpsed deer through slender pinewoods just inside the town border. Old houses in the Rhodopes are mainly of stone: new homes of brick. A meadow near Rozhen Pass hosts regular folk festivals, and a festival of Open-Air Painting is held in Ustovo and Raikovo in the first three weeks in October (and in Plovdiv in August).

Smolyan has its own Rhodope Folk Ensemble, Drama Theatre and Art Gallery, but it is in the older districts sensitively preserved at great expense that you will feel the authentic atmosphere of National Revival architecture in the Rhodopes, and a charming old stone bridge leads you from the highway to the Pangalov House (1860), with its National Museum of the Rhodopes, devoted to history, ethnography, and domestic interiors, recreated with typical rugs of goat-hair and simple yet tasteful furnishings. I found a church built in 1924 closed, and the old konak converted into a hotel, deserted in the middle of the afternoon for the employees' siesta.

The pedestrian precinct of Smolyan is enlivened by Dalchev's sculpture of Orpheus and Eurydice, lithe, looking upward, the lyre of Orpheus regrettably like a large, angular boomerang. Such mythical creatures are too beautiful to be tied down in physical terms, as if they were steers to be roped at a rodeo. In a bookshop I

Smolyan. Bridge leading to Raikovo quarter

found shelves of Marxist-Leninist orthodoxy, some language dictionaries, and some recent novels, stories and essays which explored the ideal Bulgaria, lacking in controversy, too timid to explore the possibilities inherent in *glasnost* (pendula also swing back), and providing not a great deal of intellectual stimulus in comparison with recent Hungarian or Yugoslav writing. Children's books are generally very well produced, and literacy is almost a national vanity: Bulgaria must have one of the highest true literacy rates in the world. I didn't find an edition of the poetess Elisaveta Bagriana (born Belcheva in 1893) and have only three of her poems, in *Poets of Bulgaria* (Forest Books of London, 1988), but these are enough to unveil her passionate nature (she is said to have made 'a passionate liaison' while in Britain) and her desire for total liberty:

> *Tell me, who can stop me, free thinker and free wanderer.*
> *blood sister to the north wind, to water, and to wine,*
> *lured beyond all frontiers, beckoned by steppe-lands,*
> *I who dream of open roads unseen yet, unmapped still, untrodden;*
> *tell me, who can stop me?*

Smolyan. Modern town centre

In a Smolyan café I sought out lovers, *fidanzati*, wives and still in love, to persist in a continuity of Bagriana's emotion. A young woman drinking a tiny cup of Turkish coffee raised dark, troubled eyes to a man much older, who could not take his gaze from her distinctive cheekbones, thick black hair, and full, sensuous mouth. 'Strange military review by the harbour', she said, looking up from her crossword, 'one word, eight letters'. He relaxed: 'paradoks', and flicked cigarette ash on the floor. The woman with smouldering eyes reminded me suddenly of Vera, John Updike's protagonist in his story 'The Bulgarian Poetess' who, asked whether her poems were difficult, smiled and, unaccustomed to speaking English, answered carefully, 'drawing a line in the air with two delicately pinched fingers holding an imaginary pen, "they are difficult to write". His American hero 'laughed, startled and charmed. "But not to read?" She seemed puzzled by his laugh, but did not withdraw her smile, though its corners deepened in a defensive, feminine way. "I think", she said, "not so very".'

She turned her head towards me quizzically, and allowed a single vague narrowing of her eyes to mark the encounter, before turning back to the man she faced, his shoulders relaxed in recognition of his triumph, his possession, her subjection. I left the café abruptly, like a cuckoo leaving its nest.

Pamporovo

Pamporovo, a few miles away, cradled in silent snows among age-old spruce forests, has already achieved an enviable reputation among British skiers for its amiability, from the rawest beginner to the most sophisticated racer. Safety is placed first, slopes are close to the hotels, prices are unconscionably low compared with Switzerland, and facilities are first-rate. But package-tourists, it must be remembered, make up such a vast proportion of Pamporovo's clientele that you should not reckon to stay there in private lodgings, far less a hotel, between December and April, without booking far in advance. Packaging reduces prices for everything, from rental of equipment, to room-rates and lift-rides, tuition in one of five classes (for four hours a day over six days), and bus transport to the slopes. Outside the skiing season, marvellous hikes take place in the morning, lasting anywhere from four to six hours, to Murgavets, Gela, Slunchev Bair, or Momchil Yunak. Youngsters will enjoy the video disco at Hotel Rozhen, or other discos at the Snezhanka, Prespa and Perelik. For those preferring to mix with Bulgarians, an evening can be arranged to present a timeless traditional picture, the woman of the house singing, the man playing the flute (*kaval*) or bagpipes (*gaida*). The bagpipe tradition is as strong in Bulgaria's highlands as in Scotland's. The two types of bagpipe (*jura* and *kaba*) may be made by the pipers themselves or by specialists. In the village of Gela a man who has made more than two hundred *kaba-gaidas* explained, 'One never says "Play, gaida!" but "Speak, gaida!",' because it is as though the very voice of Bulgaria is communicating.

In a Rhodope home you will be shown every room and those interested may help the hostess with the preparation of dinner, which may include *kurban* (lamb soup), *katmi* (pancakes) and *sarmi* (cabbage-leaves packed with meat). Local restaurants include the Malina, specialising in hominy, sheep's yoghourt, *banitsa* (cheese pastry) and *kawarma*. At Stoikite, 7 km away, you can eat *marudnitsi* (pancakes) and *kawarma* or fresh fish beside a mountain stream in the Vodenitsa, or Watermill Restaurant, again accompanied by *gaida, kaval* and mountain songs.

It may be boisterous, and certainly I could not indulge my favourite pastime of overhearing other people's conversation, but there is no denying the joviality of efficient bustle at Chevermeto. *Shawarma* is an Oriental dish consisting of spit-roasted lamb and the suffix 'to' is the masculine definite article. You can drink heated brandy if someone else is driving you back to your hotel, and eat crusty warm white bread in a summer sheepfold, listening to bagpipes amid a hubbub of Bulgarian voices. I drank apple juice and could just perceive my neighbours at the table through the pall of cigarette smoke. Yet even in this relaxed atmosphere, the body language of the Bulgarians remained quiet, restrained, modest, good-humoured, considerate of others, keeping like the English abroad to separate family groups. Six whole lambs were being turned on spits in the centre of the great hall when a woman of about 25 introduced the Pamporovo Folk Ensemble in both Bulgarian and English. Instrumentalists in folk costume, mainly red

Pamporovo. View from Hotel Perelik

and black, played the accordion, flute, bagpipes and drum, but were the cymbals authentic too? Dances came from all over Bulgaria, the first from the Danube Valley, in which a woman in a flat white bonnet offered bread and salt to exemplify hospitality. A soprano with a red scarf tied at the back, a red dress, gold-embroidered red tunic and red and yellow squared apron, was followed by a flautist, a trio dance for girls, two men and a girl performing a dance from Pirin, another soprano solo, another boisterous instrumental ensemble, and a humorous dance for three girls and 3 men, the latter dressed as old codgers with false noses, challenged to play blind man's buff while the girls' tinkling bells announce where they have just been. The final dance came from the Sofia district, and was received with rapturous applause, sharpened by our appetite. The first carcase was slashed off the spit and in the centre of the hall the chef's axe began to cleave the meat into portions. Everyone looked on with hungry eyes: I at least felt like a Neolithic elder waiting for the youths to serve up the day's hunting trophies. The waiters made sure that the foreign visitors, myself among them, and a handful at other tables, were courteously served first, then dealt out plates to everyone else with exemplary sleight-of-hand born of long practice.

Of course I could have dined at my own hotel, the three-star Perelik, the Orpheus, or the Panorama; and lunch half-way up the Snezhanka Tower offers unparalleled views. The natural 'Wonderful Bridges' make a fine excursion out of Pamporovo, like the Yagodina and Trigrad gorges, with caves worth exploring. Neolithic men lived on the uppermost level of Yagodina cave, but you can visit lower levels too.

Shiroka Luka

I wanted to see the ethnographic reserve of Shiroka Luka, another of those museum towns vibrant with life yet rigorously preserved against vulgar commercialisation. Many groups enjoy a special concert arranged by the School of Folk Instruments and Singing founded there in 1971; the school was one of the many cultural initiatives of Lyudmila Zhivkova's all too short career, another being the parallel school in Kotel. The five-year course (eighth grade to twelfth) includes all tuition and accommodation in boarding-houses. Competition for places is keen, as the school limits entrants to 25 a year; after graduating, most join one of the six state and amateur ensembles, and some progress to the High College of Music in Plovdiv, which specialises in training conductors and music teachers. Every student must study the piano, but other instruments are optional: the rebec or *gadulka*, the *gaida*, *kaval* and *tambura*. The Principal, Mrs. Kushleva, is one of three famous singing sisters, and she invited me to attend a *kaval* lesson on the third floor; a young undergraduate happened to be practising a Thracian tune from Plovdiv but their repertory includes folk music from all over Bulgaria. Elsewhere, tunings are different. The *kaval* tutor explained that only one kind of flute is made, but that the best examples come from masters in Kamenovo, near Burgas.

The young man, with the desires of Orpheus deep inside him, gazed through the window at ranks of pines rising like football spectators on terracing.

Bulgarian music has gained great celebrity in recent years. The Trio Bulgarka have recorded and performed widely: they are Eva Georgieva from Dobruja, Stoyanka Boneva from Pirin, and Yanka Rupkina from Stranja, lyrical yet passionate singers who are also charming envoys of their country overseas.

Who will ever forget the virtuoso clarinettist Ivo Papasov and the Orchestra Thraka from south-east Bulgaria? Or the eerie open-throat singing of Slavka Kalcheva or Yanka Uchinkova?

The name Shiroka Luka means 'Broad Meadow', an extraordinary appellation for a straggling terraced community divided by a rushing stream, with dense pinewoods scenting the air and narrow, high homes packed closely together, privacy guarded by tiny windows. But then this was a Turkish village, sheltering womenfolk from inquisitive eyes: your thick stone walls form another *purdah*. Sheep-breeding declined, the Turks moved out, and it became a Bulgarian village, with its own baker, saddler, cooper, master-builders, and smiths to fashion gates and window-frames. As I waited for a scurrying lad to summon the curator of the Ethnographic Museum, the bus from Devin to Smolyan cruised to a halt, two leather-jacketed youths alighted, and it departed with scarcely a sound. A milk-van rattled up, with an alsatian and humble mongrel in the back playing straight-man and comedian. Old men sat in the thin, deceptive sunlight of autumn, watching a lady sweeping leaves between her wooden door and the cobbled road. Their anoraks kept them snug, but their faces were screwed up in disappointment at the screeching, icy wind. Shiroka Luka's houses and contents retain as far as possible the style and atmosphere of the National Revival a hundred and fifty years ago.

The Ethnographic Museum is delightfully displayed in the Kalenjievi House: milk churns, wooden utensils for making cheese, curds and whey, ploughs. On the upper floor local costumes are exhibited beside low milking-stools, sheep-bells, crooks, bagpipes, rifles, and a fireplace so located that it could heat both kitchen and living-room. Above goathair carpets a hanging cradle; a huge trough to bake loaves for a week, with a seal blessing the bread with a cross. Women used looms in a workroom to make blankets for trousseaux; the guest-room is also covered with goathair carpets, still made today. A girl married after the age of eighteen, and by custom made her own wedding dress, wearing it until she gave birth to her first child. When she became a mother-in-law the custom was for her to wear darker clothes, and when a grandmother, dark blue and black (with an apron darker orange). On the top floor, interesting masks testified to enduring shamanism in

Shiroka Luka, Rhodopes. Houses among the pines

these mountains, some 'protecting the wearer from evil' and others worn by 'horned men' who are to be exorcised. There is still every year a 'forgiving day' when emigrants return to kiss their parents' hands in atonement for past mistakes. In a similar ritual, the bride offers the best man *banitsa* to ask pardon.

On the top floor, nowadays devoted to the history of education in the village and a poor selection of local paintings, Nikola Gyochev showed me the escape route devised to vanish into the mountains, if there were a tap on the door in the middle of the night.

Wild mountain landscapes dominated by proud spruces were blurred on the winding route to Devin spa, 20 km to the west. The two-star Hotel Grebenets serves patients at the Polyclinic and Balneotherapy Centre and holidaymakers seeking a bracing climate: hiking, hunting and fishing in the rivers Vucha and Devinska. Many of the local people make a living from timber. The drive to Dospat and its new dam is irresistible for Scots, Swiss, and any other true highlanders seeking the sublime dimension; from Dospat you should drive north to Batak for the tragic dimension.

6: RILA AND THE SOUTH-WEST

Batak — Velingrad — Bansko — Sandanski — Melnik — Rozhen Monastery — Petrich — Blagoevgrad and Pirin — Rila Monastery — Kyustendil — Zemen — Samokov, Borovets and the Return to Sofia

Bulgaria has seldom impinged on the western European mind. Neither peace nor war seems to bring the country into sharp focus. But this neglect ended abruptly on 7 August 1876, when the reporter J.A. MacGahan wrote of Batak in the *Daily News*:

Batak

'Here is what I saw. On approaching the town on a hill there were some dogs. They ran away, and we found on this spot a number of skulls scattered about, and one ghastly heap of skeletons with clothing. I counted from the saddle a hundred skulls, picked and licked clean: all women and children. We entered the town. On every side were skulls and skeletons charred among the ruins, or lying entire where they fell in their clothing. There were skeletons of girls and women with long brown hair hanging to the skulls. We approached the church. There these remains were more frequent, until the ground was literally covered with skeletons, skulls, and putrefying bodies in clothing. Between the church and the school there were heaps. The stench was fearful. We entered the churchyard. The sight was more dreadful. The whole churchyard for three feet deep was festering with dead bodies partly covered – hands, legs, arms, and heads projected in ghastly confusion. I saw many little hands, hands and feet of children of three years of age, and girls, with heads covered with beautiful hair. The church was still worse. The floor was covered with rotting bodies quite uncovered. I never imagined anything so fearful. There were 3,000 bodies in the churchyard and church. We were obliged to hold tobacco to our noses. In the school, a fine building, 200 women and children had been burnt alive. Many who had escaped had returned recently, weeping and moaning over their ruined homes. Their sorrowful wailing could be heard half a mile off. Some were digging out the skeletons of loved ones. A woman was sitting moaning over three small skulls with hairs clinging to them, which she had in her lap'.

I never try to involve myself in political and religious controversy, for that way lies no tolerance, no concord. But I have introduced the massacre of Batak to explain the resonance of 'the Ottoman yoke' and similar terms in the Bulgarian psyche, and in official historiography. Neither was Batak the only place of martyrdom: similar horrors occurred at Perushtitsa, Karlovo, Stara Zagora, Kalofer, Sopot, and Klisura... as terrible as Glencoe in our own history, or Stalin's massacre at Katyn. When shall we ever learn?

Batak Historical Museum is one of the hundred Bulgar national sights categorised as of principal importance in the guide *100te Natsionalni Turisticheski Obekta* (3rd ed., Sofia, 1987). Bulgarian tourists can obtain a rubber stamp from each site to prove they have been there, qualifying when they have the whole set for free holidays, much as visitors to Japanese temples can obtain beautiful calligraphic mementoes of their visit in a special album. I requested such a rubber stamp on a set of concertina-postcards showing aspects of early and modern Batak, such as the partisan camp called Teheran, and the Church of the Virgin Mary. The Historical Museum begins with the Besi, among the most warlike of Thracian tribes. Finds from Bezlika and Shiroka Polyana can be found near inscriptions from Despot Uvan and his wife, showing what jewellery was to be buried with them. Batak was known as Desposhovo, and to the Turks as Desposhovo Mahallesi ('Place of the Despot'). Bulgarian immigrants colonised the Turkish village in the 15th to 17th centuries and in 1592 the Krichim Monastery began to spread the usual Bulgarian words of hope towards church autonomy and national sovereignty by means of literacy, religion and cultural development. The name Batak, meaning a bog or marsh, appears by the late 16th century, when the town was ruled by an Obshtina or Council of Elders. The Turks feared and hated the town as a 'nest of haiduts' or outlaws, among whom was the Voivod Strakhil, shown here in a drawing. A saying survives that 'all the wine produced in Peshtera is drunk in Batak', but this slur can be counterbalanced by the fact that three abbots of Rila came from Batak: Yosif (1766-80), Kiril (1867-83) and Nikifor (1894-5). After the April Rising of 1876, Bashibazuks and Pomaks massacred nearly every inhabitant, as we have seen in MacGahan's awestruck account, the first to die being the priest Neicho. The museum displays the beautiful sword of Ahmed Agha, a pair of cauldrons belonging to the partisans, and two cherry-tree cannons used by rebels. Todor Zhivkov has referred to Batak as the Bulgarian Golgotha, and Ivan Vazov, in his essay 'In the Heart of the Rhodope Mountains', tells us that he could not pronounce its name without a shudder. 'I wanted to go there,' notes Vazov, 'and at the same time did not want to go. I did not want to go, for reasons rooted in the temperament of many people, especially those of the present Bulgarian generation. Fearful and sinister memories of suffering troubled the soul of the happy people and of those who were alien to it; for others who had suffered and who still bore unhealed scars it was a useless torture.' The Church of Sveta Nedelya was built in 1813 in the space of 75 days. By the old calendar then in use, the massacre of two thousand people in the church (and three thousand more in the town) occurred on 4 May 1876; by the new calendar it happened on 17 May. The church remained standing because it was made of stone, and the stout walls rose three metres high. An old walnut tree just outside the church door, a witness to the massacre, dropped an autumn leaf at my feet. Within the church you will find Vazov's poem 'Recollection of Batak', devoted to a child's account of the murder of his family. Gruesome blood-stains redden the plaster on the square columns; an ossuary below the apse bears more weight than it should be expected to support. I hurried to a peaceful bookshop on the square named for Lyuben Ganev (1927-44). There a sad man with bags under his eyes and a thin grey pullover shuffled the morning's newspapers and I bought a new notebook. Batak has a new hydro-electric dam, and is surrounded by forests of beech and oak. Holiday homes are provided for young pioneers and trades unionists.

On the road to Velingrad I found teams felling timber, in a town with a school for male juvenile delinquents and a mosque for the local Pomaks. The name 'pomak' is derived from 'pomagach' or helper. Originally, as Vazov explains in *The Great Rila Wilderness* (Sofia, 1969), the Pomaks were Bulgarian Christians from the Chepino Valley exempted from taxes in 1345 by the invading Turks on condition that every man aged twenty to thirty-five enlisted in the Turkish Army and fought in its campaigns in Tunisia, Libya and Egypt. Chepino would thus be allowed to keep its own (Christian) religion in return for military service. But in 1657 the janissaries of Grand Vizier Mohammed Küprülü were on the point of massacring the Chepino infidel when the Kara Imam Halil Hoja begged the Vizier to forgive the alleged disloyalty of the Chepino Pomaks if they converted. This was a time of drought, so the people of Chepino relied on consignments of wheat from outside to stay alive. Thus it was that the priests and mayors converted to Islam:

whoever became a Muslim was given wheat for food, and those who refused were killed or fled, after which their homes would be burned down. The fugitives sought refuge in Rakitovo and other towns nearby. The new converts demolished thirty-three monasteries and 218 churches between Kostenets and Stanimaka. These details were recorded in 1657 by Father Methodius Draginov of Korovo, possibly himself a forced convert. In the mid-19th century Muslims formed a majority in the towns of Plovdiv (which they called Filibe), Vidin, Pleven (Plevne), Ruse (Ruschuk), Shumen (Shumni), Razgrad, and Varna.

Velingrad

Velingrad consists of the old Pomak villages Kamenitsa, Chepino, and Lajane, which Vazov visited in June 1882. He wrote that Lajane occupied 'a picturesque site in a fertile and fruitful valley with many trees, much shade and refreshed by two rivers, the Lukovitsa and Bistritsa or Stara Reka ('Old River') which flowed through the two gorges. The horizon was closed by the majestic ridge of Alabak and Mileva Skala; to the north and northwest by the slope of Iliin Peak, with a clump of pine forests on its very summit and by the higher Arapchal and Ostrets, all covered with forests'. A century later, eighty per cent of all Bulgaria's pine timber still comes from the Rhodopes. Tar, furniture, and rosin for violin bows are all products of Velingrad, renamed for Vela Peeva, a Resistance fighter betrayed by a forest warden and killed in May 1944. Sanatoria and clinics are frequented by visitors seeking treatment at baths and mineral springs ranging in temperature from 22° to 90°. Carnations grown in hothouses are exported to the U.S.S.R., both Germanies, and elsewhere in Europe. Hops, strawberries, and raspberries flourish in this attractive place, which became a town in 1948 and, with a population of 30,000, attracts more than 400,000 holidaymakers every year. You can stay in Lajane's two-star Hotel Zdravets, and take a leisurely trout lunch at the Kleptuza Restaurant beside the lake in Chepino. I stopped by a tyre repair shop to talk to the residents of 146 Bulevard Georgi Dimitrov, a long thoroughfare shady with trees. The new three-storey house might have been photographed in Austria or Italy, with attractive red tiles, and white wood windows in skittishly pebble-dashed walls. 'You'll come in for a cup of coffee? No? Well, take these eggs, and remember Velingrad!' Bulgarian pop music

Velingrad. A typical new house: 146 Bul. Dimitrov

blared from their kitchen window, and a youngster of six careered on a tricycle round the yard at the side of the house, oblivious to the slight drizzle. 'Come in Stefcho!' shouted his mother, and the infant assumed instant deafness for the stubborn right to play longer. Hot mineral springs are tapped in the streets: you just fill up your bottles and jugs whenever you wish. The earliest baths date from the 16th century, and were named for the boyar Velyo, here in Lajane; the baths called Sharnata in Kamenitsa district are much hotter.

Bansko
The road to Yundola brings you, just short of the town, to the village of Sveta Petka, 1 km off the road to the left, still inhabited totally by Pomaks. Yundola itself is a beautiful hill resort, similar to Crianlarich in the Trossachs, popular among campers, hikers and ramblers in summer, and among skiers in winter. Sheep huddled in a sheepfold against gusts of wintry wind: a blizzard was forecast: snow would find its way even into these dense pine forests of Yun-

dola within a few hours. Beehives stood in small clusters like wooden receivers for insect radio. On the right a narrow railway track from Septemvri to Dobrinishte was climbing through the Rhodopes, just keeping ahead of a breathless, slowing train on the line built by the Germans in World War II to carry timber to the Fatherland. At 12.30 I pulled up in Yakoruda for a short stroll, near a sawmill. A green ambulance took the form of a four-wheel-drive vehicle to cope with rough mountain roads. Four women were carrying sheaves of tobacco-leaves; an old man hustled a dog out of the road and closed his gate behind him. Sleet slashed my face and I drove on quickly towards Pirin, and the district of Razlog. Mount Pirin, above and beyond, sat shrouded in fog, beyond signs to the ski centre and bus station. I drew up outside the two-star Hotel Pirin in Bansko, and enquired for lunch. A waitress produced white bread and a tomato, rice soup, and meat balls with chips and red pepper, with Turkish coffee to round off the welcome meal. Only 160 km from Sofia, Bansko is destined to develop as a major winter resort on the lines of Borovets or Pamporovo, but in the seven months without snow hiking offers endless summer pleasures in changing mountainous landscapes with cols and peaks, tarns and glens reminiscent of the Swiss Alps compressed into a single frag-mented pyramid. A botanist's dream, Pirin can be crossed by hardy hikers prepared to use plain hostels and to carry their own rations and sleeping-bag. The best months are May (for spring blossom) and June to August, but high winds may roar at any moment, so dress in thick trousers, anorak, and heavy-duty boots, taking all normal precautions and preferably joining a group.

The most important feature of Bansko is the new Museum of the Bansko School of Art, due to the energy and scholarship of Profes-sor Atanas Bozhkov, of Sofia University, whose team collected three hundred icons and murals in fieldwork throughout Pirin from 1976, the museum itself opening in 1986, in a former nunnery belonging to the Hilendar Monastery. This has involved a total reconsideration of Bulgarian art from the middle of the 18th cen-tury onward. Bozhkov's own *Bulgarian Art* (1964) undervalued the work of the Bansko School, which is only just now emerging from the shadow cast over it by the exuberant school of Tryavna and its sheer numbers of *dramatis personae*. Bansko, the birthplace of Paisi of Hilendar the national historian, enjoyed close religious and cul-tural affinities with Mount Athos, providing us with a complex regional art comprising many strands: the Eastern Orthodox, the Greek, the Bulgarian, and the European baroque in proportions varying with each woodcarver or painter of murals and icons. Local merchants travelled widely (Haji Vulcho visited Jerusalem in 1757) and monks passed between Bansko and the Zographou and Hilendar monasteries on Mount Athos, so there was no shortage of patrons for artists and craftsmen. Bansko-born Toma Vishanov studied painting in Vienna but by 1780 was back in Bansko, founding a school in which his own family gained preeminence, especially his son Dimitur Molerov. Room 1 of the gallery displays 'Christ' (*c*. 1830), 'Christ with Angels' (*c*. 1833) and 'Sv. Nikola' (*c*. 1835) and Room 2 copies of drawings by Vishanov (the originals being in Sofia) in a recreation of a contemporary artist's studio, with easel. Room 3 shows photographs of Toma's frescoes of 1798 for the Chapel of S. Luke at Rila Monastery rejected because his faces were recognisably those of real people, a feature offending canons of church art: neither were his warm colours and accurate perspective appreciated by traditionalists looking only for 'what had been done before'. For thirteen years the angry Vishanov did not paint again until, in 1811, he joined forces with his son Dimitur. Whereas Toma has been compared by Bozhkov with El Greco, Dimitur shows rococo tendencies in his 'Virgin of the Annunciation' (1835) for Rila. A 'Baptism of Christ' already shows the end of Byzantine stylization, and inch by inch the future is glimpsed in Dimitur's 'Raising of Lazarus', with its interesting architectural motifs, and the 'Prophet Elijah' who foretells more than he could have known in vivid yellows, reds and blues. Room 4 shows some of the later members of the Bansko School: the sons of Dimitur (Simeon and Georgi), Mihailko Yuvarov, Dimitur Sirleshtov and Kostadin Marunchev. A 'Cyril and Methodius' sets the avatars in their own partnered space. A small 'Dormition of the Virgin' (*c*. 1835) is attributed to Toma and Dimitur. The last gallery has Toma's 'Christ Blessing' and 'S. John the Baptist' (both before 1798) and two versions of 'S. John the Baptist' by Dimitur, the earlier being strongly influenced by his father but the later more individual. The large 'Christ' (1848) by Dimitur seems in a crucial way to sum up what we have absorbed so far: it is a kind of blessing on the whole careful, imaginative enterprise, restoring to its rightful place the fascinating school of Bansko. (The museum is closed on Mondays).

Snow was beginning to whiten the sky by now, as well as the

Bansko in winter

winding streets of Bansko, the sturdy stone houses defended by tiles and deeply overhanging eaves. *Debel snyag, golyam komat*, says the Bulgarian proverb: heavy snow, fat loaves, and one could well predict a bounteous wheat crop from the relentless snow that pattered without faltering. Kids came out to throw snowballs as I padded my slow, silent way along Ulitsa 9 Septemvri just short of the railway line to the Church of the Virgin Mary (1806) with its iconostasis so similar to that in Rila. But most of Bansko's monuments are to be found in a reserve bounded by Ploshtad Vaptsarov, Ul. Pirin, Ul. Otets Paisii and Ul. 9 Septemvri. I couldn't miss the Clock Tower (1850) and the adjacent Church of the Holy Trinity (1832-5), unlocked for me by a smiling, businesslike woman in a headscarf who said 'The stone columns are painted wood'. The twelve columns have stone bases, but though they cleverly dissimulate, these shafts are indeed wooden. Two old wood-burning stoves bestowed a vague penumbra of warmth around them, but chill quickly renewed its ascendancy in this active church, with frescoes and dozens of icons. The lowest level of the iconostasis is floral, the main sequence saintly and the upper borders architecturally painted, then a curved floral frieze, then another level of saints topped by a baroque golden frieze and a crucifix reaching nearly to the ceiling.

The Vaptsarov House-Museum was being gutted, with a view to a completely new display, and the Neofit Rilski House-Museum had been shut for the day, so I could see neither the exhibition devoted to the 'Bulgarian Mayakovsky', Nikola Vaptsarov (1909-42) a poet-engineer executed by firing-squad, nor that celebrating the diverse talents of the priest-educator Rilski (1793-1881), who takes the credit for building Holy Trinity Church at a time of Muslim repression.

Bansko may be the fourth largest winter resort in Bulgaria, but it resists overwhelming by incomers and especially in that delightful enclave around the Buinov, Velyanov and Sirleshtov houses divided by Ulitsa Ognev there is a sense of the past encapsulated without mummification: that kind of pent-up vigour released by your imaginative energy so evident at Nesebur.

Sandanski

Snow had caked on the roof of my car, but at least the engine rumbled into life, and I chugged off in the wake of a heavy gritting lorry, then overtook it into narrow slithery roads between dreams of heavenly snowfields and snowforests to the col of Predela, between the heights of Pirin and Rila. Beyond the icy perfection of Gradevo I turned left on a highway signed 'Thessalonika' away from 'Sofia 114 km' to the right.

The frontier-post of Kulata, on the Greek border, was insistently signed as I followed the Struma Valley almost straight to the town of Sandanski, a town of 26,000 people on the banks of the Struma's tributary, Sandanski Bistritsa. There was no mistaking the land-mark of the four-star Hotel Sandanski, rising like an Assyrian step-pyramid above the healthiest town in Bulgaria, owing its pri-macy to a yearly average of 110 cloudless days, 2,450 hours of sunshine, five foggy days, and only 66% relative air humidity.

Sandanski, void of heavy industry, is ideal whether you like walking in golden meadows, boating, abundant fruit and vegetables throughout the year, or first-rate treatment for respiratory, pulmo-nary and cardiac ailments. Mineral springs range in temperature from 42° to 81°C, and a health complex associated with the luxury

Sandanski. View from Hotel Sandanski

hotel is the largest of its kind in the Balkan states. Add to this an open-air theatre, cinemas, and a fascinating modern Archaeological Museum, and you can understand why visitors from Finland with whom I chatted in the lounge were ecstatic. 'The costs are so low, and the mountains so high!' summarised their feelings. I dined in the company of Antoinette and Ivanya, English-speaking Balkan-tourist guides from Sofia, enjoying yoghourt salad, fish and chips, baklava, and Turkish coffee. The girls were on holiday, enjoying facilities at a tiny fraction of their real cost. No, they said, they were not going on tomorrow to the Yane Sandanski chalet or – the end of the mountain road – the Begovitsa chalet, because forecast snow might drift across the road and cut off their retreat.

Next morning news broadcast from the capital recorded a temperature of -1°C and a fall of 16 cm of snow. In the invigorating air I crossed from the Spa Hotel to Bulevard Georgi Dimitrov and paid the usual pittance to enter the Archaeological Museum, where fragments of the town's long and turbulent past are posed against oblivion. The town since 1949 called Sandanski after the patriot, Yane Sandanski, is located in the lands once inhabited by the Bithynian Thracian tribe called Maidoi in Greek and Maedes in Latin. Their Maedica consisted of the Struma Valley, with modern Blagoevgrad, the upper and middle Bregalnitsa (which they called the Astibos) and the lower Strumeshnitsa (which they called the Pontos). Philip II annexed the Medians to his state: his Macedonian supremacy lasted (in the view of Maria Chichikova) to the late 3rd century or early 2nd century B.C. The Medians fought aggressively against the Roman Conquest and it was during one of these actions that the Median Spartacus fell captive in about 86, and the Romans completed their triumph in 29-28 B.C., allocating southern Maedica to the Roman province of Macedonia and the rest to Roman Thrace. The town of Sandanski was known as Desudava to the Romans in the 1st century A.D. and fell to roaming barbarians in 260-70 A.D. Justinian I, ruler of Byzantium, built an early Christian basilica here in the 6th century, and the museum is so sited that it shelters mosaics from redevelopers while connecting them with other features of the town's history. The Slav name was Sveti Vrach, 'the Sacred Healer', identifying the mineral springs known from antiquity with earth-goddess and great-mother myths prevalent throughout the region. Here are Thracian pots from the village of Hotovo (2nd-3rd centuries A.D.), mediaeval pottery fragments from the 12th-14th centuries, and marble reliefs from the necropolis of Miletarevo. With the Roman conquest, the Thracian Medi changed burial methods from mounds to sarcophagi in necropolises, as shown by a family grave from Ladarevo. The language of Thraco-Roman Desudava was Greek. Excavations continue just outside the museum itself, and – by French archaeologists since summer 1987 – at Katuntsi south of Melnik.

Melnik

Today the town of Melnik has fewer than 350 inhabitants, yet it remains adamantly a town rather than a village because of its magnificent reputation as the 13th century refuge and stronghold of the Despot Slav. Later on it welcomed wealthy Greek families evacuated from Plovdiv. In its heyday, Melnik is reported to have accommodated twenty thousand people in this ravine in sandstone cut by a tributary to the Struma, and in 1876 the figure exceeded 12,000, but in 1913, during the Balkan Wars, the town was virtually annihilated by raging fires and its trade routes were so badly damaged that the town has diminished to its present level, as a ghost town, surviving on its red wine and attractive isolation as a tourist enclave: a San Marino, another Petra.

A Byzantine chronicler wrote with some asperity that 'this impregnable town and the Bulgarians who have enclosed themselves within its confines had no fear of the Byzantines, for they realised that it would never be conquered'. Ubiquitous sandstone lent itself to the carving of grottoes by early inhabitants for themselves and their maturing wine, quarrying for patrician houses, palaces, and the 'seventy-five' or so churches noted by a 19th-century visitor, possibly with a touch of exaggeration, since only 40 were known in 1900, and after the fire of 1913 only five survive in their entirety today: SS. Peter and Paul, S. Nicholas, S. Anthony, S. John and S. John the Baptist.

In her study of the local icons, *Ikoni ot Melnishkiya Krai* (Sofia, 1980), Lozinka Koinova-Arnaudova mourns the loss of many works of art over the centuries, especially during the struggle against Greek political and religious nationalism when many icons were overpainted, and during the Balkan Wars when whole churches were burnt down. Despite these vicissitudes, she has recorded 2700 icons from 42 churches in Melnik itself, surrounding villages and Rozhen Monastery, which fall naturally into three groups. The first date from the Middle Ages and the early Ottoman period (13th to mid-16th centuries), artistic isolation during the Ottoman period (to the early 18th century) and Renaissance works (18th-19th centuries), ending in the first decade of the 20th century, when inspiration had drained away. The first group, poor in number but rich in quality and historical resonance, includes some fresco fragments (now removed to Sofia) in the Church of S. Nicholas near the fortress of Despot Slav and from the same church a late 14th-century icon of S. Anthony surrounded by scenes from his life influenced by Mount Athos artists, to judge from the white lines surrounding the brightest parts of the body and shadows over the uncovered parts of the body, traits which persisted in Melnik art to the early 18th century. During the Ottoman era, monasteries on Mount Athos organised for the various Orthodox communities, including Bulgarians, Greeks, Russians and Serbs, provided a mode for mutual support and interaction which explains the similarity between icons in museums as far apart as Ohrid and Thessaloniki, Sofia and Athens. The exhibition of icons in Melnik's S. Nicholas encompasses a wide range of styles, from the vivid 'Nativity of the Virgin' (17th century) from the church of SS. Peter and Paul to the early 18th-century tempera 'Mater Dolorosa' which already begins to exemplify Renaissance tendencies, culminating in the decoration of Rozhen Monastery (up to 1732) where each master is clearly identifiable in 'Doubting Thomas', say, or 'The Beheading of S. John the Baptist'. Full spatial awareness begins to make its presence felt in the late 19th century 'Nativity of the Virgin' brought to S. Nicholas from the church of S. Dimitur the Miracle-Worker in Golechevo.

Within the bishop's church of S. Nicholas itself, the iconostasis with its 18th - and 19th-century icons has recently been restored to great effect. The National Revival icons are interesting for two tendencies: to the ornate, and to the naive; we know the names of Lazar Argirov and Nikolai Yakov, but many other icon-painters of that period signed their works and worked both in Melnik and beyond. The other four churches were not open to the public during my visit, but I understand that the intention is to restore them as time and funds permit.

Melnik had been settled by the same Median Thracians who had settled Desudava-Sandanski, and erected a statue in their town in tribute to the Emperor Trajan, of which only the pedestal is left. The Macedonian Samuil took Melnik in the 980s, and Despot Alexei Slav was appointed by Tsar Kaloyan to rule the Struma and Western Rhodopes from Melnik (the centre from 1208), receiving the title Despot after marying an illegitimate daughter of Heinrich, then Holy Roman Emperor; when his father-in-law and wife died, and he lost influence with the Holy Roman Empire, he remarried for reasons of state, this time a relation of Theodore Comnenus of Epirus. He played off the Eastern Roman Empire against the Western, and kept a clever balance between the Bulgars whom he led and the Epirotes of Northern Greece with whom he was allied. His town rivalled contemporary Turnovo in its splendour, rising likewise in terraces, with tiled roofs: the pre-existing fortifications (we have traces datable to the 10th century) were strengthened and castles erected by boyars at strategic vantage points, with monasteries equally well defended. In 1246 Melnik fell to the Nicaeans, in 1330 to the Serbs and in 1371 to the Ottomans. By now Greek exiles had fled over the border to Melnik, and the Bulgarians were joined by Turks in uneasy isolation among sandstone peaks eroded as quickly and easily as earth's ozone layer by aerosols. The royal monastery of Alexei Slav was built in 1219-20 at the southeast side of Melnik, where you can find today the elegant white chapel of S. Zona. It was called the Holy Virgin of the Cave, after a hermit's grotto cut in the sandstone nearby, and presented with many favours by the Despot, including the land and serfs of Katuntsi, and independence from the Bishop's authority attested by a document in Greek signed by Slav and preserved in the Vatoped Monastery on Mount Athos. Another monastery, that of the Virgin Pantanassa, was erected to the north of Melnik on the road to Rozhen. Rozhen itself of course glittered as the jewel in Melnik's monastic crown.

Melnik's houses remain its chief glory today. Its first great houses arose between 1205 and 1229: stone was the material and fortification the aim. With the advent of Byzantine rule in the mid-13th century brick decoration, as we have seen at Nesebur, became more common, though it had been practised at Melnik as early as the 10th century, and the so-called Boyar's House above the two-star Melnik Hotel exemplifies this decoration. Opinions differ, but this house may date back in part to the 10th century with additions up to the 14th before its complete restoration during the

National Revival in the 19th. The Ottomans added a wall, and a tower south-east of the Boyar's House, which some believe Alexei Slav's original residence, though we have no proof of this. The golden age of Melnik arose in the 17th-18th centuries, due to the first-quality tobacco and red wine. New houses sprang up: richly furnished, spacious, with high ground floors and many-windowed upper floors. The lower floors were used for making and storing barrels of wine, the mezzanine for servants and workers, and the luxurious upper rooms for the wealthy families. Tunnels cut into the friable sandstone as wine cellars in ancient times were extended in proportion to the expansion of trade routes. The merchants' floors were built with rooms so high and ample that two rows of windows were needed, the lower row often shuttered and the upper row occasionally opulent with stained glass. A spacious hall, suitable for parties or receptions, was surrounded by other rooms, with a glassed-in kiosk or porch at one end, or possibly a balcony. An atmosphere of grandeur, different from anything you will see in Bozhentsi or Tryavna, pervades these patrician residences, to which orchestras might be invited for special occasions. Characteristics of Melnik houses include an impressive fireplace, the use of carved and painted wood on walls and ceilings, and a stone tower with open balcony, but in such narrow lanes the gardens that you will find in Zheravna, say, have been largely sacrificed to demands of uneven terrain. Forty important houses have been restored, and private accommodation is available in some of them, but the principal house-museum is that of Manolis Kordopoulos.

I left my car in the square beside the plane-trees which give the Chinarite Restaurant its name, and took lunch in the boisterous company of the Bansko Male Voice Choir, due to sing in Melnik that evening. I resisted their offers of vodka (it is a criminal offence for a driver to have *any* alcohol in his blood when tested in Bulgaria) in favour of Pepsi-Cola, and accepted the fare offered: cabbage salad, rice soup, and veal and beans. 'The plane-trees in the square seem very ancient', I ventured. A bass from Bansko spread his hands like a chief explaining a recipe: 'In Pirin we have the oldest trees in Bulgaria', he said, as his colleagues shook their heads in corroboration, 'of thirteen centuries ago: a black pine'. Their conversation turned on the World Cup match against Romania, clothes prices, and relative salaries in Britain and Bulgaria.

As you visit the houses of Dr Nikolak, Velev (a restaurant) and

Paskalev, let your fantasy fill these windy, de Chirico-blank streets outside with the long, unruly caravans of horses and camels that would leave Melnik every Monday and Friday loaded with casks and goatskins of red wine bound for Genoa and Marseilles, for Budapest and Vienna. I remembered how close I had come to Greece: the border was advertised everywhere, and you cannot hike freely in the mountains around Melnik for that reason, but must keep to the road.

I was unprepared for the Kordopoulos House, its exquisite taste, magnificence, and spatial harmony. Dated by an inscription to 1754, it was clearly erected on much earlier foundations, and retains a strongly fortified effect, with windows on all four compas points, the largest and highest house in Melnik, in 'Levantine style'. Kordopoulos was a Greek wine-merchant sympathetic to the Macedonians (he sheltered Yane Sandanski in a hide within these ample premises) and responsible for introducing healthy new strains of grape to their tired vineyards and for combating pernicious phylloxera. Detailed restoration has provided us with an

Melnik. The museum-house of Manolis Kordopoulos

authentic view of the bedroom, or Blue Room, with decorated walls, ceilings and cupboards, and of the main hall, its great frieze showing grape varieties, while dozens of flower species are painted on the ceiling and walls. The ground floor is a mazy wine cellar 180 metres in total length, where up to a quarter of a million litres of wine could be stored at any one time in a temperature constant at 13°C.

The Pashov House is later: it was occupied by Ibrahim Bey and decorated deliriously in baroque style. Now it houses the Town Museum, handily situated below the main square, and must be seen both for the house itself and for the evocation of historic Melnik in early engravings and later photographs, for the 19th-century splendours of Viennese ballgowns and lace gloves, for the pious icons and Muscovite samovar. Surely Melnik possessed the best of all worlds, including that of serene solitude. It seems unfair that a town as small as Melnik should be so much more vibrant than a town as large as Middlesbrough.

Melnik was celebrated for its ceramics in the 13th and 14th centuries, on a level with the output of Lovech, Nesebur, Turnovgrad (modern Turnovo) and Cherven (near modern Ruse). The two dominant styles were *sgraffito* and painted, especially the former, identified with excavations of coins from the reign of Isaac Comnenus (1184-94) to that of Andronikos II Palaeologus (1282-1328). *Sgraffito* wares continued to be made and exported along trade routes in the 17th and 18th centuries, until imports from Western Europe and the Middle East reduced their value.

The museum's stone monuments include a figure of Asdula, a god of Melnik apparently unknown elsewhere by that title but clearly identifiable with Dionysus. He rides a horse in a vineyard accompanied by representations of Pan and Silenus. Two tombstones show the huntress Diana, Greek Artemis, Thracian Bendis, the great goddess addressed by Aristophanes, shown as a tall young woman with a chiton and high leather hunting boots, her hair tied back so it would not impede her vision during the chase. Two running dogs help her to pursue and run down a deer. In parts of Greece she remained merely a goddess of hunting and forests; in Thrace she accompanied the deceased to the underworld, lighting their way with a torch.

We recall that the *Bacchae* of Euripides, set in Thebes, was written in Macedonia, where the wandering playwright would have been influenced by the local devotion to Dionysus. That must be one of the reasons for his unusual theme, and for his passionate identification of the two points of view: the rational, represented by Pentheus of Thebes, and the dionysiac or ecstatic, represented here by the women devotees of Bacchus and by elders such as Cadmus and Teiresias. The *Bacchae* is a fine play to read in Melnik's wind, where Dionysus 'casts his delicate curls' (*trupheron plokamon eis aithera rhipton*), drinking the red wine when 'we forget in joy our age' (*epilelismeth' ideos gerontes ontes*). Yes: give honour to the god with us (*meth' emon to theo timen didou*)! The *Bacchae* even presents us with an image for the drive to wintry Rozhen, through 'glistening arrows of snow' (*leukes aneisan khionos euageis bolai*).

Rozhen Monastery

You could walk across the mountains to Rozhen Monastery from Melnik, crossing the dry bed of the Rozhen gorge and climbing to the sandstone plateau, among jagged needles and razor-shaped peaks like chipped flints. But I preferred the main road to the village of Rozhen via Lozenitsa and Kurlyanovo, where I overtook shivering sheep carved in woolly snow. Rozhen village slept through my visit, tobacco-leaves hanging under protecting eaves like some pagan charm against the devil. In summer, the way up to Rozhen lies through wooded meadows encircled by gentle slopes. I prefer a winter blanket of frost and snow, for the climb of a thousand paces from the village is gentle and the silence Franciscan. Rozhen's charter dates from 1220, when Pirin was presented to Alexei Slav, but the monastery building was begun in 1217. I wondered about the age of the great elm, or the iron-studded oak doors. Badly-faded frescoes of the Virgin's Birth above the entrance indicate the dedication of the monastery, which retains its original fort-like plan, distant like so many Bulgarian monasteries from the nearest town. The first courtyard is overwhelmed by tall galleries of rough wooden columns and balconies resting on a stone base, sheltered from summer sun and winter snows by broad eaves covered with neat red tiles. The abbot's room adjoins the neophyte's cell and then comes the monk-grammarian's. The church, often burnt down, has existed in its present form since the 16th century, with a narthex of 1600 and frescoes in four cycles of work and one of restoration: 1597, 1611, 1728-32 and 1877 and 1982, the penultimate restoration coinciding with that of the entire church. The

Rozhen Monastery

frescoes of 1728-32 prove the most rewarding on close examination: they are to be found in the open narthex (an expressive Ladder of the Virtuous and a stylish Last Judgement) and in the Chapel of SS. Cosmas and Damian (the donor-nun Melania).

The spacious inner courtyard, with three storeys of rooms for visitors and monks, could be used as a meeting-place for pilgrims. The triple-naved church is supported by four wooden columns with a wooden ceiling, tiled roof and no dome, the pulpit on the left and throne on the right. The hundred and fifty mural scenes have not been restricted to the canon. On the southern wall, with a cycle of the Virgin's life and the Passion of Christ, the best fresco is the Raising of Lazarus; the northern wall illustrates more miracles of Christ and various ecumenical councils. I found it astonishing to see the charming low-key stained glass style here that I had just seen in a wholly secular environment at Melnik. On the western wall S. Zosimas gazed at me severely: what right had I to interfere with his line of vision? The same thought had occurred to the Archangels Michael and Gabriel beside the door. Rozhen Monastery is still active with three monks, but may be visited from 8 to noon, and from 1.30 to 6. The quality of the Revival iconostasis by Debur and Samokov carvers is as 'miraculous' in its excellence – plasticity, vivacity, humour – as the allegedly wonder-working icon of the Virgin and Child (1670) from Mount Athos, haloes and hands covered in silver, framed in 1790. The narthex paintings had been an index of national origin at the International Court of the Hague, because under the stratum of 1732 it was found that a cycle dated 1511-1601 had Bulgarian inscriptions, so the Greeks dropped their case. It is suggested that the fine top layer is to be removed to the monastery museum in order to reveal the whole lower layer for posterity.

The museum itself shows a number of smaller icons effective more in facial individuality than in the conventional treatment of hands. A 16th-century Virgin and Child still pursues the Byzantine suggestions of Cimabue, but I enjoyed an eccentric 17th-century S. George, with a little Turk in a turban. An old kitchen still keeps its bread oven intact, and a serving-hatch leads to the refectory, but there is another kitchen on the first floor. I was shown, by one of the three monks still in residence, the scriptorium where the *Glosses on Job* were written by Rozhen scribes in the 14th century; the MS was taken by Patriarch Dosifei in 1674 to Jerusalem's Church of the Holy Sepulchre. Under drifts of snow lay the grave of Yane Sandanski, freedom-fighter and a leader of the Internal Macedonian Revolutionary Organization, uniting in one hidden symbol tempestuous past and stormy present.

Petrich

Just north of the Greek frontier and just east of the Yugoslav border, Petrich is a town of 25,000 people on the site of a Thracian settlement overlain by the Roman town of Petra. A health spa amid chestnut forests, Petrich offers treatment for arthritis, rheumatism and cardio-vascular ailments with accommodation at the two-star Hotel Bulgaria. In the lounge a leather-jacketed youth smoked a cigarette with the dedication of a Trappist monk to silence. Local agriculture is broadly based, from cherries, melons, peaches and grapes to peanuts and tobacco. As well as the Roman fortress of Petra, archaeologists have found near Klyuch the remains of a fortress of Tsar Samuil (993-1014), whose capital was Ohrid, on the modern frontier between Albania and Yugoslavia. Striding away from me in the glittering snowfield I made out two men in the middle distance: confederates, trackers, hunters?

Blagoevgrad and Pirin
Roughly halfway between Sofia and the Greek frontier must have seemed an appropriate place for a settlement, and the Thracians established one at Skaptopara, or 'Mountain Market', where hot springs obligingly gushed forth. The Romans built thermal baths, and the Turks restored them in 1502, when the place's name is recorded as Gorna Jumaya, half-Bulgarian, half-Turkish, but still 'Mountain Market'. Above the town the snowladen sky stared luminously, as though ready to disseminate fresh anthems to the radiant, expectant white world below.

From Jamaya or Pazarishte ('Bazaar'), the town was renamed in 1950 after a Macedonian Marxist called Dimitur Blagoev (1856-1924), who founded the Bulgarian Social Democratic Party in 1891 and the Bulgarian Communist Party in 1919. Political heroes in Communist countries play the same rôle as saints in non-Communist countries, but a modern hero is less durable, as the place named after Stalingrad will prove. They reverberate in street-names too, recur in films and stories, becoming the stuff of legend and romance. They become an inspiration to school children. We all need heroes: in art, football, fashion, politics, but in peacetime the need for heroes should diminish and generally does unless fomented by organized media and a controlled educational system. We lose a part of our self-importance when our heroes fail us, in their private lives or public *volte-faces*. We cannot easily reconcile hero-worship with the foibles of power or the weakness inherent in human nature. Anthony Blunt a spy yet in the Royal favour? Rock Hudson a homosexual?

Yet there *is* something heroic about modern Blagoevgrad, with its spotless Macedonia Square and determined industrialisation: tobacco, machinery, timber, cotton.

The town possessed only 3,500 inhabitants in the 1830s, but today that figure has increased twenty-fold. You can stay at the three-star Alen Mak Hotel at 1 Bul. Vaptsarov, or in the heart of a pine forest at the two-star Bor Hotel. The Parangalitsa nature reserve, 30 km northeast of Blagoevgrad, offers invigorating rambles among spruce and white pines and a chance to see eagles, jackals, foxes and bears. The botanical gardens prove a delight in all seasons. The city itself has an evocative Varosha, or old quarter, with a new District History Museum which opened in 1981. In the evenings one might choose the Drama Theatre, cinemas or the Pirin Ensemble, and eight-day stays based in Blagoevgrad introduce visitors to Pirin songs and dances in some depth through an organised course. The town is the base for a Chamber Opera established in Sofia in 1971 as the Youth Chamber Opera by students of the Bulgarian State Conservatory; its repertory of shorter works suited to 19 instrumentalists and 11 singers includes Glück and Haydn, Monteverdi and Galuppi, Donizetti and Stravinsky.

Rila Monastery

If you have no car, you can visit Rila Monastery very pleasantly on a Balkantourist excursion from your hotel in Sofia. It is more fun by public transport, and of course then you can stay as long as you like which is just as well if, like me, you view Rila as a wonder of the world in the same collection of slides as S. Mark's Square in Venice or the Potala Palace in Lhasa. Stay the night in the new three-star Rilets Hotel, which also hires out ski equipment for beginners' slopes nearby and makes a convenient starting-point for hikes to the chalets of Skakavitsa and Grunchar, and the seven enchanted Rila lakes. Half a dozen buses leave Sofia for Rila every day from the Uchna Kucha terminus on Bulevard 9 Septemvri; the 7.30 train from Sofia to Petrich stopping at Kocherinovo Halt is met by a bus for Rila and other local destinations.

From Blagoevgrad I followed the Struma Valley under gradually darkening skies until, entering Kocherinovo, lightning speared surrounding snow as suddenly and crudely as a death sentence read out at a children's party, and I shivered, lonely for the company of my wife. Many storks nest here in summer, but they had flown south many months before. I passed a 'bookshop on four wheels' of the type that serves localities with a town bookshop and in a few minutes came to the village of Rila, founded in 1816-19 but burnt down in 1833. It was rebuilt in the same style, but higher up and stronger. The Ribarnika restaurant and trout hatcheries, like the Chinarite at Melnik, is part of the KOP co-coperative, as opposed to Balkantourist's chain of restaurants. The Drushliavitsa river foams angrily in the gorge, mist rising endlessly, restlessly at this height of 1250 metres. I was anxious to see the monastery museum before it closed for the evening, but I need not have bothered: the women acting as ticket-sellers and custodians tactfully left me to pore over splendid books and icons long after official closing-time. The history of Rila Monastery is shown in documents, beginning with the paean to Rila from Father Paisi's *Slav-Bulgarian History*, written in 1762 and circulated in manuscript but not printed until 1845, in Budapest:

'Of all the glories of Bulgaria, where there were once so many monasteries and churches, in our time Almighty God has left whole only the Rila Monastery, to survive through the prayers of the Holy Father Ioan...'

Paisi's Ioan was Ivan (876-946), who decided on a hermit's life at the age of twenty and found a cave in which to live and worship in the wilderness, attracting by his reputation for sanctity a group of disciples who would build a hermitage, some four km east of the present monastery, where you can find the saint's tomb, his cell, and a small church dedicated to S. Luke. Serbs too followed Ivan Rilski, and Serbian saints are depicted with Bulgarian and other saints in the main church today. Suffering under the Byzantines, Rila rose again, but was damaged first by avalanche and then by fire in the 14th century. An autonomous ruler, one Dragovol Hrelyo, reconstructed the monastery on its present site in 1334-5, adding in the middle of the great courtyard a five-storey tower 23 metres high, with a frescoed chapel dedicated to the Transfiguration of Christ. Tsar Ivan Shishman presented a Charter to Rila in 1378 to confirm all its earlier rights and granted the monastery more lands and the adjacent villages. The copy is here: the original in Sofia. Even the Ottomans chose to ignore the threat posed by Rila monastery as a cradle of Bulgarian Christianity and a focus for nationalism, in the mistaken belief that Rila lay too far off the beaten track, but the monastery was attacked in the mid-15th century, leaving intact only Hrelyo's central tower. In 1469, Sveti Ivan's relics were brought to Rila from Turnovo, a factor which led to increased zeal on the part of scholars and theologians attached to Rila, among them Vladislav the Grammarian. Ties with Russian monasteries were made and strengthened throughout Ottoman times, such as the contract of 1466 between Rila and the Russian monastery of S.

Panteleimon on Athos, and visits by Rila delegations to Russia in 1558 and 1584. Ottoman depredations tormented the monks at frequent intervals, but the present monastery took shape from 1816 to 1846, mainly under the guidance of Alexei Rilets (interrupted by the terrible fire of 1833) and it was as recently as 1961 that the east wing was restored to show major treasures in suitable surroundings. Most of the books were lost in the fire of 1833, but magnificent icons remain. Portraits of Sv. Ivan were painted at Zemen, Dragalevski and SS. Peter and Paul at Turnovo. Here is the original 14th-century walnut door from Hrelyo's Tower, in which one room was maintained as a prison-cell for disobedient monks. I wondered idly how a monk normally desiring chastisement could be punished further – by reducing his diet to zero? Rila's relations with Moldavia, Romania and Serbia are indicated by ecclesiastical garments, books and crucifixes. Lithographic stones shown used to produce prints for pilgrims, and an English-made printing press, brought from Vienna in 1865, still provides pious images of S. Demetrius and his horse drawn by Toma Sider, some bilingual in Greek and Bulgarian (SS. Sava and Simeon). An exhibition is devoted to the life and times of Neofit Rilski (1793-1881), who created secular and religious schools for national awakening. Tiny crucifixes with silver and gold decorations are dwarfed by a superb naive linden crucifix carved by the monk Raphael incorporating 36 scenes with more than 600 figures, mainly from the New Testament, on the double-sided masterpiece. Raphael studied under no master and attended no school. The impact of his single-minded reverence is all the purer for lacking technical *maîtrise*: I do not recall being so affected by any man's homage to the visions that formed a greater part of his daily life than did the petty world outside. When we hear that Raphael died blind, having been unable to finish it due to failing eyesight, we remember the pathetic fable of Our Lady's Tumbler in mediaeval French *fabliaux*, giving all that he possessed.

Rila's icons displayed in the museum date from the 14th century to the 19th, the earliest being a half-length portrait of the patron saint in tempera, sombre and monumental. A late 17th-century 'Sv. Ivan with Scenes from his Life' is memorable for the pilgrimage made by Tsar Petur, on a silver background.

Popular prints began to be sold at Rila from 1791, financed by a certain Milcho Stankovich and imported from Vienna for local sale. They were cheap enough for every pilgrim to afford one, and even to buy more for friends and relatives, who would keep them as a relic in the family iconostasis. The metal plates engraved abroad would subsequently be run as required on the monastery press. In 1816 the businessman Manasi Georgiev commissioned from Moscow a block depicting the Dormition of John of Rila, and the engraver added the Russian emblem and the monogram of Tsar Alexander I, a symbol not lost on Bulgarian Christians under Ottoman imperialism. The earliest known prints engraved at Rila (as opposed to being merely printed there from plates engraved elsewhere) date from 1836 but it was in the 1860s that the monk Kalistrat, having studied in Belgrade, opened a modern graphic studio, with the introduction of lithography. The studio closed in 1922.

Night had fallen, and I stumbled along the road to the Hotel Rilets in a bitter wind that cracked like a whip around my exposed hands, neck and face. I dreamt of a pilgrim with a staff, who was myself, and also Ivan Rilski, with a long protecting beard, and a black hood, like that black monk of Chekhov's story. Ivan the Terrible greeted me, his eyebrows black as night. I woke up, sweating, hailstones tapping at the window like a beggar's pebbles. Next morning, after a reviving coffee, I crossed from the wooded hotel by bridge to the other side of the Rilska gorge, and walked a few hundred metres to the monastery, passing on my left the railway line with a steam engine stranded perpetually; the last service for Kocherinovo left Rila many years back. I entered through the back gate: brigands are no longer feared in Rila Monastery.

What does one see in Rila? Scampering schoolchildren, on a winter excursion from lessons in Sofia, see an immense courtyard; a snowfield in which to run and shout for the hour or so during which they leave the warm boredom of their coach. A middle-aged woman in thick brown coat and scarf, standing in the souvenir kiosk at the foot of Hrelyo's Tower, sees a couple of tourists, a hubbub of excited children, and a slow priest against a familiar white gallery. That black-bearded, black-robed priest, huddled in thoughts of the next service and importunate visitors, scans the ground for patterns of stone he has recognised at every season of the year for the last forty years. I? I see impossible staircases exercising the wit of the Dutch artist Maurits Escher, who wrestles with fish that transmogrify to birds and back, and water that rushes along neat channels forever uphill. I shall piece together sky and figures, pious wood-

Rila Monastery

block prints and icons shot with radiance. Nobody sees everything, for we each see what we consider important and ignore the rest, sometimes unconsciously. Though I prepared for Rila by reading whatever I could find, I could not evaluate the details of the service recognisable to a theologian; or assess chalices and church plate with the judgment of a goldsmith. I have always envied an artistic woman's sensitivity to slight variations in musical timbre, visual similarities, tactile values, emotional atmosphere: I fear my reactions are always too coarse, too easily satisfied by immediate pleasure, too wary of silence or calm.

Rila juts arrogantly like a fortress above its gorge, surrounded by mountains where beech and pine vie for pre-eminence. Roughly quadrilateral, it seems (though is not) mediaeval and its central tower, the only mediaeval structure, adds to each novel vantage point a new and fascinating perspective. That massive stone exterior is lit by many small windows and crowned like any village by ranges of red-tile roofing pitted with white chimneys. The interior views are its glory, as tier after tier of arcaded gallery rises from the flagstones, bold red stripes enlivening cells and church alike, black and white check sparkling up elegant walls, the rough grey stone of Hrelyo's Tower interfering with each vista like a grey grandfather coughing above your conversation.

You wander at will along open galleries, which protect monks from rain but not from mountain winds. Room 96 gives access to a majestic library. On the second floor, Room 79 was labelled the home of Archimandrite Leonid. I overheard a French guide telling a distinguished marquise that the church is getting too cold, so in a week's time all services will be held in rooms above, where baptisms are normally conducted. Room 78 was labelled the quarters of Hierodiakon Pamphili and Room 77 those of Hieromonakh Vitali. I tiptoed past the open door of Room 73, belonging to Archimandrite Evtimii, and he sneezed. 'Na zdrave!' I called out in the appropriate Bulgarian response, but acknowledgment came there none. Icicles hung from guttering with transparent innocence, but a nudge would have sent one aiming straight through the skull of a little old woman swathed in a dark green coat below in the courtyard.

Wealthy towns such as Teteven and Koprivshtitsa endowed rooms where their own pilgrims might stay while at Rila, and the poet Ivan Vazov stayed in the Chirpan Room while writing 'The Great Rila Wilderness' in 1891. 'The Chirpan Room was near the kitchen; and this desirable proximity was precious to guests who came to stay three weeks in this mountain desert without bringing food for so long and who tended to have appetites like wolves. Because, frankly speaking, where would one have an appetite if not here, where the air is pure and invigorating, scented with pine and full of oxygen, where the Rila river swarms with trout, where the

Kocherinovo wine is delicious and all cares are forgotten? This blessed room was entirely laid with carpets, some of delicate weave. All of them, as well as the cushions, were gifts to the monastery from peasant pilgrims. From such pilgrims came the bedding of the hundreds of other rooms and cells at the monastery.' (Nowadays, the Synod Board sells off presents from donors.) 'On the rafters near the door, one above the other, there were water jugs, candlesticks, and washing utensils, while a large wardrobe in the wall contained mattresses and blankets... Outside and around the monastery were the bakery, the stables, a mill, the smithy, the carpenter's shop, granaries, and all manner of sheds and huts so situated that, when seen from above, all the buildings and tiled roofs gave the impression of a small town hidden in a wilderness'.

The kitchen mentioned by Vazov remains structurally intact in the northern wing, its piercing cone 24 metres high penetrating each succeeding storey by means of ten rows of arches, at their summit a tiny holed dome for a chimney. Massive cauldrons give some idea of the numbers to be fed in past decades. The Ethnographic Museum delights the eye with its embroidery, carpets, jewellery and ornaments, pots and pans, local and imported furniture. I almost forgot: do sample fresh bread from a bakery just outside the Samokov Gate: remember Vazov's warning about a sudden increase in appetite!

Rila's stronghold protects the main sanctuary, the hub of religious life, at the centre of the compound, mingling in its eclectic style Italian domed churches, cruciform churches in the Athos manner, its three naves enhanced by two chapels and three apses. The open gallery, striped to match the lines above it, presents a curious analogy to Granada's Alhambra.

Strange that such a majestic Church, the Assumption of the Blessed Virgin Mary (1834-7) should seem so completely overwhelmed by the grandeur of surrounding mountains, as if San Pietro in Vaticano were relocated in the foothills below Tivoli. Within, the wonderful frescoes by painters of the National Revival gleam in the sun's rays as they move from scene to scene. Most of the paintings are by the renowned brothers Dimitur and Zahari Zograf, with contributions by Dimitur's son Stanislav Dospevski, all of whom we have found elsewhere, and by Ivan Nikolov and Kosta Valyov of Samokov. Look too for murals in the two inner monastery chapels, the Cemetery Church (1795), the Church of S. Luke (1799), and

Toma Vishanov-Molera's Church of the Shroud of the Holy Virgin (1811).

Murals in the main church are on three levels: at the top the twelve apostles; the lives of Jesus and Mary, and saints; and religious festivals. The relics of Sveti Ivan can be seen just to the right of the door. The Russian imperial coat-of-arms salutes you above the centre doors, as incongruously as the flag of monarchical Libya on the cover of my book *Tripoli*. History makes fools of everyone. Iron beams between columns protect the building and its congregation from Samsonic destruction. Side-chapels are devoted to Sv. Nikola and Sv. Ivan. The cross-shaped domed church replaces the conventional narthex with a charming frescoed open gallery, echoing those around it much as the Florentine baptistery respects the lines of S. Maria del Fiore. Portraits of donors remind us of the immediate connection between nationalism and Orthodoxy in the Revival: Theodor and his mother Rada; Metropolitan Jeremiah and Lazar Arsenovich; Petko Hristov and his wife Rada; Vulko Chalukov and his wife Rada; Lulcho Stefanov and his wife Gena; Grandfather Yani and Grandmother Stefana.

No iconostasis in Bulgaria can be compared with Rila's masterpiece of 19th-century Samokov woodcarving, gilded for splendour but interesting especially for its thirty-six scenes blending into a pattern bordering on ecstasy: martyrs, kings, saints and prophets are surrounded by a delirium of flowers, birds, vines and arabesques. Hreljo's throne dates to the 14th century.

The Seven Lakes of Rila may be approached either from the Rila side (between 2 and 3 hours) or from the Malyovitsa side, via Govedartsi from either Borovets or Samokov. The seven interconnecting lakes are situated on plateaux rising from 2100 to 2550 metres: Sulzata (the Tear); Okoto (the Eve), Bibreka (the Kidney), Bliznaka (the Twin), Trilistnika (the Clover-Leaf), Ribnoto (the Fish) and Dolnoto (the Lower). It is usual to spend the night at the Sedemte Ezera Hostel by Ribnoto Ezero. The way down to Vada, along the banks of the Cherni Iskur, takes another hour, and in two hours more you can reach the Malyovitsa complex.

Kyustendil

I looked at my watch, and suddenly realised that I could leave Ivan Rilski's wilderness at three o'clock in the afternoon and still reach

Sofia in time for Verdi's *Don Carlo* at the National Opera, curtain up at seven. But my objective was quite different: to cross from the Rilska valley by way of the Struma valley to the health resort of Kyustendil. I turned off the main road to Sofia and headed for Boboshevo on the Struma, lunching at the Struma Restaurant on the main square, now well below the snow line. Unpolluted air stung my face as I looked around. An old woman, possibly bereaved of a husband, was trudging with her head down, and a heavy shopping bag dragging her down on her right. I felt like comforting her, but all the condolences in the world would prove useless, and her pale, watery eyes (as they looked unseeing through me) could not fix on anything in our imperfect world, but wandered away like a ghost on a battlefield.

For consolation I drove out to Boboshevski Monastery, 3 km to the west, a foundation dedicated to Sv. Dimitur in which S. John of Rila passed some time as a novice, according to his *Life* by Patriarch Euthymius. Hidden within a forest on the eastern slope of Mount Ruen, the church is decorated with 15th-century frescoes, including an animated Last Judgement and a cheerful if disproportionate S. Demetrius on Horseback, fitted uncomfortably into an arch. Christ Pantocrator in the nave is by contrast profoundly still and dignified, in a milieu far removed from the quotidian world of the facing apostles and prelates on a green ground.

From Boboshevo I saw Skrino signposted 5 km away, and was tempted to visit the birthplace of S. John of Rila himself, but I resisted. What could a cluster of modern tiled houses tell me about a 10th-century saint? Yet I regret never having seen Skrino. Might a clue to a man's mission towards sanctity, poverty and celibacy not appear in a clap of thunder? On the outskirts (a Bulgarian once reasonably translated the lower slopes of a mountain as its footskirts) of Nevestino, I slowed up for a row of braggart geese that wobbled along the road in well-disguised anxiety. Yesterday they had evaded the regiment of foxes, but what of today? Nevestino's new bridge is not a patch on the wonderful Kadin Most (Bride's Bridge), a span of five granite arches built from 1463 to 1470.

Kyustendil and its region has been occupied since the Neolithic Age, notably at Kremenik between about 6,200 to 5,000 B.C. You can visualise the ascent of man hereabouts in the converted Mosque of Ahmet Bey (1575) within inhaling distance of Turkish baths still

Kyustendil. Ahmet Bey Mosque (1575), now a museum

being used during my visit.

Horn and bone tools as well as ceramics represent the advent of the Copper Age before 4,000 B.C. Very few finds characterise the local Bronze Age (1100-1200 B.C.) but the Iron Age, here extending to the first century B.C., assumes the confidence of dexterity. The Thracians of this fertile valley protected by mountains on all sides quickly discovered the healing properties of its mineral springs rising to 74°C in treating inflammation and diseases of the joints, nervous system and spinal cord, and gynaecological problems. Today there is a hydropathic medical centre in such favour with Scandinavians that the only leaflet I could find on current treatment was in Finnish.

But it was with the Roman occupation of the newly-named Pautalia in 46 A.D. that the city rose to real prominence, becoming a trade and agricultural centre in the 3rd and 4th centuries. The Roman Emperor Marcus Ulpius Traianus (98-117) spent much time and energy pacifying the Danube territories (98-9, 101-2 and 105-6) and Trajan was apparently cured of a skin disease here, so

Pautalia was honoured with the title Ulpia to recognise its contribution to the imperial wellbeing. Rivalling Serdica (modern Sofia), it possessed a sacred precinct to the god of health Asklepios-Aesculapius, with temples and baths on the foothills of Mount Osogovo. Stockbreeding flourished; so did pottery, jewellery and stonecarving. Only the eastern gate of the original 29-hectare Roman fortress area has so far been excavated, but we know that Byzantine walls strengthened the town during Justinian's reign. Thermal baths, like those we have seen in Varna, must have looked rich and opulent, with an arch-and-vault hypocaust system, recreation halls and a palaestra for gymnasts. Aesculapius was not the only deity worshipped here: we have testimony to cults of the Thracian Horseman/Mithras, Apollo and Artemis/Diana, Zeus and Hera.

The Archaeological Museum displays a 2nd-century bronze of Hera, and a 3rd-century votive tablet to Apollo, making tangible these dreams of past worship. The Bulgarians named the town Velbuzhd (according to records of the time of the Emperor Basil, 1019) after a feudal chief, but in the 14th century intertribal warfare led to the seizure of the town by a Serb called Konstantin Dragash, so the Turks who defeated him and razed the Byzantine fortress called the town 'Konstantin's Land' or 'Konstandili', a name which ended up as Bulgarian Kyustendil. The Turks transformed the region into an orchard, cultivating the apples, pears, cherries and plums still freighted to Sofia markets, as well as tobacco; today hothouses also produce peppers, cucumbers and tomatoes.

You can stay at the three-star Velbuzhd Hotel on Bul. Dimitrov, or at either of the two-star hotels: the central Pautalia on Ploshtad Velbuzhd, or the even more pleasant and quiet Hisarluka, in Hisarluka Park, 2 km from the centre but linked by bus and in summer by tourist train. Private accommodation is also available and, as always, greatly to be recommended. After visiting the Asclepion and fortress on Hisarluka Hill, you can visit 12th-century Church of Sv. Georgi, the 14th-century Pyrgos Tower and the parish church of 1849, now used for exhibitions of children's art. Many people enjoy the paintings of locally-born Vladimir Dimitrov (1882-1960), called the 'Master' and the Dimitrov Art Gallery has a large permanent show of his works. I remain unmoved by his reiterated self-portrait in brash colours applied in broad, facile strokes. His typical canvas is a pretty woman in full face against a back-

Kyustendil. Across the main square

ground of apples: almost a pastiche of woman as fertility symbol, as 'Bulgarian Madonna'. It is unfair to think of Van Gogh's 'Sunflowers' when looking at Dimitrov's approach to the same subject: unfair but irresistible. I preferred the temporary exhibitions of modern Chinese art, the book illustrations of Nikola Milchev, but in most cases here a functional approach to art has overcome the aesthetic approach, leading to the inevitable dilution of inspiration. Three women guarding the shiny new gallery watched me suspiciously, switching off lights as I left one part and entered another level. Between visitors they seemed to stand stock still, not breathing, emerging into real life again only when someone else had to be charged twenty stotinki for a ticket.

Zemen

Next morning the temptation to sit around the main square in the brittle wintry sun and watch clerks and shop assistants on their way to work held me in Kyustendil beyond nine, but I wanted to traverse the mountainous heights on the way to Zemen before lunch. Past Baikal I encountered no other vehicle on the snowy roads, though bulldozers had preceded me. I drove slowly along icy roads precipitous and dangerous but gradually thawing. Past a piggery, I met two yoked bullocks with a load of timber, and then shortly after Blateshnitsa, in the valley, I arrived in the charming railway town of Zemen, and strolled around aimlessly, watching boys playing football, and scarved women entering and leaving shops. A restaurant advertising a menu in the window appeared deserted, so I asked a taxi-driver, who recommended the Zemenski Kale near the centre. There I consulted the chef. 'Rice soup', he ticked off on his fingers as if instructing a seven-year-old in the principles of arithmetic, 'meat balls, French potatoes, bread, cold drink, no coffee, o.k.?' A military gentleman was weaving an impenetrable smoke-screen with the avid assistance of two other joky smokers: I could hear them, but I could not see them.

The same taxi-driver was waiting for me, in hopes of a fare, as I paid the bill. I felt guilty: I should have told him before that I had a car. 'The monastery of S. John the Theologian?' He pointed straight up into the sky, and I understood. I would be in the mountains, among deciduous forests far from the valley town. And so I came to the most exquisite church in the Balkans: simple, modest, intimate, ravishing in its frescoes. Following restoration work (1970-4) led by Bonka Ilieva, Velda Mardi-Babikova has indicated a dual origin for the church frescoes, the first cycle dating from the 11th-12th centuries (surviving only in insignificant fragments), and the second from 1354, at the expense of Despot Deyan of Velbuzhd. The church is unique in Bulgaria in its almost perfect cuboid form, with three high apses on the inner eastern side, the whole capped by a high domed cylindrical drum in the centre of a tiled roof. On the south and west walls appear portrait frescoes of Konstantin Deyan, his wife Doya, and their two children. Doya's elegant headdress and robe are not only beautifully drawn, but represent a capital moment in the documentation of mediaeval costume, as we have seen in the Boyana Church above Sofia. The artist's eloquent draughtsmanship, typical of the Macedonian School, excels in individuality, as we can see in the faces of the sleeping disciples in the 'Garden of Gethsemane' and vigorous powers of composition, as in 'The Kiss of Judas' with a detail of Peter tearing off a soldier's ear in the bottom right-hand corner. 'The Last Supper' depicts Jesus twice, turning to both left and right

Zemen. Monastery Church of S. John the Theologian

(once with bread, once with wine) to ensure that neither group of disciples will be ignored. A full-length portrait of Sv. Ivan Rilski appears at the lowest level.

The monastery itself was ravaged during the Ottoman epoch, and not rebuilt until the 19th century. It remained an active monastery until 1968; now old cells are now being reconstructed as rooms for foreign-language students.

If you have the chance to take the train from Zemen to Kyustendil, the Zemen Gorge will enchant you along twenty km from just beyond Zemen town to Ruzhdavitsa, 16 km north of Kyustendil.

There is no road along the gorge, so if you want to see the Struma in its foaming progress through limestone heights, fantastic crags and scarps, you must take a train that chugs over bridges and through nine tunnels. Wherever soil persists, apple-trees are planted: then at the third tunnel you look up to find on the right bank the Gulubinski Skali, friable rocks in which wild pigeons nest, and on the left bank the rows of Samotvorskite Kukli, or 'Self-Made Dolls', and then a ruined fortress belonging to the mediaeval town of Zemlun, centred near the monastery above modern Zemen but extending its tentacles through the gorge wherever invaders might be spotted and ambushed. Next comes the tiny hamlet of Polska Skakavitsa, and waterfalls crashing more than 50 metres to the Struma. A mediaeval watchtower crowns a rock above the eighth tunnel and near the ninth you can see the Shagava, a tributary of the Struma, and finally you come to Ruzhdavitsa, before the gentle valley of Kyustendil.

Samokov, Borovets and the Return to Sofia
From Zemen I planned to see Samokov, that great centre of National Revival art and craftsmanship, and passed through Kalishta, Debeli Luk, Izvor, Kolosh, Zhedna, Bobovdol, crossing highway E79 near Stanke Dimitrov. I filled with petrol at a filling-station which bore the sign *Visok profesionalizm na vsyako rabotno myasto* (High professionalism in every workplace), a typical exhortation to constant effort.

Between fields of tobacco I noted a road off right to Sapareva Banya, a resort nestling in foothills under an evening sun. Potatoes and hops were growing in the countryside before Samokov, though the town today is famous for linen, wool and cotton plants in addition to the traditional crafts of woodcarving, carpets and ceramics. 'Samokov' means ironworks and from mediaeval times foundries used local deposits of ore and energy from the Iskur to provide the Ottoman Empire with much of its iron. The town has only 27,000 inhabitants now, but in the 17th century Samokov exceeded Sofia in population and prestige, and it seems only decent to allow yourself two or three days to explore the town, which once possessed more than a dozen mosques and numerous fountains. I parked near the bus terminal, and wandered among passengers standing in a queue for tickets, sitting on suitcases waiting for their bus, or buying fruit from stalls at the back. Behind trestle tables, flower-sellers chatted among themselves, for trade was slack. Samokov is not geared for overnight accommodation, unfortunately, so one has to try 10 km away in Borovets, which is organised for group bookings. 'Bor', the pine-tree, gives its name to the royal resort founded in 1897, with eight ski runs at Sitnyakovo, four at Yastrebets, and five at Markujik. Skiers at all levels can find runs to suit their prowess, and all-in packages to include accommodation and the hire of equipment can be bought abroad. The ski school has no age limit, and the season extends from late November to mid-May. Hotels are available on three levels: the first comprises the three-star Rila above the pine forests; and below the fir trees are the three-star Moura, Breza, Ela and Samokov; the second level comprises the three-star Bor and Musala, and the two-star Edelweiss, all surrounded in the resort's original location by spruce and fir; the third level consists of two three-star holiday villages of wooden villas, the Yagoda of Finnish type with saunas for men and women, and the smaller Malina. The two-star Edelweiss, hung with icicles, provided a heated single room and an excellent dinner in heady surroundings. In the dining room, a handsome woman of fifty sat alone, a black handbag complementing her stubbornly black hair. She chain-smoked avidly, taking food as a kind of unwelcome additive to cigarettes. Her face was crossed by furrows betraying constant emotional turmoil, as if two armies had dug in for a long battle behind her hair, arrogance vying over the years for supremacy against petulance but in the end neither would give way, stubbornly clambering across wrinkles and creases of their own making.

The following morning I strolled around this charming resort, known as Chamkoria when founded by Prince Ferdinand; if you take the gondola lift up to Yastrebets you will see the former royal hunting lodge. I returned to Samokov's Historical Museum (closed on Mondays) at 4 Ulitsa Barumov. Here are objects of iron, brass, copper, silver and gold, cameos, textiles and embroidery. Models show the operation of furnaces and foundries (of which the last closed in 1919), and in the hall I found Osmanli inscriptions in marble, headstones and weapons. Samokov was a centre of sheep-breeding and the making of woollen *abbas* or long coats; of glazed pottery, and of glass. Nikola Karastoyanov operated the first printing press in Bulgaria here from 1827. Here are the palette, artist's materials and personal effects of the artist Nikola Obrazopisov, whose house is situated close to the Nunnery, off Ul. Sotirov.

Personal belongings of Zahari Zograf are also on show with his icon of 'S. John the Baptist', or 'precursor' as his title translates from Bulgarian. An original portrait of his brother Dimitur is by his son Stanislav Dospevski.

The local artist Hristo Dimitrov had been trained first in both Mount Athos and Vienna in the late 18th century, and when he returned to Samokov he taught religious and secular painting to his sons Zahari and Dimitur Zograf and lesser figures. Our vision of the Bulgarian mural is largely theirs, for they, with Ivan Obrazopisets (1795-1854) and his son Nikola, were responsible for the decoration of Rila Monastery's main church and chapels as we see them today. Old Hristo never broke free from tradition, but Zahari took liberties, portraying himself as we have seen at Preobrazhenski, Troyan, and Bachkovo and daring to depict living people in contemporary dress. His nephew Zafir Dimitrov Hristov continued to extend the family's range, using the name Stanislav Dospevski, as witness a 'Nude' (1856) in Plovdiv and a portrait of his wife (1869) in Sofia.

Defying Tsar Ferdinand, socialists created the Samokov Commune in 1910 and this essay in self-government endured until 1912, but a second Commune arose in 1919 and a third in 1923. A separate Museum of the Samokov Commune recently opened near the main square.

Woodcarving has always been connected with Samokov since Father Antoniou came from Mount Athos in 1793 to carve the iconostasis for the Metropolitan Church of the Virgin Mary, a late 17th-century building. The carver Atanas Teladuro completed both wings of the Metropolitan iconostasis before beginning work on his masterpiece: the iconostasis of the principal church at Rila. Its details are well worth examination, particularly the scene 'Adam delved while Eve span', a moustachioed Adam crouching in toil.

The Church of the Birth of the Virgin Mary known locally as the Belyo Church after its sponsor, a foundry-owner, lies 3 km from Samokov on the road to Borovets. Dating from 1869, it was frescoed by Nikola Obrazopisov and assistants, a vigorous 'Massacre of the Innocents' exemplifying the naive piety of the time. There was nobody else there at all during my visit. The almost complete abandonment of Bulgarian Orthodoxy in these sceptical days reminded me of Sacheverell Sitwell's suggestion that 'all religions alike would seem to be fogs or miasmas or exhalations given off and induced by the human fear of death'.

The Convent of the Holy Virgin (1772) rises between Ulitsa Sotirov and Ulitsa Zuibarov, a high cross tiny above the yoked entrance door and cobbled street. The present church on the site (1837-9) possesses murals on part of the vault, but my favourite work is an icon of a strapping Archangel set against a scene remarkably reminiscent of contemporary Samokov, by an unknown 19th-century local artist. Desks for the liturgical books, iconostasis and the bishop's throne are all finely carved. But it is the sense of tranquillity in the cobbled yard and path shaded by broad eaves and overhanging branches that one recalls after emerging into the sunny morning light again. On the other side of Ulitsa Sotirov stands one of the many period houses which form an integral part of Samokov's past and present: that of the Hajipenov family, with a carved wooden rosette in the centre of a ceiling. Similar houses on the convent side of Sotirov include the Hajilalov, also 19th-century, with a graceful colonnaded portico, the Obrazopisov (1861) and the Gerov. By crossing Ul. Patriarch Evtimii you will come to Ul. Zahari Zograf, with the houses of Maximov (1879), Esov and Bosev, before arriving at the Metropolitan Church.

The large Church of Sv. Nikola (1861) dominates Ul. Sotirov beyond the Hajipenov and Marchin houses; its icons on the iconostasis are more successful than the overly attenuated columns on the northern side of the church.

As well as mosques and churches, 19th-century Samokov boasted a synagogue off Ul. Dondukov, finished in 1860, with traditional woodcarving and frescoes.

In the corner of the bus terminal a splendid Ottoman public fountain or *cheshma* of 1662 is topped by a tiled roof. Close by is Bairakli Mosque, newly enclosed and restored from the Old Mosque reconstructed in 1845 at the expense of Mehmet Husref Pasha, using local muralists whose names have been recorded: Ivan, Risto, Kosto. Stained glass windows are surrounded by floral decorations I felt more apt for a patrician residence, say one of Ferdinand's lodges in Borovets, than for a mosque. Windows in the domed drum provide more light than two ranks of windows illuminating the square building; a portico with eight columns at the front and yoked arches gives a bizarre impression of a church narthex. The brickwork on the minaret may be pleasant, but is not authentic to judge from my photo before the 1961 restoration. Altogether, I

Samokov. Bairakli Mosque (reconstructed in 1845)

suppose my most cherished recollection of this charming and unexpected mosque is the painted mosque and saffron-clouded landscape in the mihrab, painted curtains hanging above it and falling to
the side as if the view had just been unveiled to public gaze. The
Bairakli Mosque is closed on Wednesdays but, guiltily assuming
Bulgarian hospitality to be as great as my effrontery, I asked, one
Wednesday, whether a key-holder at the nearby Historical Museum
could let me into the mosque, confessing that I collect mosques as
ardently as I collect Bulgarian literature. The curator, smiling
patiently, despite my incoherent Bulgarian shook his head in
approving agreement as at a willing but stupid sheepdog. 'Yes', he
said.

I drove back to Sofia across the river Palikariya, which pours into
the artificial Iskur Lake. The Iskur Dam (1948-55) assures electric
power for Sofia and provides water sports from the resort of Stur-
kelovo Gnezdo (Storks' Nest). All that survives of the submerged
villages of Kalkovo, Gorni Pasarel and Shishmanovo is Kalkovo's
school, now converted into a hotel. The Pancharevo gorge huddles

259

between the Plana and Lozen heights, the former concealing the Urvich Monastery, and the latter both the Lozen and the German Monasteries. The Urvich or Kokalyan Monastery dedicated to the Archangel Michael is situated close to the castle of Urvich, destroyed by the Ottoman invaders after their victory over the forces of Tsar Ivan Shishman. Another monastery, devoted to S. Nicholas, once active near the castle, was never rebuilt, but the Kokalyanski endured repeated raids: the monastery was last restored in 1858 and the stone church some time after Liberation. The Germanski is of hoary antiquity, from the First Bulgarian State, in a secluded slope of the Lozen Mountain 15 km east of Sofia. Though the monastery buildings are recent, earlier Samokov icons, the episcopal throne, and part of an ancient iconostasis are to be found in the stone church of 1885. The Lozenski is located 5 km southeast of Dolni Lozen. Like the others, the monastery – probably belonging to the Second Bulgarian State – became a centre of learning in the 17th century, before the Ottomans devastated it again. The present church of 1821 has a single nave and apse with three domes and high octagonal drums, and shows the donor, Abbot Kyriakos of Vratsa, in a portrait of 1868, the year when the vaulting was replaced by the domes we see today. The artists from Samokov, including Nikola Ivanov Obrazopisov, concentrated on Bulgarian saints and ecclesiastics such as the obvious S. John of Rila and Cyril with Methodius, together with lesser figures such as Onuphrius of Gabrovo and S. Constantine of Sofia. The view from Lozenski ranges far and wide. Lake Pasarel is the second lake on the Sofia road, the third being Lake Pancharevo, with its power station and resort. Balnea Caesarea has been exploited for its baths since Roman times; the translation into Bulgarian was Bani Tsarevi, from which it is a mere slip of the tongue to Pancharevo. Pancharevo Lake has a restaurant, the Lebed, with a floating stage for summer shows, including rock bands, variety acts, local (*shopski*) folklore, and two hundred dancers.

A few kilometres farther on comes the turning to Sofia International Airport, and the highway leading to the centre of Sofia. Which is where it all began. If I have learned anything in Bulgaria, it is that the indomitable cordiality of the people reaches out to the end of the last winding lane before the path disappears in woodland. From Ahtopol on the Black Sea to the narrow alleys of Kovachevitsa and other Pirin villages; from the stormy rocks of

Belogradchik in the northwest to the silent stones of Pliska in the historic heartland: every hour in the plains and forests of Bulgaria I consider well-spent. It is not only that the values of hard work, communal spirit and immediate generosity appeal to me; it is more that the dignity of the people has not allowed them to be swept along by crazes such as consumerism, advertising (which they rightly distrust), and punk fashions. Once Bulgaria was a land of villages with a few towns. Now towns are expanding and rural communities contracting. But ties with the land persist: townees take holidays with their relatives in the country and vice versa. Goods obtainable only in urban centres are taken by friends to the countryside; they return laden with fresh fruit and vegetables. I have come back laden with fresh memories.

Bulgaria exceeded every expectation, and yet I have to admit a kind of defeat. I have still not found the time to walk enough in the Rhodope mountains, in Pirin National Park, or in the hills around Zheravna. I have never been inside the 19th-century mansions of Panagyurishte. And I regret more than anything missing Teteven, of which the national poet Ivan Vazov could write, 'I should consider myself a stranger to my native country if I had not been to Teteven. Nowhere have I found a place so enchanting.'

Perhaps you, reader, will go to Teteven, and tell me what it was like...

USEFUL INFORMATION

When to Come

The Black Sea Coast hosts the largest number of visitors to Bulgaria by far, and you should not attempt to secure accommodation 'on the off chance' during July and August, for there will be none available. Package tours starting in mid-April and continuing to mid-October are priced so competitively that at the time of writing it often pays you to book a package even if you only intend to use the hotel in question on the first and last night, hiring a car to travel every other day, a method highly to be recommended, especially if you yourself have booked hotels in advance. Camping is popular, as are chalets and cottages; private accommodation is not only cheap but allows you to see the Bulgarians at home and experience their radiant welcome; and inter-town buses and trains cost very little indeed yet are reliable and very frequent. There is a great deal of domestic tourism throughout the year, so accommodation is likely to be your biggest problem, and a Dormobile or similar vehicle allowing you to sleep anywhere you want is the best possible solution, though it is a long drive through Europe to the fringes of Istanbul!

Winter resorts such as Vitosha (just outside Sofia) and Malyovitsa normally enjoy snowfall from early December to February, though your travel agent will be able to let you have the latest news. Hiking in the mountains can be enjoyed throughout the rest of the year, and rambling in the hills lower down the slopes and throughout so much of unspoilt Bulgaria will offer ideal relaxation for those seeking a return to gentler, slower times.

Over the last few years average daily temperatures in Fahrenheit through the years have been as follows, with the Black Sea being exemplified by Varna, and the mountain resorts by Borovets:

	Black Sea	Mountains
January	35	30
February	42	33
March	43	40
April	53	48
May	62	58
June	70	65
July	75	70
August	75	73
September	68	61
October	60	54
November	50	42
December	38	33

Altogether, I judge spring and autumn the best seasons, avoiding extremes of climate and crowds which do not harmonise with the tranquil way of life characteristic of Bulgaria from Koprivshtitsa to Arbanasi. Roselovers should known that the Annual Rose Festival takes place in the Valley of the Roses in the first week of June. Cruises along the Danube on the *Sofia* and *Rousse* begin at Passau and end up at Ruse, calling at Melk, Vienna, Bratislava, Budapest and Belgrade. Ruse holds a music festival in March, Varna in June, and for chamber music the place is Plovdiv, the time September.

The number one tour operator from Britain to Bulgaria is Balkan Holidays, 19 Conduit Street, London W1R 9TD; from Ireland, Balkan Tours, 5-6 South Great George's Street, Dublin and 9-10 Lombard Street, Belfast BT1 1RB. Other major operators to Bulgaria include Intasun, Global, Schools Abroad, Enterprise, Ingham's, Falcon, Phoenix and Sunquest. You might decide on specialists like Contiki, Duggan Holidays, Golden Circle, Ramblers Holidays (only in the mountains), Thomas Cook (only cruises), Saga Holidays (only coach tours, for the over-60s), Sovereign Holidays (only cruises), and Sunseeker Holidays (only Sunny Beach). Peltours (4 Winsley Street, London W1N 7AR) specialise in providing packages incorporating vouchers towards accommodation anywhere in Bulgaria, a system I strongly recommend.

The most expensive packages, corresponding to high season, are January-February and mid-June to early September. If you choose to spend one week at a centre and another week touring, a 'Discover Bulgaria' or a 'Wine and Dine' tour, both offering full board and coach travel, can be booked with many operators, including Balkan Holidays, Trafalgar Tours, Cosmos and Swan Hellenic. Inter-Church Travel (45 Berkeley Street, London W1A 1EB) provide a 9-day 'Frescoes and Icons' tour, and opportunities with other operators include eight-day gourmet courses in Bansko and Kyustendil; carpet-weaving in Chiprovtsi, pottery and woodcarving in Troyan, icon-painting at Rila; five days by donkey-cart through Pirin; an eight-day hike in the Balkan Range; folkdancing in Blagoevgrad; and game-hunting for roe deer (May to October) wild boar (June to January), wolves, jackals, and foxes. Sportsmen might like an eight-day riding course in Shumen, a ten-day tennis course in Slunchev Bryag, Zlatni Pyasutsi, Albena or Druzhba, and 8-day or 15-day fitness programmes in Black Sea resorts, Pravets, Sandanski and Pleven.

How to Come

Most visitors (about 80%) visit Bulgaria by road, which allows them to see the magnificent landscapes from the Danubian plain to the Rodopi and Pirin mountains; from the so-called 'Old Mountain', or Stara Planina (known to the Turks as the Balkan range) to the old towns and new villages near Burgas such as Sozopol and Pomorie. An increasing number of tourists arrive by scheduled and charter flights, especially to the Black Sea, which accounts for nearly half the hotel accommodation in the country, predominantly in July and August. The airports at Varna and Burgas receive Black Sea visitors direct, without having to change at Sofia, in a season extending from mid-May to mid-October. Among European cities offering direct flights to Sofia are London, Paris, Amsterdam, Brussels, Madrid, Copenhagen, Munich, Frankfurt, Milan and Rome.

Internally, regular flights link Sofia with Gorna Oryahovitsa (for Veliko Turnovo and Central Bulgaria), Vidin, Silistra and Ruse in the north, and Varna, Turgovishte and Burgas in the east.

By rail, Sofia is connected with Moscow by daily departures via Pleven, Ruse, Bucharest and Kiev; with Warsaw, Berlin (via Budapest and Prague); with Istanbul and Ljubljana, with Thessaloniki and Athens. There is a first-rate domestic rail service.

By road, the E-80 crosses Europe from La Coruña, Toulouse, Nice, Genoa, Rome and Dubrovnik, continuing to Edirne and

Istanbul; the E-70 from La Rochelle and Lyon passes Turin, Verona, Trieste, Zagreb, Belgrade and Bucharest to end up in Ruse and Varna; and the E-79 crosses Romania from Oradea and Craiova, touching Vidin and Botevgrad before continuing to Thessaloniki.

Driving in Bulgaria is pleasant on three counts: you can go where your fancy leads you; the roads are emptier than in Western Europe; and because of the total ban on drinking any quantity of alcohol no matter how small, the roads are safer than anywhere else I know. The speed limit is 120 kph on motorways, 80 kph on other roads outside built-up areas, and 60 kph in built-up areas unless signs are posted to the contrary. You will want to learn the Cyrillic alphabet if only for the road signs. Petrol coupons may be bought at the borders, at Balkantourist hotels and motels, and at some travel agencies overseas. You may drive on your current national licence as long as you can prove insurance cover for third-party liability, and show Green and Blue cards, the latter being available at border checkpoints. If you belong to a motoring organization affiliated with A.I.T. or F.I.A., the Shipka Travel Agency provides free road aid on breakdowns requiring an hour's work or less, and repatriation of damaged vehicles. Costs of labour are much lower than in Western Europe.

You can drive your own car, but the journey through Europe is very long compared with the size of Bulgaria and my advice is to hire a self-drive car (limited or unlimited mileage as you prefer) at the airports of Sofia, Burgas or Varna; at the Grand Hotel Sofia or Vitosha New Otani in Sofia; at the Novotel in Plovdiv; or at the Black Sea in the major hotels in Sunny Beach (Slunchev Bryag), Burgas, Golden Sands (Zlatni Pyasutsi), Albena, Druzhba and Varna. Otherwise you will not have easy access to monasteries and museum-towns off the beaten track.

Taxis are plentiful and can be hailed in the street, hired by phone, or awaited in a taxi-rank. The charges are very low and the drivers exceptionally honest: they do not expect to be tipped.

Many towns (like Plovdiv and Melnik) have old pedestrian precincts and many others (such as Pleven and Vidin) have created new pedestrian precincts with shopping centres, fountains and gardens where the traditional promenade can take place on summer evenings or on holidays. Where you do not have to walk, buses, trams and (in some cities) also trolley-buses make a convenient alterna-

tive, and at kiosks you can buy tickets which are a standard price
and usable on any type of urban public transport. Trams and trolleybuses link outlying housing estates with city centres between
about 4 a.m. and 1 p.m., though most bus lines stop around midnight. At kiosks you may be able to buy street maps and postcards,
but the supply is erratic, and you might have to explore bookshops
with stationery departments for local maps and guides.

Accommodation

Package tours stay at expensive, well-appointed hotels of international calibre such as the Ambassador or International at Golden
Sands and the Globus or Kuban at Sunny Beach. Though hotels are
ranked by their number of stars, I did not detect much difference
between the 5-star, 4-star and 3-star, and the food at the 2-star
Hotel Moreni on Vitosha, above Sofia, was the best I tasted in
Bulgaria.

To see the real Bulgaria, however, there is no substitute for
taking rooms in private accommodation. The problem is that of the
150,000 beds in private houses and flats, nearly 75% are at the
seaside, and most of the others are in major cities, so in the countryside there are fewer opportunities to meet Bulgarians in their
own homes. Of the ninety-odd campsites, 35 are beside the sea, and
especially by the Black Sea and in mountain resorts, you will also
find abundant chalets and cottages, any of which can be booked at
one centralised booking system for all accommodation: Balkantourist, 1 Vitosha Blvd., Sofia, a foreign-trade corporation with the
Bulgarian Association of Tourism and Recreation, 1 Lenin Square,
Sofia.

You can book any type of accommodation at a Balkantourist
information or tourist bureau, and also reserve tickets for major
performances, buy transport tickets, rent a car and change money,
though you should check whether the rates are better at a bank or
supermarket first. Young people will use Orbita Youth Travel
Agency, 45a Stambuliiski Blvd., Sofia as well as Balkantourist. In
this connection, they might be interested in work camps requiring a
forty-hour week from the 18-30 age-group volunteers, who are
offered board, lodgings, clothes and a small travel allowance. Outside the U.K. you can apply for this chance (before the end of May)
to the National Committee for Voluntary Brigades, 11 Stambuliiski
Blvd., Sofia. Within the U.K., you apply to Quaker Work Camps,

Friends' House, Euston Road, London NW1 2BJ, or to the International Voluntary Service, 53 Regent Road, Leicester LE1 6YL, and must attend an orientation meeting.

Restaurants

Package tours provide meal coupons valid at any Balkantourist establishment, not necessarily in hotels, which gives you a very wide choice. Compared with any North American or Western European experience, however, restaurants in Bulgaria are extraordinarily low-priced, and your budget will easy cope with a few unscheduled meals off the beaten track. For breakfast you may find a hot egg dish ('hamniks' is a dish naturalised by long usage in Bulgarian), but most offerings will be cold, with several kinds of cheese, cold meats, yoghourts, white bread (why never any brown?) and jam or honey. Lunch and dinner will emphasise salads, a choice of soup, and a small range of meat dishes led by pork, lamb and veal, with the occasional chicken, and fish obtainable chiefly near the Black Sea and lakes.

The Bulgarians are aware that service in restaurants is still very slow, and are constantly trying to solve this, but the main problem seems to be limited choice, both in ingredients and in treatment. Chefs generally have no experience of cuisine beyond Bulgaria's borders, and kitchens are understaffed. You may be able to encourage a head waiter to produce a fairly rapid lunch, but dinner is another matter, for numerous groups large and small fill most well-reputed restaurants every night, staying long to listen and dance to the (often very noisy) band, with its incongruous mixture of western pop, Bulgarian pop, heavy metal, 'easy listening' of the Dean Martin generation, and the occasional local folk song.

I found the quickest solution to be self-service restaurants, and buying fruit from private-enterprise stalls by the roadside, or in markets (*hali*) and shops (*hranitelni stoki*, *gastronom* or *magazin*). The *patisserie* or *sladkarnitsa* displays attractive cakes bordering on the ecstatically sweet and provides coffee, normally Turkish in a tiny cup, very strong with grounds in a thick sediment, a legacy from five centuries of Ottoman rule, like the *baklava*. Ice-cream is another obsession and speciality of Bulgaria.

It is a criminal offence to drive with *any* amount of alcohol in the blood, which must rile the oenophile, for Bulgaria is justly renowned for its cognac, apricot brandy, and red and white wines and they taste better, as usual, in their place of origin than after travelling.

Passports and Visas

You must be in possession of a full passport, but package-tourists do not require a separate visa each at the time of writing: it is however advisable to check the current position with your local travel agent, or the Bulgarian National Tourist Offices abroad, (in the U.K.) at 18 Princes St., London W1R 7RE; in the U.S. at 161 E. 86th St., New York, N.Y. 10028; and in Canada c/o Bulgarian Trade Mission, 1550 De Maisonneuve West, Montréal, Quebec. In the Netherlands, the address is 43 Leidsestraat, 1017 NV Amsterdam; in West Germany you could try 1-3 Stefanstrasse, 6000 Frankfurt/Main 1 or 175 Kurfürstendamm, 1000 Berlin 15; in France the address is 45 Avenue de l'Opéra, 75002 Paris, and in Belgium it is 62 Rue Ravenstein, 1000 Brussels. It is worth stressing that anyone planning *individual* tourism, including individual deviations within package tours, must have a visa at present, and must have a rubber stamp from the hotel reception at both arrival and departure there, failing which a fine may be levied on leaving the country.

Apply for longer than you need in case of delays (the fee will be the same), and allow at least three weeks before departure.

Customs and Currency

You may neither import nor export Bulgarian leva, and you should keep receipts for hard currency changed into leva so that you can change back (into a currency that may not be what you prefer) at the point of departure. Allow time for this. There are 100 stotinki (100 means 'sto') in a lev, and at present the highest denomination of notes is 20 leva. Always double-check, because these matters have a way of changing overnight, but at present there are three official rates of exchange: the base rate subject to weekly review, the 100% premium available at all Balkantourist offices and hotels, and a premium rate far above this which I found in banks and major department stores such as the Sofia Central Universal Supermarket (TsUM). I exchanged sterling travellers' cheques for leva while in Bulgaria, and was offered either US dollars or Deutschmarks on leaving, when I produced my receipts. A vigorous black market exists, but I urge you not to be tempted into illegal deals, no matter how attractive the offer. Quite apart from the criminal offence involved, the cost of living is already so low in Bulgaria that there can be little if any good cause to risk your liberty for a few extra leva.

Customs searches are not likely to worry the foreign tourist. You may bring in and take out at the moment 250 cigarettes, 2 litres of wine, and 1 litre of spirits. On entry, declare radios, tape recorders, TV sets, cameras and typewriters; on departure, declare gifts and purchases totalling in excess of 50 leva – the only question customs officers asked me was 'Have you any leva?'. There is no restriction on the import or export of any hard currency.

Embassies

Britons and Commonwealth citizens use the British Embassy at 65 Bulevard Tolbuhin (tel. 88-53-61 and 87-83-25), except that Canadians use the U.S. Embassy at 1 Bulevard Stamboliiski (tel. 88-48-01, -02, and -03). The Belgian Embassy is at 19 Frédéric Joliot-Curie St., ap. 6 and 8; the Netherlands at 19a Denkoglu St., the French at 29 Oborishte Bulevard, and the West German at 7 Henri Barbusse St.

Health

In Sofia the Clinic of Foreigners can be found at Mladost 1, 1 Evgeni Pavlovski St. (tel. 75 361), but elsewhere the main hotels have a doctor on call and some even a modern medical centre, especially those at places like Sandanski or Kyustendil with a very long reputation as a spa. No charge is made for consultation and treatment in emergencies; longer treatment will be charged for (always reasonably) if Bulgaria does not have a reciprocal agreement with the Government of the country to which the patient belongs.

Speaking (and Reading) the Language

Bulgarian is very close to Serbo-Croat, the main language of Yugoslavia, though it has affinities with all the other Slavonic languages. Closely akin to Russian, it shares the Cyrillic alphabet (with a few minor differences) and if you prefer not to spend time learning the language, rest assured that a knowledge of the alphabet alone will take you a long way in Bulgaria. You will recognise at once, for example, 'telefon', 'muzei', 'hotel', 'galeria', 'kino', 'teatur', 'pet-rol' and of course the names of cities, towns and villages on road-signs, maps, and leaflets. I have transliterated Cyrillic consistently for the most part, though 'Sofiya' is given its traditional Italianate form. The soft sign when a vowel is shown as 'u' in 'Turnovo', on the analogy of 'Bulgaria', and when a consonant as 'y', the pronunciation of 'Kolyo Ficheto', the self-taught master-builder.

BULGARIAN ALPHABET

А а	a	К к	k	Ф ф	f
Б б	b	Л л	l	Х х	h
В в	v	М м	m	Ц ц	ts
Г г	g	Н н	n	Ч ч	ch
Д д	d	О о	o	Ш ш	sh
Е е	e	П п	p	Щ щ	sht
Ж ж	zh	Р р	r	Ъ ъ	a, u
З з	z	С с	s	Ь ь	
И и	i	Т т	t	Ю ю	yu
Й й	y	У у	u	Я я	ya

Few textbooks exist, and the only dictionaries I have found had to be hunted down in a dozen bookshops because they sell out so quickly. The *English-Bulgarian Dictionary* (2 vols., 1987) by Maria Rankova and others is published by the Nauka i Izkustvo Publishing House, Sofia, who also issue one-volume *Bulgarian-English* and *Bulgarian-French* dictionaries. In the absence of a teach-yourself style grammar with a key to exercises, the only convenient grammar is *A Course in Modern Bulgarian* (2nd ed., 2 vols., 1983) by Milka Hubenova and others, from Slavica Publishers, Inc., P.O. Box 14388, Columbus, Ohio 43214. To learn Bulgarian through the literature, you might like to know that Sofia Press has produced a multilingual version of Hristo Botev's *Immortality* (1988), and the great historical novel by the national poet Ivan Vazov, *Pod Igoto* (10th impression, 1988), can be studied side-by-side with the English translation, *Under the Yoke* and the French version *Sous le Joug* (both Sofia Press).

Russian is the commonest foreign language taught in Bulgaria, followed by English and French.

Words and Phrases

English	Bulgarian
Good morning (first thing)	Dobro utro
Good day (until evening)	Dobur den
Good evening	Dobur vecher
Goodnight	Leka nosht
Yes, no	Da, ne
Please tell me...	Molya, kazhete mi...
Thank you	Merci *or* blagodarya
What is the time?	Kolko e chasut?
Do you speak English?	Govorite li angliiski?
I don't understand you	Ne vi razbiram
Excuse me	Izvinete
Where is Dimitrov Street?	Kude se namira Ulitsa Dimitrov?
Straight on	Na pravo
Here, there	Tuk, tam
To the left	V lyavo
To the right	V dyasno
How much do I owe?	Kolko tryabva da platya?
Speak more slowly	Govorite po bavno
Goodbye	Dovizhdane
I wish to exchange money	Iskam da obmenya pari
How far is it to Plovdiv?	Kolko e daleche do Plovdiv?
A first-class ticket to Varna	Edin bilet purva klasa za Varna
When does the train leave for Gabrovo?	Koga trugva vlakut za Gabrovo?
Please, help me?	Molya, pomognete mi!
A single room, with bath	Edna staya s edno leglo sus banya
Toilet	Toaleta (M for men; Zh for women)
Entrance; exit	Vhod; izhod
How much does it cost?	Kolko struva?
What is this called?	Kak se kazva tova?
Open, closed	Otvoren, zatvoren
No smoking	Pusheneto zabraneno
Under repair	Na remont
Vacant, occupied	Svoboden, zaet
Today, tomorrow	Dnes, utre
Yesterday	Vchera

Numbers and Days of the Week
1 edin, edna, edno 2 dva, dve 3 tri 4 chetiri 5 pet 6 shest 7 sedem 8 osem 9 devet 10 deset 11 edinadeset 12 dvanadeset 13 trinadeset 14 chetirinadeset 15 petnadeset 16 shestnadeset 17 sedemnadeset 18 osemnadeset 19 devetnadeset (from 11 to 19 'nadeset') is often contracted to 'naiset') 20 dvadeset 21 dvadeset i edno 30 trideset 40 chetirideset 50 petdeset 60 shestdeset 70 sedemdeset 80 osemdeset 90 devetdeset 100 sto 120 sto i dvadeset 200 dvesta 500 petstotin 1,000 hiliada 1st purvi purva purvo 2nd vtori vtora vtoro 3rd treti treta treto

Monday	ponedelnik	Friday	petuk
Tuesday	vtornik	Saturday	subota
Wednesday	sryada	Sunday	nedelya
Thursday	chetvurtuk		

Months and Seasons

January	yanuari	Winter	zima
February	fevruari		
March	mart		
April	april	Spring	prolet
May	mai		
June	yuni	Summer	lyato
July	yuli		
August	avgust		
September	septemvri	Autumn	esen
October	oktomvri		
November	noemvri		
December	dekemvri	Christmas	koleda

Holidays and Festivals

January 1	New Year's Day
May 1-2	International Labour Day
May 24	Day of Bulgarian Culture and the Slavonic Alphabet
September 9-10	Socialist Revolution Day
November 7	Great October Revolution Day
January	Winter Music Festival, Plovdiv

February	New Bulgarian Music, Sofia
	Throughout Bulgaria, Wine-Growers' Day on the 14th
March	International Music Festival, Ruse
	Folk Arts and Crafts, Veliko Turnovo
April	Days of Bulgarian Symphonic Music, Plovdiv
May	International Fair (Light Industry), Plovdiv
	Satire and Humour Biennale, Gabrovo (odd-numbered years)
June	International Book Fair, Sofia (even years)
	Bulgarian Culture Days, Zlatni Pyasutsi
	International Ballroom Dancing Competition, Burgas
	International Music Festival, Varna
July	International Ballet Competition, Varna
	Bulgarian Culture Days, Albena
August	International Folklore Festival, Burgas (even years)
September	Arts Festival, Old Plovdiv
	International Fair (Heavy Industry), Plovdiv
	Arts Festival, Sozopol
October	Bulgarian Film Festival, Varna (even years)
November	International Dance Competition, Ruse
	Jazz Weeks, Sofia
December	Musical Evenings, Sofia

Things to Remember

Bring your own camera equipment and enough films; very few foreign-language newspapers and magazines are obtainable in Bulgaria; the time is two hours ahead of Greenwich Mean Time; local 'summer time' applies from early April to late September; a nod of the Bulgarian head usually means 'no' and a shake 'yes', but the opposite is not unknown, so beware! To dial 'fire!' in Sofia and Plovdiv, Ruse and Varna, the number is 160; 'ambulance' is 150; and road aid from the Union of Bulgarian Motorists 146. Electricity is 220 volts. Museums are usually closed on Mondays; on other days they could be open from 8 to 6 or 6.30 in summer, closing earlier in winter, and some close for lunch. Shops close on Sundays;

on other days they are usually open from 9-1 and 2-7.30. Laundrettes and dry cleaning services are very rare, but you can get laundry done (well and cheaply) at all major hotels. Large rail stations have twenty-four hour left-luggage offices marked 'garderob', to adapt the French term. If self-catering, pack your own favourite brands of tea or coffee, which will be unobtainable in Bulgaria, like brown sugar or artificial sweeteners.

To join the British-Bulgarian Friendship Society, write to the Secretary, c/o Finsbury Library, 245 S. John St., London EC1V 4NB. As well as films, parties, lectures, and opportunities to meet Bulgarians on exchange visits, the Society organises general and special-interest tours with full board that often cost less than the return flight London-Sofia-London. Typical tours in any given year might emphasise birds, wine, art and architecture, education, medical treatment, textiles and embroidery, folk-dancing, and music.

Books and Maps

My favourite history of Bulgaria is Crampton's, but this could be supplemented on the archaeological side by D.M. Lang's *The Bulgarians from pagan times to the Ottoman Conquest* (London, 1976) and Mercia Macdermott's *A History of Bulgaria, 1393-1885* (London, 1962); the latter enjoys cult-heroine status in Bulgaria for her sympathetic biographies of Vasil Levski, Gotse Delchev, and Yane Sandanski. If you want to know how an orthodox communist views his country's history, Dimitur Markovski's *Bulgaria: a brief historical outline* (Sofia, 1988) will give you an insight into how children learn a certain interpretation of their past in schools and pioneer camps. There is a dearth of travel books about Bulgaria, and certainly nothing to compare with such masterpieces as *Black Lamb and Grey Falcon* (London 1941) by Rebecca West concerning Yugoslavia (in 1937). Stowers Johnson wrote a personal narrative misleadingly entitled *Gay Bulgaria* (London, 1964), mercifully unaware of the interpretation that later generations would place on his title. My favourite Bulgarian travel book is by Ivan Vazov: *The Great Rila Wilderness* (Sofia, 1969), incorporating also his essays 'In the Heart of the Rhodope Mountains' and 'A Recess of Stara Planina', on a walk up to the Promised Rock not far from Sopot.

For up-to-date brochures and maps, your local Bulgarian National Tourist Office will provide a selection, though the current free *Motoring across Bulgaria* (printed in English) reflects the 1983 *Putna Karta* ('Road map') in Cyrillic letters which has merely been reprinted, and hence does not include the major new international freeways crossing the country. Hiking maps of mountain regions are published by the Bulgarian Tourist Union, 30 Stamboliiski Bulevard, Sofia 1000.

Town plans can sometimes be found in kiosks or bookshops or stationery stores, but if all else fails basic town plans of Sofia (large and small scale), Burgas, Varna, Veliko Turnovo, Vidin, Plovdiv, Stara Zagora, Shumen, Pleven and Ruse can be found on the other side of the *Putna Karta* (again, only in Cyrillic). Sectional maps of Sofia appear in Mihailov and Smolenov's *Sofia: a Guide* (Sofia, 1966), which lists routes of buses, trams and trolleybuses in the capital.

INDEX

276

Asenovgrad, xi, 192, 206-8, 223
Asparuh, *Khan*, 1
Assumption Monastery, 107-8
Atanasova, Y., 163
Athos, Mount, 58, 78, 106, 151, 208, 225-6, 232-3, 239, 257
Augusta. *See* Hisarya
Augusta Trajana. *See* Stara Zagora
Aurelian, *Emperor*, 73
Austria and the Austrians, 115
Avars, 33, 114
Avramov, 176

Bacchae, 236-7
Bachkovo Monastery, xi, 9, 166, 192, 208-10
Baev, G., 169
Bagriana, E., 212
Baikal, 253
Bakurianisdze, G., 208
Balabanov House, 194-5
Balchik, 147-9, 152, 161
Balkan Bulgarian Airlines, ix, 135, 161
Balkan Holidays, 263-4
Balkan Range, 1, 2, 107, 183, 264
Balkan Sheraton Hotel, 72-3, 76, 78, 101
Balkan Tours, 263
Balkanski, N., 126
Balkantourist, x, 149, 163, 168, 172, 174, 179, 230, 266
ballet, 273
Balnea Caesarea. *See* Pancharevo
Baltata, 150
Bani Tsarevi. *See* Pancharevo
banitsa, 130, 219
Bansko, xi, 224-8, 264
Bansko School of Art, 225-6
Banya, *nr.* Hisarya, 55; *nr.* Sunny Beach, 161
Banya Bashi Mosque, 81
Barakov, V., 90
Barov, A., 100
Barovo, 72
barracks, Vidin, 117
bashi-bazuks, 54-5, 60, 63, 221
Basil, *Emperor*, 251
Batak, xi, 220-3
baths. *See* under the names of towns, *e.g.* Kyustendil; and resorts, *e.g.* Narechenski Bani
Baudouin II, *Emperor*, 14
Bayazit I, *Sultan*, 115
Bazarovo, 134
Bazev House, 64
Bdin. *See* Vidin
beaches, 150, 161-2, 175. *See also* under the names of resorts, *e.g.* Albena
bears, 210
Beckett, S., 97

278

Danailov, S., 96
Danchov, G., 197, 200
dancing, folk, 215-6, 274
Danube, 84, 113-5, 118, 134, 140-1, 263
Darroch, R., 38
Daskalov, H., 41-2, 45
Daskalov, S.T., 200
David's Bookshop, Cambridge, ix
days of the week, 272
Debeli Luk, 255
Debelyanov, D., 62, 64
Debur School of Art, 63, 126, 174, 204, 239
deer, 48
Delchev, G., 274
Delchev, K. *and* C., 89-90
Denev, B., 26
Deneva, S., 200
dervishes, 146-7, 194
Desposhovo. *See* Batak
Dessislava, Maria, 103
Desudava. *See* Sandanski
Desyov House, 61
Devetaki, 131
Devin, 80, 161
Devin spa, 217, 219
Deyan, *Despot*, 253
Didier, C., 54
Dikilitash, 161
Dimanov, L., 90
Dimitrov, G., 83, 112
Dimitrov, H., 257
Dimitrov, V., 84, 128, 251-2
Dimitrovgrad, 187
Dimitur, *Haji*, 182
Dimitur, *Sveti*, 20
Dimovo, 120
dinner, 267
Diocletianopolis, 53
Dionysopolis, 148
Dionysus, 236-7
Divinova, 99
Djagarov, G., 117-8
Dobcheva, M., 90
Dobreisho, *Pop*, 73
Dobrich. *See* Tolbuhin
Dobrinishte, 225
Dobroplodni, S., 11
Dobrovich, D., 74, 84
Dobruja, 12, 141, 143, 148, 181, 217
Dobursko, 88
doctors, 268
Doganov House, 63
Doirentsi, 131

Etropole Monastery, 65-6, 74
Etura Open-Air Museum, xi, 38-9
Euripides, 236-7
Euthymius, *Patriarch*, 15, 20, 26-8, 200, 208, 249
Evdokia, *Sister*, vii, 28
Evstatieva, S., 94
exchange, 268-9
Ezerovo. *See* Smolyan

Falcon Holidays, 263
Fandukov, S., 123
Felmer, 96
Ferdinand. *See* Mihailovgrad
Ferdinand, *Tsar*, 206, 256-7
festivals, 111, 272-3
Fichev, N.I., 23-4, 27-8, 35, 39, 128-9, 132, 141
Filaretov, S., 179
Filevo, 190
Filibe. *See* Plovdiv
First Bulgarian State, 1, 73, 189, 192, 260
fishing, 135
Fo, D., 200
Fol, A., 159
folkdancing, 215-6, 264
food and cooking, 11, 55, 70-1, 74, 95, 110, 118, 134-5, 170, 176, 206, 214-5, 225, 234, 241, 253, 264, 266-8
football, 49, 201
Forev, H., 52
foxes, 264
Freedom Park, Sofia, 94-5
frescoes, 27, 31, 39, 53-4, 57-8, 62, 77-8, 103-6, 108-9, 133-4, 141-2, 152, 165, 208-9, 237-8, 247-9, 253-4, 264
Friendship Bridge, Ruse, 139-40
Friendship Bridge, Sofia, 95
Fugard, A., 200
Furtunov, S., 38

Gabe, Dora, 84, 144-5
Gabrovo, xi, 22, 35-9, 46, 274
Galin, A., 97, 182
galleries, 24-6, 38, 46-7, 51-2, 83-5, 89-91, 126-8, 131, 139, 144-5, 159, 169-70, 180, 187-8, 194, 200, 211, 225-6, 251-2
game-hunting, 48, 110, 124, 142, 206, 264
Ganchev, K., 183
Ganev, L., 222
Garkov House, 61
Garudis, M., 145
geology, 119-21, 161
Georgi, *Haji*, 196
Georgi, *Sveti*, Sofia, 78
Georgia, U.S.S.R., 208
Georgiadis House, Plovdiv, 196-7
Georgiev, E., 99

Ingham's, 263
Intasun, 263
Inter-Church Travel, 264
Internal Macedonian Revolutionary Organisation, 82, 239
International Fair, Plovdiv, 201
International Voluntary Service, 267
Irinopolis. *See* Stara Zagora
iron, 255
Iron Age, 72, 189, 250. *See also* Thrace and the Thracians
Isaac Angel II, *Emperor*, 12
Iskur Dam, 259
Iskur Gorge and River, 67, 107-8, 124, 255
Islam, 80-1. *See also* mosques; *and* Turkey and the Turks
Isperih, *Khan*, 140
Isperihovo, 192
Istanbul, 56, 62, 86, 135, 140, 161, 178, 264-5
Istros. *See* Danube
Ivailo, 15, 26
Ivailovgrad, 72
Ivan Alexander, *Tsar*, 15-16, 23, 26, 105, 114, 164, 210
Ivan Asen I, *Tsar*, 23
Ivan Asen II, *Tsar*, 13-17, 20, 23
Ivan Asen III, *Tsar*, 15
Ivan Rilski, *Sveti* (S. John of Rila), 20, 27, 58, 78, 242-9, 254
Ivan Shishman, *Tsar*, 15, 16, 105, 122, 126, 242, 260
Ivan Stratsimir Shishman, *Tsar*, 114-5, 119
Ivanko (boyar), 13
Ivanov, A., 131
Ivanov, G., 130
Ivanov, I., 159
Ivanov, I.G., 185
Ivanov, S., 51, 84, 95
Ivanovo, 15, 132-4
Izvor, 255

jackals, 264
Janissaries, 125
jazz, 273
Jelal ed-Din Rumi, 146
Jerusalem, 23, 208, 239
Jewish Museum, Sofia, 82-3
Jireček, K., 176
John of Rila, S. *See* Ivan Rilski, *Sveti*
Johnson, S., 274
Justinian, *Emperor*, 12, 73, 89, 114, 124, 141, 192, 230, 251

Kableshkov, T., 62-3
Kailuka, 124
Kalamis, 172
Kalcheva, S., 217
Kalenjievi House, 218
Kaliakra, 148-50
Kalishta, 255

Mithras, 110, 119, 124
Mitov, A., 84, 87, 90, 95, 196
Mitrev, A., 108
Mlachkov House, 61
Moesi, 118
Mogila, 109-110
Molerov, D., 226
Molière, J.-B.P. de, 96
Momchilov, P., 81, 89, 95
monasteries, ix, x, 107. *See also* under the names of monasteries, *e.g.* Troyan
months of the year, 272
Moore, H., 90
Moreni Hotel, Vitosha, 101
mosques, 8, 70, 80-1, 89, 95, 115, 165, 186-9, 192, 201, 249-50, 258-9
Mota, *Baba*, 25
mountains, 262-3, 266. *See also* under the names of mountains, *e.g.* Pirin; and resorts, *e.g.* Pamporovo
Mrkvička, J., 38, 76, 84, 90, 131, 196
Muglish, 50
Murad I, *Sultan*, 15, 114-5
murals. *See* frescoes
museums, 22-5, 32, 35-6, 38-9, 45, 49, 51-5, 58-60, 66-7, 71-4, 80-1, 85-9, 91-4, 109-13, 115, 117-8, 121, 123, 126, 130, 135, 139, 141, 144, 146, 149, 153, 157-9, 165, 167-9, 172, 178, 183, 186, 188-90, 190-2, 194-200, 205-6, 209-11, 221, 225-6, 228, 230-2, 237, 241, 247, 249-51, 256-7, 273
music, 85, 140, 164-5, 170, 196, 200, 217, 272-4
musical instruments, 179, 196, 214-7
Muskoyani House, 168
Mussmann, A., 70
Mussorgsky, M., 77

Narechenski Bani, 210
Natalie (jeweller), 171
National Archaeological Museum, Plovdiv, 190
National Archaeological Museum, Sofia, 80
National Army Theatre, Sofia, 97
National Art Gallery, Sofia, 83-5
National Assembly, 85
National Committee for Voluntary Brigades, 266
National Ethnographical Museum, Sofia, 83
National History Museum, Sofia, 69, 71-4, 150, 165
National Library, Sofia, 44, 65
National Museum, Sofia. *See* National History Museum, Sofia
National Opera, Sofia, 70, 94
National Palace of Culture, 67, 91, 99-101
National Revival, 41-2, 84, 103, 112, 149, 157, 167, 174, 178-9, 188, 190, 196-7, 211, 218, 232, 234, 247, 255
Natural History Museum, Sofia, 85
nature reserves, 140-1, 150, 240
Naum, *Sveti*, 3, 8, 17
necropolis, Varna, 153, 159
Nedelya, *Sveta*, Sofia, 76, 112

Turkey and the Turks, 53-5, 88, 119, 122, 124-6, 138-40, 143, 146-7, 160, 187-8, 220-3
Turnovgrad. *See* Veliko Turnovo
Turnovo. *See* Veliko Turnovo
Turzhishki Monastery, 108
Tvorcheski Dom, 194

Uchinkova, Y., 217
Union of Bulgarian Artists, 90-1
Union of Bulgarian Motorists, 273
University of Sofia, 98-9
Updike, J., 213-4
Urumov, V., 90, 100, 169
Urvich Monastery, 260
Ustovo, 211
Uzana Hunting Lodge, 48
Uzunjovo, 187, 190
Uzunov, D., 84-5, 90, 100

Valley of the Roses, 49-53, 60, 134, 161, 196, 263
Valyov, K., 247
Vanlian, M., 145
Vaptsarov, N., 92, 228
Varbanov, M., 100
Varna, xi, 72, 100, 109, 112, 135, 138, 152-61, 164, 178, 223, 262-5, 273, 275
Varosha, Blagoevgrad, 241
Varosha, Lovech, 130
Vasileva, D., 51
Vazov, I., 12, 44, 55, 89, 91-2, 96-7, 123, 206-7, 221-3, 246-7, 261, 270, 274
Vazovgrad. *See* Sopot
Velbuzhd. *See* Kyustendil
Veliko Turnovo, x, xi, 1, 12-26, 72, 85, 87-8, 112, 115, 125, 129, 236, 242, 264, 273, 275
Velingrad, 223-4
Velkov, I., 164
Venedikov, 191
Venets, 176
Venkov *family*, 42
Verdi, G., 170, 249
Vereia. *See* Stara Zagora
Vesin, J., 38, 90, 196
Vetovo, 135
Vetren, 50
Vezhinov, 97
Vida, *Baba*, 115-6
Vidin, x-xi, 1, 42, 82, 90, 112-9, 141, 223, 264-5
Vienna, 135, 139, 243
visas, 268
Vishanov *family*, 226, 248
Visigoths, 34
Vitali, *Hieromonakh*, 248
Vitanov *family*, 42, 47, 58
Vitosha, xi, 67, 101-6, 167, 262
Vitosha New Otani Hotel, Sofia, 101, 265
Vodenicharski Mehani, 105